Contents

Preface

From the moment I heard the story of Mary Bryant (née Broad) I wanted to write a book about her. In fact her escape from Botany Bay in an open boat is one of the greatest escapes stories of all time.

Although it is based on truth, I have embellished many parts of the story to help bring Mary to life in terms of our modern world. I began visiting her home town, the fascinating seaport of Fowey, in 1983. I wandered the streets Mary would have frequented, visited the late eighteenth-century buildings she might have visited, drank at the pubs her contemporaries may have drunk at, prayed in St Fimbarrus Church, sailed out through the heads on a boat as she could have done, clambered downs the cliffs to the beaches and walked over Bodmin Moor inspecting the Hurling Stones near the Cheese Wring rocks and felt the magic of that ancient realm. I also talked to many of the local Fowey townsfolk who knew her story, including some carrying the name of Broad.

Although I have used records wherever possible, I have had to assume many things, imagine most of Mary's childhood, her fishing trips with her father William, attraction to the moor and relationship with Richard Thomas and of course re-create the dialogue — although in some cases this is based on documentary records from the day. I have also embellished the robbery scene to make it more dramatic, and her time in prison. But having re-enacted the voyage of the First Fleet myself for Australia's 200th birthday in 1988, sailing from London to Sydney, I based Mary's voyage on my own experience and the journals of First Fleet officers, including my ancestor who sailed with Mary, naval Lieutenant Philip Gidley King (later Governor of New South Wales). I also re-created her life in the colony on the day-by-day journals of the early colonists.

The basis for her escape voyage was the 'Memorandums' written by her fellow escaper James Martyn and the journals of the captain and surgeon of HMS *Pandora*. I based her return to London on contemporary newspaper reports and the papers of James Boswell. Her reunion and marriage to childhood sweetheart Richard Thomas are derived from the records in the parish churches of St Bartholomew in Lostwithiel and St Breage which confirm a marriage between a Mary Bryant and a Richard Thomas.

In short, I have tried to tell the story in a way that is true to the spirit of Mary and her great triumph.

Jonathan King
August 2004

Acknowledgements

I thank Mary Bryant née Broad for giving me and the world such a great yarn.

I also thank Jane King (my Mary Bryant) who lived with the project for 21 years and my four mini-Mary Bryants who researched the book in Fowey and encouraged the author throughout — Lowanna, Bryony, Mollie and Charlotte.

Others to whom I'm grateful include sailing and dialogue writer David Iggulden who made it happen and was the main support writer; reader and reviewer Louise Pfanner; Paddy Boxall a first class courier; and illustrator John Spooner from *The Age* newspaper.

Those who inspired me include Burnum Burnum (aka Harry Penrith) who passed on the secrets of the Aboriginal plants and wildlife that might have sustained Mary and her escape gang; the 1988 First Fleet Re-enactment Expedition leaders and directors of the Oceania Foundation, Wally and Trish Franklin; the First Fleet

Re-enactment Expedition sailor and scriptwriter of Channel 7's 1988 *First Fleet Rite of Passage*, John 'Vanya' Lind; the director of that documentary, Dick Dennison, and his shipmate Mark Norris.

To the BBC's Chris Ralling; historical scholars and writers Michael Hast, Fai Hast, Everett de Roche, Patrick Edgeworth and Russell Hagg, I give my thanks.

Those who helped me in England include Arthur Venning, former Editor of the *Cornish and Devon Post*; the townspeople of Fowey; Ian Shepherd and Oscar Morse of the *Cornish Guardian* (who checked relevant chapters); and film director John Dollar.

Finally, thanks to Simon & Schuster's Jon Attenborough and Julia Collingwood, my editor Robyn Flemming and the proofreader Ian Tonkin.

'I confess, that I never looked at these people without pity and astonishment. They had miscarried in a heroic struggle for liberty after having combated every hardship, and conquered every difficulty.'

CAPTAIN WATKIN TENCH, MARINES
CAPE TOWN, 1792

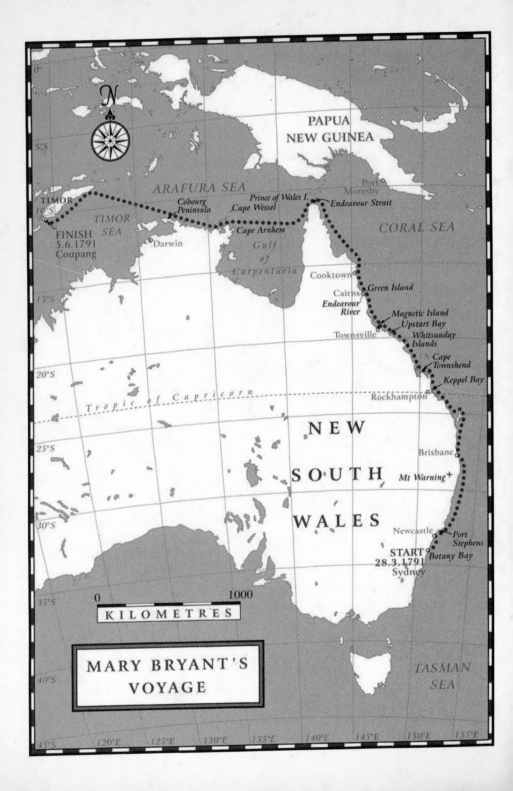

Prologue

London, 1892

Mary Bryant (née Broad), an illiterate 27-year-old, sat in her Newgate Prison cell in the summer of 1792 awaiting death by hanging. Her thoughts turned to the stories her father, William Broad, had told her as a young girl of the champion of the underclasses, Jack Sheppard. The outlaw had not only escaped from Newgate and every gaol in which he had been imprisoned, but had also escaped from the gallows at London's Tyburn Hill in the 1720s.

The story went that Sheppard had been taken by horse-drawn cart to the scaffold, where crowds of onlookers craned to see the notorious escapee. Two hooded executioners standing at his side placed the hangman's noose around his neck. A man of the church read out a few words from the bible, no doubt consigning Sheppard's soul to the fires of hell. Then the signal was given.

The driver of the cart lashed the horse, which lurched forward. Sheppard was left hanging.

Just then, two men leaped forward from the crowd. As the bigger of the two lifted Sheppard to slacken the noose, the other slashed the rope with a sword. Sheppard was then passed from hand to hand over the heads of the crowd and into a waiting coach that whisked him away from death's door.

Mary Bryant had no reason to expect a last-minute reprieve. A convicted criminal and escapee herself, she faced the worst punishment the law could throw at her. But she had evaded death and imprisonment in the past. She had journeyed halfway around the world — and back again — in the most difficult of conditions. She had survived cruel tempests at sea and the loss of her children and husband. But she had not lost hope that she would once again see her dear father and her beloved Richard Thomas.

Mary's thoughts were interrupted by the sound of the turnkey unlocking the heavy door to her cell.

'Mary Bryant?' he called.

'Aye. 'Tis Mary Bryant,' she replied.

'Gen'l'man to see you.'

The turnkey escorted her into an adjacent, less gloomy cell where a well-dressed, rather portly man stood clutching a newspaper.

'Mary Bryant?' the visitor asked.

'Sir,' Mary nodded.

'I am James Boswell, a defence lawyer. I read of your

predicament and have taken an interest in your case. Do you know when it is to be heard?'

'I 'ave 'eard 'tis the morrow, sir.'

'It's possible I may be able to help you,' Boswell said.

'What? 'Elp me?' Mary said. 'But why, sir? I 'ave no money for 'ee at all?'

'I have no need of payment. But what I have heard of your adventures fascinates me. I think I can save you from the gallows, but first I need to know everything that has happened.'

CHAPTER 1

Robbery on the King's highway

*Mary Broad, from a Cornish fishing family, is forced by poverty
to engage in robbery on the king's highway. She is arrested and
tried with her accomplices at the Exeter assizes. Her
imprisonment separates her from the man she loves, a young
Cornish farmer named Richard Thomas.*

On 20 March 1786, a 20-year-old Cornishwoman stood
before the Exeter assizes on a charge of highway robbery.
The penalty, if she were to be found guilty, was death.

Some time prior to March 1786, Mary Broad, in the
company of Catherine Fryer and Margaret Shepherd, stole from a

Miss Agnes Lakeman 'one silk bonnet value twelve shillings and other goods valued at eleven pounds eleven shillings'. Following their capture, the three women were held in Plymouth Gaol, from where they were taken by cart to Exeter to appear before Sir James Eyre and Sir Beaumont Hotham on charges of robbery on the king's highway, a capital offence.

Mary Broad had been baptised on 1 May 1765, the first child of Grace and William Broad, fisherfolk of the Cornish village of Fowey. They say she was born with a caul covering her face, which was said to bring good luck and preserve one from drowning, for Mary never feared the sea.

Mary's father was a sailor when he could get the work, a fisherman when he could not, and a smuggler whenever the chance arose. Tall, thin and wiry, he wore a fisherman's smock and a cap pulled down over his black hair. His craggy face, with his strong Cornish nose, was as lined as the rocks that guarded the harbour mouth. But his sky-blue eyes were clear and gentle, and his ready smile as sunny as a mid-summer's day. Mary's mother, Grace, worked as a domestic servant and took in washing. She was short and small-boned, and worn out from years of hard labour. But with her brown hair and brown eyes, and a chalk-white face, she had been, in her youth, something of a beauty.

Neither William nor Grace had been taught their letters. But William, like his forebears, had always owned boats, had never feared a storm at sea, and held a fine reputation for bringing in a good catch come rain, hail or shine. In times gone by, it was said, when the fish weren't biting, the Broads could locate (if not help cause) a bountiful shipwreck. In fact, they were Cornish wreckers, one of the families who had always known the rocky coasts off Fowey's harbour well enough to lure a ship aground and get the cargo stowed before daylight brought in the revenue officers, the despised 'preventative men'. Their beat, which stretched from Gribben Head in the west to well beyond Blackbottle Rocks to Pencarrow Head in the east, had yielded many treasures over the years — casks of brandy, hogsheads of madeira, French spirits and bales of silk. But the Broads were never as ruthless as the notorious 'Black Humphrey', who erected false beacons on the rocks by night and claimed, 'A wreck is not a wreck if a man, dog, cat or parrot escapes.'

It was also rumoured that the Broads were skilled smugglers who brought the finest silks and brandies across from Spain, France or the Low Countries. It was no easy task to unload the small boats in the rough seas off Coombe Hawne beyond the harbour mouth.

Families had to be adaptable and keep their wits about them if they were to be able to feed their children in the harsh times of the 1760s. There hadn't been enough work to go around since the Seven Years War ended two years before Mary was born, as many soldiers had been laid off and were looking for work. To make matters worse, many cottage industries had been forced to close down, as machines in the bigger towns were now doing the work of people at home in the villages. According to the gossip at Fowey's King of Prussia Inn, a protester against the industrialisation of work, Ned Ludd, had been executed in Yorkshire and his followers, branded 'Luddites', had been sentenced to 'transportation beyond the seas' — to the American colonies, from which far-flung land there was little chance of them ever returning.

High above Fowey was Bodmin Moor, from which ground the River Fowey issued forth. Fowey children were brought up to respect its many traditions and folktales that went back to the time of King Arthur. Dozmary Pool was said to be the lake into which the sword Excalibur had been thrown. These legends, and the landscape itself, with its many mysterious tors dotted among the heather, made the moor a very special place. In her teenage years, Mary Broad would spend much time up on the moor, fascinated by the stone formations, especially the circle of Hurling Stones (said to be rebellious young maidens turned to stone by a bolt of lightning flung down by an angry God displeased they were dancing on the Sabbath). She was also fascinated by the old burial mounds, and the native herbs, in whose medicinal and other uses she developed a keen interest.

Just after Mary's birth, Grace had followed the local custom of passing the baby through the hole that pierced the centre of the Holy Stone, a large stone that stood on the moor. It was said that this ritual kept the local babies safe from diseases such as rickets and from disasters such as being lost at sea. Grace made the acquaintance at the holy stone of another young mother, Ruth Thomas, who also wanted to give her baby son, whom she called Ricky, the protection said to be provided to newborns by the Holy Stone.

As Grace passed the tiny bundle, wrapped in her shawl, through the hole into Ruth's outstretched arms, she said: 'Now Mary is blessed an' guarded by the spirits of the moor.'

From the moment that William Broad, who had been at sea at the time of Mary's birth, first held his daughter in his arms, he felt a great tenderness and love for her. 'Well, now, thee's made a fine catch, Gracie, tho' a boy would've 'elped me in the boat,' he'd said, picking up the baby. 'No. Ah'm glad this 'un didn't get away.'

He carried Mary to the window, where he looked deeply into her eyes — they were as grey as the stone walls that held the sea back from the village. 'You do 'ave somethin' to tell us with the faraway look, don't you, my pretty? A message from another world, is it, with them eyes of yourn? Well, I'll make sure you'll fear naught of anyone,' he whispered, handing the bundle back to Grace, 'so you can keep that look forever.'

Over the next six years, William and Grace had three more surviving daughters, Elizabeth, Jane and Dolly. Another daughter, Grace, and a son, William (named for their parents), both died in infancy. With so many mouths to feed, life at 30 Lostwithiel Street was a struggle. Grace worked whenever she could, often with a baby strapped to her back. Mary, as the eldest, also had to help earn money from around the age of ten. As it was cheaper for William to have his daughter help him on the boat than to share the catch with others, he began taking her out with him and training her in the ways of fisherfolk. Besides, from the mid-1770s, many of the local sailors had enlisted to fight against the rebel American colonists and Fowey was short of deckhands.

Mary's birthday coincided each year with the May Day celebrations. The bells of St Fimbarrus would ring out and the townsfolk would dress up in colourful costumes and dance the 'Obby 'Oss dance, during which a make-believe monster known as the 'Oss pranced around the town square. A week later, the villagers took part in another ritual, the Faddy dance; again, everyone dressed in their Sunday best and danced through the narrow streets to the beat of a drum and the rhythm of a strolling band.

But there was nothing Mary loved more than setting off from the busy town quay with its pubs and inns and escaping the crowded village. She would perch up on the bow of her father's boat watching the seagulls circling above, with the sea breezes blowing her brown hair off her face as they searched for another catch. True to her caul, she never felt seasick. Neither was she frightened by even the roughest of seas, but just rode with the boat as it pitched through the waves.

Although not able to pull in nets, by the time Mary was around 12, she was as helpful to William as his former crew. Moreover, William far preferred his daughter's company to any male crew. A true salt, more at home in a boat than on land, he soon taught Mary all he knew about his beloved boats, fishing and the sea. And he couldn't have had a more adoring or responsive shipmate. Once he explained a landmark, she had it forever. William said to Grace that he believed Mary's eyes were grey because she had taken in the granite colours of the stone houses of the town.

'A boat of your'n gives you freedom, my gal,' he loved to say, as he set off for the heads with Mary coiling the anchor rope and stowing the painter. 'Not a body can hold you down. You come an' go just as you fancy. You 'old your fate in your 'ands,' he would say, pulling out his old pipe. 'In teachin' you to handle a boat, ahm teachin' you to handle yourself. There's always a livin' on a boat. An' if things get passin' 'ard ashore, now, you'm get to your boat an' away. Once at sea, there's nobody to stop you.'

In time, Mary learned to steer with the tiller as her father ferried folk over to Bodinnick with an incoming tide or across to Polruan with the outgoing tide. She soon proved to be a valuable deckhand, throwing out the lines, hauling in the catch and packing away the fish. She loved the heaving swell beneath their boat as they sailed down past the Blockhouse ruins from which, her father told her, a chain had once been strung to control the ships entering the harbour. Or when they were abreast of Coombe Hawne, William would tell her of the legends of St Catherine's Castle as the boat slipped past the old ruins on the western shore.

There were, of course, times when William wouldn't take his daughter — in particularly bad weather, or late at night, or when he was 'meetin' foreign gentlemen', as he would describe his smuggling activities. Mary knew not to ask questions about these meetings.

While her father taught her the lore of the sea, of boats and of seamanship, Grace taught Mary to sew and cook, and to make infusions from the herbs she loved to collect up on the moor. She also instilled in her daughter an appreciation of the local history and folklore. Neither parent thought it necessary to have any of their daughters taught their letters and numbers at Fowey's private grammar school; and in any case they could never have afforded the fees.

Late one summer afternoon, Mary was returning to Fowey after gathering herbs on the moor. A young farmer she encountered on the way offered her a lift in his wagon. He was taking his vegetables to sell at the Lostwithiel market the next morning, he said.

'D'you hail from Lostwithiel, farmer?' Mary asked him.

'Aye,' he said, looking her in the eye. 'Our farm is close by, at Trewindle. Where be you from?'

'Fowey,' Mary replied, a little self-consciously. 'I am Fisherman Broad's first daughter.'

'I'm a Thomas, first son of James and Ruth. Richard Thomas, at your service.'

The young man touched his cap, making Mary blush. With a start, she remembered her mother telling her about meeting Ruth Thomas and her baby son at the holy stone, just after Mary's birth. She looked at him now, perched on the bench at the front of the wagon and flapping the horse's reins. She felt sure they hadn't met since then, as she would have remembered his tall, thin frame, his kind and open face with its ready smile, his coal-black hair, and his deep brown eyes as rich as fresh-ploughed earth. They didn't say much more during the journey, but Mary was touched that, on alighting from the cart at his turn-off, he gave her a cabbage for her family.

On arriving home, Mary pretended that she had found the cabbage, and didn't mention her meeting with Richard Thomas. Grace wasn't well, and was spending most of the day in bed where her worn body was racked by terrible coughing fits. Mary and her younger sisters took care of the housekeeping and cooking.

Over the following days, Mary's thoughts turned often to the young man she had met on the moor. She started to take an interest in her appearance and took special care with her clothes. She had reached her full height of five foot four inches and was the picture of health. Though petite, she was well proportioned, with an animated, engaging and open face. Her grey eyes were striking; her brown hair straight and silken. Although not conscious of it, she had caught the eye of most of the young men of Fowey.

A week after their first meeting, Mary returned to the moor, but there was no sign of Richard. She timed her next visit to coincide with Lostwithiel's market day and left home at a time when Richard should have been returning to the family farm. This time she was in luck and their paths crossed; again, he offered her a lift. Mary found the young farmer easy to talk to and soon became attracted to him.

Richard had the same inner strength as her father, which made him seem calm and capable. At night, Mary would lie awake in the bed she shared with her young sisters, remembering the way Richard had looked at her. He made her feel that she could trust him with her innermost thoughts. Perhaps he was *the one*, she began to think.

Mary filled in for her mother, whose health remained very poor, until the washing and cleaning jobs dried up as news of

Grace's ill health spread. Her father was away at sea, having taken a job on a merchant ship. Mary became very worried. Without her mother's wages, they couldn't buy enough food. The family's future seemed desperate. Although Mary had worked in domestic service, she hated the work. She would have to find some other way to provide for the family, she realised.

One Sunday evening, Mary made her way to the moor for the annual Harvest Moon Festival held within the Hurling Stones circle. She had planned to meet there some of her girlfriends from Fowey, who were also eager to enjoy the annual ritual which, it was believed, would usher in a good harvest. But it was Richard Thomas who was uppermost in her mind.

As night fell and the piper piped his tune, people began to dance. Mary joined in with a group of young men and women who were dancing together around a huge replica of a sheaf of corn. When she saw Richard on the other side of the circle, her breath caught. He saw her and gave her a broad smile. After the dance ended, they moved towards each other. For the next dance, the dancers formed a human chain. Mary was thrilled when Richard's hands encircled her waist.

Exhausted, the dancers collapsed on the grass by the roaring bonfire, where they refreshed themselves with mugs of French wine. Impulsively and emboldened by the wine, Mary pulled Richard to her and kissed him deeply. She could feel that he adored her and wanted her in return. Just as their passion threatened to engulf them, one of the village elders carrying a flaming torch called to them to make up the numbers for the final dance of the evening. They broke apart but looked at each other longingly. For the moment, they had to join the other dancers, but there was no turning back now. Things would never be the same again. Mary knew that it was just a matter of time before she and Richard would be lovers. It was as if they were now promised to each other.

The first opportunity that the young couple would have to be alone together again would be the following Sunday, as Richard had to return home that night. He was contracted to work on another farm all week. Mary had promised her mother that she would find some work to help feed the family, but she had no idea what she would do. Perhaps it was time to try something different? As she settled by the remains of the bonfire with her friends to sleep, her thoughts were of her next meeting with Richard.

Mary's first priority, on the morning following the Harvest Moon Festival, was to put some food on her family's table. She set off across the moor heading for Fowey. Nothing stirred, apart from the occasional lark hovering above a clump of heath that housed its nest.

Not long after she had left the Hurling Stones and passed by St Cleer on her way to Liskeard, where she hoped to get a lift with a farmer heading southwest towards Lostwithiel and Fowey, she saw the smoke of a fire. As she drew closer, she could see two figures cooking something in a pot.

'What brung you so early to the moor, friend?' a tall, black-haired woman of about 30 years of age, dressed in a long black overcoat and a pretty dress, called out as Mary approached.

'I'm hopin' to find a cart travellin' to Fowey,' Mary replied. She noticed the woman's white, thin-featured face and her piercing dark eyes. 'I must get some work,' she added. Having not had any breakfast, she grew hungry at the smell of the broth the woman was stirring over the fire.

'Fowey be a fair distance,' the woman said, dipping a mug into the pot, 'an' you with no food, I be bound. Here, have some broth, girl.' She handed Mary the steaming mug. 'I be Cath'rine, an' this'un's Marg'ret,' she said, pointing to her companion, a broad-faced, red-haired woman with blue eyes and freckles who looked about 25. Mary noticed that the coat and dress she wore were well made and expensive.

'I should keep goin',' Mary said, suspecting the motives of the pair, but her hunger overcame her doubts. 'But it do smell good, an' 'tis true I've no food.' She sighed and seated herself on a log by the fire. 'I'm Mary, Mary Broad.'

Mary explained to her new acquaintances that she was in urgent need of paying work.

'Well, now, Mary Broad,' Catherine said thoughtfully, with a glance at Margaret. 'If'n it's work you're after, you could do worse than come with us. A certain situation we'em be contemplatin'.'

'What sort of situation would that be?' Mary asked warily. ''Twill be work enough for three?'

'Aye, plenty enough, I'm thinkin'. We'em buyin' an' sellin' a parcel of expensive clothin', you might say,' Catherine said.

'Where'bouts, then?' Mary asked.

'The town o' the toffs,' Margaret said, stirring the embers of the fire with a stick and pointing to the southeast. ''Oity-toity Plymouth Town. There be twice the work and thrice the money than your Fowey.'

'O' course, that be if'n you *do* want work,' Catherine added. 'We know Plymouth an' 'er folk right well. It is only half a day's journey by cart. We'll be there this afternoon an' we can fix you with a situation. Why, you'll make more money one day in Plymouth than one month in your piddlin' Fowey and be back 'ome afore week's end, eh.'

Mary thought about the women's offer. They both had fine clothes already. Perhaps they worked in the clothing industry? They also seemed to have plenty of food in their bags, so they must be earning money. She certainly needed some quick cash, but there was something about the women's offer that made her feel uneasy. Then she pictured her ailing mother and thought of the food she could buy if she had some money. And if there was anything to spare, she might be able to buy something pretty to wear when next she saw Richard. She broke her silence, agreeing to join the two women on their journey to Plymouth.

After dousing the fire, the trio walked to Liskeard, where Catherine paid for three seats on a cart that was headed for the Saltash ferry. On the journey Mary learned that the women's full names were Margaret Shepherd and Catherine Fryer, but not what sort of work they did in the clothing business or what work she might find with them.

After catching the ferry across the lower reaches of the River Tamar, from Saltash to the Plymouth side, Catherine and Margaret said they wanted to get something to eat at St Budeaux. They would then walk into Plymouth, instead of going by cart, they explained to Mary.

Mary followed her companions to the King's Head, a rowdy public house with stables set back from the road. It was full of drinkers and drunks, prostitutes and stable hands, many of whom greeted Catherine and Margaret by name. As Margaret and Mary made themselves comfortable by the fire in a back room of the inn, Catherine went off to speak with the drivers in the stable. An old waiter brought them some bread, cheese and ale. Catherine soon returned and nodded to Margaret, who returned the nod.

A middle-aged man with a limp appeared beside their table. 'Understand you'll be workin' late tonight, ladies.' He giggled drunkenly. 'Ere's a little Dutch courage for you.' He slurped a tot of brandy into their tankards of beer and then stumbled away.

'Thank 'ee kindly,' Catherine called after the man. 'Naught wrong with a bit o' Dutch courage.'

'I thought that were a French bottle?' Mary said, recognising the French brandy that her father smuggled into the country from time to time.

'Only a sayin', m'dear: "Dutch courage." 'Ave'n 'ee heerd tell of 'ut?' Catherine then looked around before lowering her voice. 'They's sayin' there's a toff lady from Launceston comin' down by coach on the 'ighway tonight on the Callington coach. Only the driver, an' all her goods for passage to France.'

'So, she's easy pickins, then, isn't she?' Margaret said.

Mary was shocked. 'You're not goin' to …? I thought you worked in a clothing business?'

'We do, dearie, but 'tis our own!' Catherine cackled. She pushed Mary's tankard towards her. 'You want money for your dear old mother, doan you?'

'You know I do, but …'

'So, you're goin' to help us, then. Good. 'Tis the job we promised.'

Mary dipped her head and took a sip from her tankard.

'Mind you,' Margaret said, 'it may be we'll make enough tonight to feed that family of yourn for a year.'

'But you can't stop a coach on the king's highway. Not two women.'

'That's why you're here, ducky. Two an' one make three, doan it?' Catherine said. 'One to 'old the driver, one for the toff, an' one for the goods.'

'Hold the driver?' Mary asked, forgetting herself and taking another sip from her tankard. 'Hold 'im with what?'

'This little beauty,' Margaret hissed, pulling back her smart overcoat to reveal a pistol.

Mary had pictured herself buying and selling clothes in a busy Plymouth marketplace, not engaging in highway robbery! She couldn't imagine stopping a horse-drawn coach in the middle of the night. Yet, she was torn: she was now a long way from home, and once they got the money she could return to Fowey and no one should be the wiser. She took another sip. The brandy and ale was a strong, heady combination. These women were tough, she realised. But her family needed food. Her head started to spin; she felt both frightened and a little excited by the turn of events.

'Now, Mary Broad,' Catherine said, standing up and leaning over her. 'What's it to be? Do 'ee 'ave the 'art to help yer poorly mother, or not?'

'If you swear not to harm the old lady,' Mary said. She stood up herself with a little difficulty. 'Otherwise, I want no part of it.'

'Course we sharn't hurt 'er,' Catherine said, pinching her arm. 'On my word. I doan want to hang, girl.'

Her word may not be worth much, Mary thought, but it appeared to be decided.

By the light of the taproom fire, Catherine and Margaret discussed how they would stop the night coach. Their informants had told them the time to expect the coach and the name of the sole passenger, a Miss Agnes Lakeman. They had done it before, Catherine explained with increasing merriment. There was nothing to it — once they produced a pistol, that is.

They would wear stage masks, Catherine said, so they wouldn't be identified. While Margaret and Mary held up the coach, Catherine would relieve the passenger of her fine clothes. Nor could they be traced, as Miss Lakeman was taking passage to France early the next morning and wouldn't be around to give evidence. All that Mary would be required to do was stand guard with one of the pistols. Mary knew that this was highway robbery, for which the punishment was death.

'Gettin' dark,' Catherine said, looking out of the smoky window. 'Best be startin'.' Picking up her bag, an empty sack and two lanterns, one of which she handed to Margaret, she led them out into the warm summer night. They walked down the moonlit road back towards the ferry.

''Tis 'ere when the coach is slowest,' Catherine explained. 'After it starts from the ferry, they come roun' this corner slow-like afore they start trottin' along. An' we stop 'em with this.' She pointed to a log lying beneath the hawthorn hedge. 'Give us an 'and, Marg'ret,' she ordered. The two women rolled the log out from under the hedge. 'We'll lay it 'crosst the road when we hears the horses a-comin'.'

Catherine explained that both the coach driver and the horses would see the log. At this late hour, they would be the only travellers and should be easy to rob. Margaret then drew out her pistol, which glinted in the moonlight, making Mary's heart skip a beat. She showed Mary how to cock and, if necessary, fire the pistol, which she boasted she had stolen from a drunken ensign home from the war against the American rebels. Used to handling oars, anchors, nets and lines, Mary picked up the technique immediately.

'But I'll not be usin' it,' she warned them, 'not to shoot, anyway. Only for stopping the coach.'

'As you please, dearie. As you please,' Catherine said.

With the log in place, and a lantern lit but shielded from view, the three women waited by the hedge, where they were barely visible in the moonlight. For a while, the only sound that Mary could hear was a nearby night owl and her own heart beating quickly. Then Catherine hissed, and soon there was the snort of a horse, the thud of hooves, and the sound of coach wheels turning on the road. Catherine and Margaret opened the lantern and placed it in front of the log. The three women looked at each other, then put on their masks. In silence, in the night shadows, they were ready to make their move.

In what seemed to Mary a matter of seconds, the postillion lantern appeared, swaying in the dark, followed immediately by the outline of the large coach. The driver shouted when he saw the illuminated log blocking his path. Then he was upon the log. 'Hold you, hold!' he called to the two horses, pulling back on the reins. 'Whoa, whoa, whoa.' The animals whinnied; he shouted again, a foul oath to the sky.

'Who goes there?' he called in what sounded to Mary like a French accent. 'In the name of the king, clear yon log from the highway. This is punishable by death. I carry the Royal mail.'

'Stand and deliver,' Margaret shouted, stepping forward from the shadows at the nearside of the coach. Her pistol, its hammer clearly cocked, was pointed directly at the driver.

'What? Just for a woman in a dress?' he scoffed. The horses stamped their feet impatiently.

'Nay, driver — not one, not two, but three pretty maidens at yer service!' Catherine shouted.

'Oh, that's your game? No, you don't,' the driver said, lifting his whip and lashing it towards Margaret. It became entangled in the hedge, whereupon Catherine sprang forward and pulled it from his grasp.

'Highway robbers!' he shouted. 'You'll hang for this!'

'Aye! An' you'll be shot if yer doan stop there!' Catherine cried, pointing her pistol at the driver's face. 'Stop where you are!' Calling to Mary behind her, she ordered: 'Keep 'im covered, girl. I'll greet 'er ladyship.'

Stepping forward in what seemed to her a dream, Mary held her pistol with two hands pointing straight at the driver, a big, round-faced man with a moustache. She was grateful for the mask she wore.

'In God's name,' the driver swore, dropping the reins and raising his hands. 'Three o' the country's worst bitches!'

'Hand over your arms!' Margaret barked.

'Damn your eyes,' the driver spat. But he removed a pistol from its leather holster on the seatback and tossed it on to the roadside grass. 'You'll hang for this, ye witches — all three of you.'

'Your purse an' your coin, woman,' Catherine said, after wrenching open the door of the coach. There was a cry from within.

'Sharply, now, we doan 'ave all night. Put your bonnet, scarf an' jewellery into this sack 'ere. Or I'll blast you to kingdom come!'

Mary caught sight of the old woman in the moonlight as she stepped down to remove her jewellery and finest clothing before handing over her travel box. Mary thought she was so beautifully dressed, she could spare the items that Catherine was taking.

Meanwhile, the horses stamped the ground, making the harness rattle and the coach wobble. The driver kept his hands raised, but continued to curse his assailants.

Then Catherine, flinging a final insult at the driver and warning him not to try and follow them, rejoined Margaret and Mary. She tossed the now-bulging sack over her shoulder. ''Tis time to disappear,' she hissed. Extinguishing the lantern, she led them through a hole in the hedge to a sheep path that wound its way across the fields and to a disused stable.

Safely inside, Catherine removed her mask and grinned at her accomplices. 'Well, now. We'em done it! An' a good haul, betimes.'

''Ow's your nerve, Mary?' Margaret asked, laughing.

'In God's truth,' Mary said, 'I'm not sure. 'Twas all a blur.'

'Aye. You did fine, Mary Broad. Just fine. An' you can see why we needed the three of us,' Margaret said.

'What if they recognised us?' Mary asked nervously.

'We was masked,' Margaret said.

'As long as we're not betrayed,' Mary said.

'By who? Nay, we'll never hear o' that lot again,' Catherine said. 'An' you'll be fine, Mary. 'Tis a long way from Plymouth to Fowey. You'll never see 'em again.' She stooped to open the sack. 'Let's see what we 'ave, an' then share the load.'

Catherine tipped from the sack a purse full of coins, jewellery, a shawl, a fine pair of London silk gloves, a parasol, a coat and a silk bonnet.

'Here,' she said, handing Mary a handful of heavy coins and the bonnet. 'For your troubles, dearie. A fine silk bonnet, pretty enough to catch a sea-captain. Silk it is, an' sure to fetch a shiny shillin' or two at any market. Oh, an' I'll have me pistol back.'

''Tis fine silk, too,' Mary said, thinking of the valuable bales of silk that her father had smuggled into Fowey over the years. 'That'll do me, Cath. I'll sell that quick enough for a pretty penny to feed my family.'

The spoils divided, Mary and her companions agreed it was best to go their separate ways and lie low for a while. If Mary ever wanted more work, Catherine said, she could always get word to her through the innkeeper at the King's Head, where they had supped earlier.

Catherine and Margaret headed off in the direction of the market town of Tavistock. Mary, shaking now with the shock of what they had done, headed towards home, the coins and bonnet hidden inside her clothing. She felt she had never held anything as fine, feminine and soft as that silk bonnet.

On the day following her return home, Mary went to see Richard, who was working at Woodland Farm, not far from his father's farm at Trewindle and near where the St Neots River ran into the River Fowey. She couldn't wait until Sunday night to see him; her news was too important. Besides, anything could happen between now and then.

She found him stacking hay in the barn.

'Mary!' he exclaimed. 'What brings you here?'

'Oh, Richard,' she sighed. 'Events have turned, much to the worse. I must speak to you.'

'Come, then,' he said, taking her arm and leading her into the barn. 'What ails thee?'

'Well, I must show you this.' She produced the silk bonnet and, as he watched, placed it carefully on her head. 'What do you say?'

He gazed at her lovingly. 'Suits thee well, lass. It shows off thy pretty little pink lips. Makes 'ee look like an angel.'

There was a long silence.

'But how come you by that bonnet, girl?'

Mary told Richard all that had occurred since she had seen him just a few days before.

'God in heaven, lass,' Richard said, tenderly taking her hands in his. 'I fear for you. An' us. Highway robbery is punishable by death.'

Mary reassured him that she wouldn't be recognised and that all would be well, so long as he stood by her. She had only wanted to help her ailing mother and young sisters, she explained. She prepared to take her leave. 'We'll talk more on Sunday e'en,' she said.

'Till Sunday e'en, then, my pretty, bonnet-wearing Mary,' Richard said. 'But if 'ee needs help, then 'tis me to ask. I want to help all I can.'

'I won't forget your sayin' that, Richard,' Mary said. She hid the bonnet in her clothing and followed Richard to the barn door and out into the bright sunlight.

'But be careful who ye sells bonnet to,' he called after her as she set off down the road to Fowey. 'Only sum'un ye can trust, Mary.'

As she headed home, Mary came up with a plan. 'I must ask the fishermen to sell the bonnet to them sailors who are only visitin' — the way Father gets rid of smugglers' goods.'

The next morning, after preparing a meagre meal for her mother and sisters, Mary set off to find a buyer for her contraband goods. She headed for the King of Prussia public house, where she knew that some of her absent father's friends would be having a tot of rum after a night of fishing. I can trust them, she thought. They could tell her who was visiting the port, and who was about to leave. She pushed open the door into the old inn and sat down on a stool beside one of her father's oldest friends, James Tregare.

'Why, 'course I'll help William's daughter,' old Tregare said kindly when she explained her predicament.

'Thank you,' Mary said.

'But if you be wantin' to sell some clothin', I'd take it to old Jim Matthews,' he continued, taking a pull on his pipe. 'He's travellin' all the while on the coaches, he is. Tell 'im your ma's poorly now and yer father's still away.'

'Does he know people who are buying goods, then?' Mary asked.

'Aye, he does. He knows people from here to Lunnon who will buy and sell,' Tregare assured her. 'Fact, he'll be back tonight, so come back then, girl, an' I'll show 'im to you. But bring what you sell, mind. He won't be interested, otherwise.'

'And he can be trusted?' she asked.

'Aye, far as I know, Mary. Far as I know.' He took a last drink from his tankard and turned back to the bar.

Returning that night with the bonnet concealed beneath her gown, Mary again found James Tregare in the smoky bar. They would have to wait for Matthews, he explained, who was due to return from Launceston any moment by coach. When Matthews eventually appeared in the doorway, he spotted Tregare and made his way across the room towards where they sat at the bar. After ordering Matthews a drink, Tregare introduced Mary to his regular drinking partner, explaining that she had something to sell. Matthews was interested, but suggested that they all go out to the stables where they could talk in private and Mary could show him the goods.

When he saw the bonnet, he put on a traveller's glove and inspected it closely. 'Very pretty,' he said. 'Pure silk and all — just the bob for a lady of Lunnon. An' I doan doubt it 'as a good pedigree. Hails from a good home, you might say,' he said with a wink.

''Tis true,' said Mary impatiently. 'But what's its value, pray?'

'Barely worn, as 'tis,' Matthews mused, turning the bonnet over thoughtfully. 'For you, 12 pence — one round shilling.'

'Is that all?' Mary asked, looking at Tregare, who raised his eyebrows.

''Less I can sell it to a traveller with French customers,' Matthews said. 'Likely he would pay a little more — perhaps double. I know you're in hard times, girl. Make it one silver shilling now. But come back Friday night when I'm meetin' him, an' I'll see what I can do for you betimes.'

'I'll take the shilling till then,' Mary said, holding out her hand, 'as a down payment.'

'Down payment, eh? We'll see. For now you've pennies in the hand, no questions asked. Never any questions, mind, when

Jimmy Matthews takes your goods, eh James?' he said, turning to Tregare. He reached into his coat-tail pocket for the coins.

Mary felt uneasy. 'No questions — your word?'

'Good as is,' said the fence, handing over 12 copper pennies and taking the bonnet, not really answering her question.

The next day, Mary bought enough food to last the family until her father was due to return home the following week. She also arranged for the local surgeon to visit her mother, but he was able to do little other than to prescribe a soothing mixture for her throat.

In the hope that Matthews would have another shilling for her from the sale of the bonnet, Mary decided on the Friday evening to return to the King of Prussia. Again she felt uneasy, but another shilling would make all the difference; it was worth taking the risk, she decided. Tregare was nowhere to be seen in the bar, and Mary went to wait for him out by the stables, as they had arranged.

Suddenly, there was a commotion as a coach pulled up. Two men alighted, one of whom Mary was surprised to see was Jim Matthews. Before she could say anything, his companion called out in a voice that sounded vaguely familiar: 'That's her, right enough! 'Tis same clothes 'n' all. Grab er, man. 'Elp me grab her!'

Matthews and the other man sprang forward and took hold of Mary's arms. It was then she recognised the French accent. Her accuser, who went by the name of Marcel, was the part-French, part-Cornish coach driver she and her accomplices had held up on the moonlit king's highway just a few nights before. Mary's heart sank as Matthews sent word for the parish constable to be fetched.

The previous day, Matthews had offered to sell the bonnet to Marcel over a beer at the nearby Old Lugger Inn. In addition to driving coaches from Launceston to Plymouth, Marcel also drove them to Fowey and happened to be in town. He had quickly realised where the expensive silk bonnet had come from and reckoned he would get a bigger reward from Agnes Lakeman if he returned her bonnet than if he sold it to a buyer in England or France. He would also get a handsome fee for turning the thief over to the watchhouse and for giving evidence against her in court. He licked his lips. Marcel offered Matthews a share of his reward from Agnes Lakeman if Matthews would agree to take him to the thief. They both stood to gain more by turning her in. The agreement struck, the two rogues had shaken hands and finished their drinks.

When the parish constable arrived at the King of Prussia, reeking of cheap wine and unsteady on his feet, he took one look at Mary and said, 'Aye, she's one of 'em smuggling Broads, ones that've done wreckin' an all. We'll jest put her in yon watchhouse.'

Mary was marched to a room behind the stables that was used as a lockup. The constable roughly pushed her into the room. 'Ben gettin' away wuth ut fer too long, yer bleedin' Cornish wrecker, you — they'll take care of 'ee at Plymouth Watchhouse, girlie.' He locked the door and stumbled off into the night.

In despair, Mary looked around her. The room was bare apart from a rude bed and a bucket. It had one window set very high in the wall. There was no way for her to escape. Mary sat on the bed and tried to collect her thoughts. What would her mother and sisters think when she didn't return home? Thank goodness her father was due home soon. Then she thought of Richard. She *had* to get out before Sunday. What would he think if she failed to meet him as planned? Distraught, she couldn't think of anyone who could help her. No one knew where she was. She would have to help herself, but how? She decided that she must try to get a message to her family before she was taken to the Plymouth Watchhouse.

When, some time later, there was a rattle at the door and the sound of keys, Mary's heart skipped a beat. The door opened to reveal a guard with some bread and water. She recognised him as Dunstan, the 'village idiot'. She knew that Dunstan loved his drink, and a plan quickly came to mind. She offered to give him the cost of a bottle of rum if he would send a messenger to nearby Lostwithiel Street to fetch her sister Dolly, who should be at home.

After what seemed like hours, Dunstan returned with Dolly, whom he agreed to let into the lockup for a few minutes in return for the coins Mary had promised him. The sisters looked at each other for a second, then flew into a hug.

'Mary, Mary, what are you doin' here?' Dolly asked anxiously.

'Oh, Dolly, I must go away now, an' I want you to look after Mother till Father returns next week,' Mary replied.

'But why, Mary? Come home now. Mother needs you, she does. She's still sick in bed,' Dolly said.

'Dolly, listen to me. I can't. You must do as I tell you.'

Mary sat her sister down on the bed and explained that she must tell their parents that Mary had stolen a bonnet from a rich

31

woman in order to buy food and medicine. She would be taken to Plymouth, where she would have to appear in court.

''Tain't fair, Mary,' Dolly said, beginning to cry. 'Mother's sick an' needed the med'cine.'

'I know, Doll,' Mary said, wiping Dolly's tears. 'There's a lot not fair for poor fisherfolk like us. But I'm a Broad an' I'll not go under. But you must help me.'

She told Dolly the name of the prison she thought she would be taken to in Plymouth. Dolly must ask the minister of St Fimburras, the Reverend Tobias Salt, to write a note explaining what had happened and have it delivered to Richard Thomas at his family's farm before Sunday night. That was everything she could think of. After a final hug and some shared tears, Mary asked Dolly to be brave, as they might not see each other for a very long time.

On waking up early the next morning, Mary realised that she hadn't just been having a bad dream; her predicament was real. When a hungover Dunstan opened her door, she saw waiting outside the parish constable and the driver, Marcel, with an accomplice. 'We 'ave a liddle journey in mind for thee, we do,' Marcel said. And before Mary could reply, he marched her straight to a waiting coach that he was taking to Plymouth. He pushed her up the steps and into a seat, then locked the door. 'I 'ope 'ee enjoys scenery on way to Plymouth,' he said sarcastically.

Sitting stony-faced in the carriage and refusing to show any emotion, Mary wondered as they drove through the villages she had known all her life when she would see them again. She swore to herself that she would return as soon as she was able. The further they travelled along the country roads towards Plymouth, the stronger her resolve became. By the time they reached Plymouth, she had promised herself to return at all costs.

Mary was bundled out of the carriage in the town square and escorted straight to the Watchhouse, where she would be held until the mayor was ready to formally charge her with highway robbery. She was unceremoniously ushered into an ill-lit room. The first thing that hit her was the stench of unemptied buckets and unwashed bodies in the airless room. As her eyes adjusted to the gloom, she saw other women sitting on the straw that covered the floor or lying asleep in corners. Then she heard a familiar voice.

'Bless me! You too, Mary?' said Catherine Fryer. 'I thought you was far away by now. How come they got you?'

'You said them masks'd work fine!' Mary said bitterly.

'Aye, we've all 'ad bad luck,' said Catherine. 'There be a rat in every inn'd betray you for a florin or two.' She spat on the floor.

'An' Margaret?' Mary asked.

'There, asleep,' Catherine said. She pointed to a bundle in a darkened corner.

'They took the three of us, then,' Mary said, shaking her head at the calamity.

'Bastards!' swore Catherine. 'We was dobbed by that limpin' rat from the King's Head. Spies for the coach, the cripple!'

'An' so much for us never hearin' from that driver again,' Mary said. 'He caught me, red-'anded, thanks to a two-faced fence name of Jim Matthews.'

Some time later the three women were brought before Thomas Nicolls, mayor of Plymouth. A clerk read out their charges. The driver Marcel took great delight in swearing an oath that he had seen all three commit the crime. This satisfied the mayor, who gave his name as the authority committing the women to trial for highway robbery. This trial, he told them, would be held at the convenience of the judges when they held the next county assizes at the closest court at Exeter.

Mary hoped that her extenuating circumstances would help to reduce her sentence. After all, some people were transported to the American colonies for theft, although she had heard that the colonists were now refusing to take convicts, having won their war for independence against England. At the present time, then, there was nowhere to send those convicts who were banished beyond the seas instead of being hanged.

After their committal, the three highway robbers were placed in a cold and crowded cell in Plymouth Gaol, along with other prisoners, to await their trial. The turnkeys said they were allowed a limited number of visitors while awaiting trial, but none after sentencing. Mary had no way of knowing whether Dolly had managed to get word to Richard, so she was mightily relieved some days later when a turnkey called her name and said she had visitors. She followed the turnkey to an outer room where, in the brighter light, she saw Richard's tall straight figure, cap in hand, standing in the centre of the room.

'Mary!' he cried. He took the dishevelled-looking figure in his arms. 'Oh, Mary! Are you alright?'

'Aye, Richard, right enough considerin',' she said, holding him tightly until the turnkey motioned for them to separate.

'Your Dolly came to the farm with letter from Reverend Salt an' told me you was taken,' Richard said. 'What a bastard is that Matthews. I'd like to deal with 'im. You was only helpin' your family.'

'An' missin' Sunday, too, Richard. I so wanted us to be together.'

'Aye, Sunday. No matter. I'll wait for you, Mary.'

'We doan have long now,' Mary said, reassured by Richard's promise. 'Listen, Richard. I'm hoping the judge will take pity on my sick mother and pardon us.'

'I got somethin' for ye, to keep in the leather pouch I know ye keep at yer breast,' Richard said. He took a penny from his pocket. 'See, it breaks in half down the middle. I cut it with me axe. Half is for you, Mary, and t'other half is mine. 'Tis like the old Bodmin sayin': "If yer take half a penny away you can't die till you bring it back to its mate." You see?' he said, pressing Mary's half of the coin into her hand.

'Oh, Richard,' she said, looking at the coin. 'It'll pull me back to you.'

'Aye, and it's a special penny for you, Mary. I know you don't know your numbers, but it's 1765 — your birth year — and that's written right under King Georgie's head,' he said, pointing to the date.

'That'll care for me while I'm inside, Richard. But I want you to care for my mother and father, till I get back.'

'Aye, 'course,' he said, taking her hands. 'But your father's here right now. I brought him down. He's waitin' outside and wants to see you — wants to see you on his own. Cut up and all — yeah, he just got back from sea. But I'll go and get 'im an' I promise to come down when I can from the farm and see to your ailin' mam when he's fishin'. I'll bide till you come back, Mary.'

'An' I'll carry you inside me till I get out,' she promised. 'I'll come back, I promise. Oh, Richard, you will give me the strength I need.'

'Afore you know it, we'll keep that promise we made up on the moor,' he said, turning to go. And with a long, lingering look, he turned and walked out the door to freedom while Mary waited for her father.

'Mary,' is all William Broad said as he appeared in the doorway, a fisherman's cap covering his tousled hair, and moist eyes shining from his craggy face. Shoving his pipe into the pocket of his navyblue smock, he put his huge mariner's arms around her, hiding her inside his embrace like a baby.

'Father,' she murmured into his chest.

'You needn't done it, girl. I got back earlier from that trading voyage with good-enough pay to put food back on the table.'

'I'm sorry,' she said. 'I was so worried about Mother.'

'Well, I love you for it, my darling daughter, and now it's done we just gotta get you home,' he said.

'I'm hopin' they'll hear my plea about Mother bein' sick an' all and you away, and let me come back home.'

'Well, I need you, girl. I'm gonna lose your mother afore 'ee get out of this dungeon here,' William said in a choked voice. 'I'll be needin' my Mary for company, not to mention some help with the boat, that I've taught you so much about. Don't want that to go to waste, do we?'

'Well, let's pray the judges have some heart,' Mary said boldly.

'Speakin' of heart, now,' William said. 'That Richard who brought me down here on his cart — he's a fine lad. You make sure you don't lose 'im, then.'

'I won't forget him, Father. Tell Mother I'll always love her. And when I get back, I'll stand by you and take her place looking after you till I die.'

'Yet, it was me who always said that we Broads look after our own and I'd keep you from harm's way. But doan forget what Jack Sheppard did and try to escape yourself.' he said, seeing the turnkey approaching. He got ready to leave.

'I won't forget a thing you taught me, and I will behave as a Broad through and through, till I get back to your side, Father. I promise,' Mary said. She watched her father being led out, then turned to confront her fate inside. The visits from Richard and her father had strengthened her resolve.

So in the cold winter month of March 1786, Mary Broad, Catherine Fryer and Margaret Shepherd were taken with other prisoners by cart from Plymouth Gaol to Exeter. Although they set off before first light they did not arrive till after dark, making it a long and cold journey in the chilly open air. They were also all chained for the duration of the journey. They were placed in a large cell, again with a stone floor and straw bedding. On 20 March, the three women were escorted into the court before the two judges who were conducting the assizes for Lent, Sir James Eyre and Sir Beaumont Hotham.

One by one the three women stood in the dock while the judges read out the cases against them. The coach driver, Marcel, who was also representing Agnes Lakeman, now in France, gave his evidence. Further evidence was given by Jim Matthews in Mary's case, and by the limping informant from the King's Head in the cases against Catherine and Margaret. All three informers were being paid by the court for their evidence.

Although they had been given the opportunity to defend themselves, none of the three accused had the means or ability to hire a defence lawyer or to organise independent character witnesses. Their pleas to the judges fell on deaf ears. Mary's hopes that the judges would show compassion for her situation had come to naught. She steeled herself for their verdict:

'Mary Broad, Catherine Fryer and Margaret Shepherd, for feloniously assaulting Agnes Lakeman, spinster, in the King's Highway, feloniously putting her in corporal fear and danger of her life, and feloniously taking from her person and against her will in the said Highway one silk bonnet value twelve shillings and other goods valued at eleven pounds eleven shillings, her property — found Guilty of Highway Robbery, each guilty party to be hanged by the neck until dead.'

CHAPTER 2

Saved from the hangman's noose

*Mary, stunned by the verdict, is flung into a dank cell to await
execution. Her luck turns at the 11th hour, when her death
sentence is commuted to transportation. However, the place to
which she is to be sent is a distant land of bloodthirsty savages
from which there could be little hope of return.*

After their death sentences were handed down, Mary and her
two partners in crime were taken back to Exeter Gaol
where, with other condemned felons, they would await their
deaths. It was a terrible turn of events. Not only had Catherine and
Margaret's ill-conceived plan backfired, but it now looked as if it

would claim all three young lives. There seemed little chance of getting a reprieve. Before England had lost its war against the rebel American colonists a few years earlier, many death sentences had been commuted to transportation. But with the loss of the American colonies, the government now had nowhere to dump its felons. With prisons full to bursting, space had to be found in the gaols as quickly as possible. So, as the taunting turnkeys warned, the three women might be 'turned off' any day soon to make room for others.

At the news of their bleak prospects, Catherine and Margaret sobbed uncontrollably. Mary, by contrast, found an inner strength that enabled her to face her destiny with some dignity. There was no possible means of escape from the stone fortress; even Jack Sheppard couldn't have cracked this one, Mary thought, looking around her. And there was no chance now of saying goodbye to her dying mother, her beloved father or her three sisters, let alone her dear Richard. Exeter was a long way from Fowey, and condemned prisoners weren't allowed visitors. In any case, Mary didn't want them to learn the worst; it would break their hearts, as would a farewell meeting before she was hanged. It was best to let them think that she was in prison serving out her sentence. Everyone knew that the wheels of justice turned slowly. When she was given the date of her execution she would dictate a farewell letter, but until then she would spare their feelings. Her half of the 1765 penny Richard had given her gave her comfort. But even as her fate looked likely, Mary clung to her faith that something would save her.

While Margaret and Catherine refused to be cheered up, Mary found a kindred spirit in one of the older male prisoners, James 'Paddy' Martyn, whom she had met while walking around the exercise yard. He was a short, stocky Irishman from County Antrim, aged in his mid-thirties, with long black hair that was already going grey. He was a stonemason, he said, and it was true that his rugged face looked as if it had been fashioned by a sculptor, though it frequently broke into a kindly smile. When Mary asked what his crime had been, he said with a lisp: 'I been nabbed for nothin', lass — just for pinchin' a few screws and bolts. Oh, and a bit of old lead and iron.'

'They doan sound valuable,' Mary said. 'Why they hangin' 'ee for that?'

'I won't hang!' Martyn spat. 'But truth is, lass,' he said, dropping his voice to a whisper and looking over his shoulder, 'the owner of that there metal, this English toff — name of Lord William Viscount Courtenay of Powderm Castle, no less — has a house not far from here, an' he has first-class connections with His Majesty's judges and wants me turned off.'

'Bastards,' Mary said. 'The toffs have got the whole country sewn up. It's like the old toff I pinched the bonnet from — she wouldn't miss it, but the courts give me a death sentence. It stinks.'

'Take heart, my Mary,' he said, as they took another turn around the stone courtyard. 'They would have hanged us off by now if they were going to, mark my word. Something's in the wind, I can feel it — I read all newspaper I can lay my hands on an' things is changing. I also keep records in me diary, 'cause I'm a writin' type. I'm markin' off the days in 'ere and I defend meself in me trials, I do. You see, the government's gettin' softer since losin' the American colonies.'

'Why is that, James?' Mary asked.

'Government can't justify hangin' so many young people for such small crimes anymore. Things is changin', they is,' he said mysteriously as they returned to their cells.

'I'm prayin' for a miracle,' Mary said. 'I've got to get back to Fowey before my mother dies, or if I'm too late for that I've got my father to care for. I know he'll be alone when my mam dies and will need me.'

'Yer poor gal,' Martyn said kindly.

After a pause, as if to gauge Martyn's trustworthiness, Mary added: 'An' I left behind my man, as well. Richard Thomas. I love him. He promised he'll be waitin' for me.'

'You'll get back in time, lass. I know it,' Martyn reassured her. 'An' if this Richard is the man for you, why, he'll wait for ye.' He paused and looked around. 'But if you ever have a chance to get out of here and need help, James Martyn is at your service, to be sure.'

Deeply touched, Mary smiled back at him. She recognised that she had her first real ally if ever any opportunity to escape should arise.

The weeks dragged on, and still there was no date announced for her execution. James might be right about the changing times, Mary thought. There was no word throughout the spring. Even when the first anniversary of the robbery came around in the summer of 1786, Mary still didn't know if she would hang. By now her dress was becoming threadbare and dirty from lying on the floor on straw mattresses that were rarely changed. Her shoes, nibbled by rats when she was asleep, were full of holes. Catherine had obtained a needle and some thread from a turnkey with whom she had spent the night, so they were able to patch the worst of their clothes.

Meanwhile, as James Martyn had predicted, circumstances outside the prison were indeed changing, as the broadsheets and newspapers were reporting. Some of the turnkeys who could read would pass the news on to the felons. They recounted that the new prime minister — 'William Pitt, the younger', as he was known, having followed his father into the job a few years earlier — had started to reform the prisons. In fact, the turnkeys reported, a penal reformer by the name of John Howard was always in the papers calling for more humane policies towards felons who had been sentenced to hang. Having visited many gaols and interviewed a number of inmates, Howard told the newspapers that capital punishment was too cruel for petty thieves, who often stole through poverty and desperation. He recommended continuing the transportation of felons, rather than executing them, and challenged the government to find a new dumping ground for felons to replace the American colonies.

Then, in September 1786, Charlie Spence, a bespectacled and friendly turnkey when he wasn't in his cups, brought a copy of *The London Chronicle* into the prison. Calling Mary over to the bars of her cell, he indicated that he had something of interest to tell her. Charlie had taken rather a shine to Mary and sometimes brought her extra rations of water and bread.

'Well, me darlin', I have some good news.' He held up the newspaper and grinned. 'Your sisters tell me you don't read nor nothin', not knowing your letters an' all, so I'll break the good news to you first, I shall.'

''Bout what, Charlie?' Mary said nervously, fearing that a date had finally been set for their execution.

'You lovely ladies might be settin' off for a little holiday instead of swingin' from a gallows,' he said, laughing.

'Now, what do you mean exactly?' she demanded. 'Are we swingin' or what?'

'No. On the contrary, me darlin'. This 'ere article says that our esteemed secretary of the colonies has found a new home for you, 'cause it seems our tender-hearted prime minister don't want you hanged.'

'Pray, tell where, Charlie,' Mary said.

'Let me see,' Charlie said, squinting at the newspaper. 'Called Botany Bay, it says. An' it's an island with savages in the South Seas, it is — so you won't be lonely, Miss Mary.' He laughed again.

'If that be true, Charlie,' Mary said, ''Twas kind of you to tell me first. I'll tell the others.'

'And don't forget, me darlin', now you owe Charlie a favour, you do.' He fixed her meaningfully with his eyes.

'I understand, Charlie,' Mary said, hoping to have left Exeter Gaol before she was forced to compromise herself to a turnkey.

Mary told James Martyn the news during their next walk around the yard. 'You wait,' he said. 'Mayhaps we Exeter felons will be the first lot sent to this Botany Bay.'

Mary passed on the news to the women's cells. Within seconds they were all a-buzz with the development. Most of those condemned to hang could now be transported instead. Over the following days, more news filtered into the cells. It seemed that the government had been debating this move for some time. When Charlie brought in the next day's newspaper, he told Mary that, apparently, Botany Bay had been discovered some 16 years earlier by the famous Captain James Cook but, according to the paper, the government hadn't taken any interest in the place until the American colonies were lost.

'Mind you, Mary Broad,' Catherine announced pessimistically one morning as she sewed a patch on her dress. 'The guv'ment will prob'ly work us to death anyway. Some say we'll be cuttin' down trees and farming to grow food, so it'll just take a little longer to work us to death than by hangin' us.'

'Or else,' Margaret chipped in, 'the savages will spear us in the vitals, so that'll be even quicker and save 'em wastin' money on rope.'

'Now, listen,' Mary reassured them, ''tis good news. We are now of more use alive than dead. The savages doan have guns like our solders. Might be a long way from home, but 'tis better than being hanged, an' who says we have to stay there forever? I doan. People have journeyed to the South Seas for a while now — and back.'

Some weeks passed before the prison authorities officially confirmed that death sentences passed on Mary, Catherine, Margaret, and many of the other female and male felons waiting to be hanged, had been commuted to 'transportation beyond the seas' for seven years. Those who had been given a reprieve broke out into spontaneous shouting and swearing.

There was plenty to talk about. No one knew where this Botany Bay was located. Some said it was to the west, heading past the Lizard and then past the Americas; or south and then east past the Indian colonies. All that they knew was that their passage would be by sea. They had all heard of the dreadful slave ships used by the companies of Bristol and Liverpool, but surely, they thought, they wouldn't be put into slave ships by their own countrymen? Charlie Spence told Mary that there would be no danger of that happening, as a certain William Wilberforce was talking about stopping the slave trade. It was against God's will, he claimed. But still no one knew where they would sail from — Plymouth, Southampton, Portsmouth or London, maybe — but certainly not Fowey.

Mary felt relieved that she hadn't let her father and Richard know about her death sentence. But now that she had something to hope for, she decided to send them a letter. Once she knew when and from where they would sail, she would ask Catherine to write the letter.

A few days later, Charlie staggered up to the bars of Mary's cell. He told her that he had been drinking with one of the older gaolers, who had heard that the felons would be transferred to a hulk called the *Dunkirk* at Plymouth. 'But the good news, my little pretty,' Charlie added with a gleam in his eyes, 'is I is goin' too — extra pay an' all — to keep an eye on my Mary Broad and her fellow convicts. 'Cause that be what they callin' you now. Convicts.'

'What do you mean?' Mary said suspiciously. 'Your post is here.'

'As was and ever shall be, Missy, but some honest soul has to make sure none of you lot escape till yer put on a ship to them savages what are waitin' for their dinner,' he laughed.

'But why would they pay you extra to go from Exeter to Plymouth?' Mary persisted.

'There ain't 'nough of us respectable turnkeys to go around seeing as how there is so many of you nasty felons crowding His Majesty's gaols,' he said, pulling himself up to his full height. 'It's a priv'ledge for me, it is, an' I ain't never been to Plymouth. If yer lucky, I'll be on your cart,' he said with a smile.

'Time will tell, Charlie, time will tell,' Mary said absentmindedly, carrying on with her sewing. She thought to herself, 'That's it. I'll get Spence to send my letter from Plymouth, which is a lot closer to Fowey, even if I have to pay for the favour his way.'

The next week, Mary and the other felons were put in the same cold chains that had been used for convicts transported to America before the war and led outside the gaol into the bright daylight. The snorting horses were harnessed up and the women loaded on to the open carts. They were driven through the streets towards

Plymouth, escorted by beady-eyed gaolers and turnkeys, including Charlie Spence who seemed to be enjoying his day out. With all the upheaval, Mary was relieved to see James Martyn nodding to her reassuringly from one of the male carts as if saying, 'See, I told you we wouldn't get turned off.' She smiled back, pleased that her mentor was going on the journey with her.

When Mary's cart reached Plymouth, memories of that dark night of the highway robbery and of her first confinement in the watchhouse flooded back. As they moved through the town towards Sutton Harbour, she could see why they were leaving from this port. Naval and merchant ships were everywhere. Sailors were drinking in the inns and taverns, and dancing with women in all stages of dress and undress. Morris dancers entertained the drinkers, there was cockfighting to cater for the gamblers, and street sellers shouted to the passersby above the din. Mary had never seen such a bustling port. Soon they reached the harbour, where they were loaded straight into longboats and rowed out to the hulks. The harbour water was polluted by garbage, slops, human waste, dead dogs and cats, as well as human body parts.

Mary, Catherine and Margaret — all still in chains — were taken with the other women to a large and imposing hulk silhouetted against the sky. As they approached, Mary, the fisherman's daughter, looked to the stern where she could see the name of the boat. 'What does it say?' she asked Catherine.

'Well, let me see now,' Catherine said, pushing up the front of her bonnet. 'I'm like your eyes, Mary Broad, aren't I?'

'I just want the name, that's all,' Mary whispered impatiently, aware that a turnkey was watching them.

'All right. It looks like *Dungeon*,' Catherine said, sounding uncertain.

'You've been too long inside, Cath,' Margaret chipped in. ''Tis *Dunkirk*, it is.'

'*Dunkirk*,' Mary repeated to herself, noting just how far from shore the hulk was moored. It was too far to swim, especially through the filthy water with its rotting flotsam and jetsam that included the occasional corpse in a shroud.

On arriving at the starboard side, Charlie Spence and the other turnkeys offloaded the convicts one by one on to the gangplanks, ordered them up on to the main deck and then took them below to their cells. The cells were smaller than those in any of the gaols Mary had seen, but the air was better and the deck was wooden, not stone. Nor was it covered in stale urine and muck. The hulk gaolers also removed the convicts' chains once they were in the cells, warning them not to try and swim for it. From the sound of male voices through the bulkheads, Mary realised that there were also male convicts on board — it wasn't surprising, she thought, with all the work they would have to do in Botany Bay. She felt sure that James Martyn was in one of the men's cells on board.

The next day a heavily tattooed sailor who called himself Crispy came down below under the watchful eye of Charlie Spence, who was now supervising meals. Crispy, who had been with the *Dunkirk* when she was a fighting ship, was now carting water to the convicts. This endearing old salt told Mary and her companions that the ship had been paid off by the navy because it had been heavily damaged during the American war. The government had taken it over, he said, as a temporary gaol moored a few hundred yards out to sea. Crispy assured them that no one had ever escaped, as all the cells were below-decks in sealed-off holds between the bulkheads. He also warned them the bulkheads were filled with nails running across the boat from side to side in between decks, and the guards could fire through loopholes between the decks if the convicts caused any trouble. Nor could they get out on to the deck, he said, as the hatches were well secured by crossbars, bolts and locks, and were nailed down from deck to deck with oak stanchions. There was also a barricade of planks about three feet high, armed with pointed prongs of iron on the upper deck abaft the mainmast, to prevent any connection between the convicts and the guards and ship's company. They could never get out, Crispy told the convicted women, as sentinels were also on guard at different hatchways, and there was a guard always under arms on the quarterdeck of each hulk in order to prevent any improper behaviour among the convicts. The only way out of these convict hulks, Crispy warned, was in a shroud tossed overboard.

Although impressed by Crispy's warnings, Mary still thought she could have escaped had it not been for the poisonous harbour water. She knew that when a convict died, a gaoler came to the cell and wrapped the body in a black shroud, which he then sewed shut. He would then leave the cell and find a second gaoler to help carry the shroud up on deck, where it would be lowered over the side. Mary hit on the idea of crawling into one of these shrouds. After a dead convict had been placed inside and the first gaoler had gone for help, she believed she could remove and hide the corpse, get into the shroud, and have her cell-mates sew it closed before the guards returned. They would then carry her up on deck and toss her into the water. Using a concealed knife, she could cut open the shroud and swim for the shore. But it was a long swim, especially through that disease-ridden water, and she decided to bide her time.

'Ye know that scheme of yourn about gettin' outta 'ere?' Crispy whispered to Mary one evening. He had formed a relationship with Catherine and was regularly sneaking into the women's cell to lie with her.

'What scheme?' Mary asked, alarmed.

''Bout goin' out in one of 'em shrouds the lads sew up the dead-uns in,' he replied.

'No, I don't know,' Mary said.

'Well, Cath told me 'bout it, she did. I'm sorry to know an' all. Anyways, it won't work. I tell yer why,' he said, leaning in close to Mary.

'Pray, talk,' she said, giving nothing away.

''Cause, lass, the last thing they do 'afore throwin' body over the side is a final stitch right through the nose, ta make sure corpse inside is really dead.' He noticed Mary wince and pulled back with a laugh. 'It's an old seaman's tradition, ut is.'

On 7 December 1786 a breathless Charlie Spence came puffing down below-decks into the gloom and told Mary excitedly that he was headed back to Exeter. The ship they were to be transported on, the *Charlotte*, had just sailed into port that day. They should ready themselves, he said, as they would soon be transferred to the transport. 'I'll miss every one of you lovelies — especially my Mary,' he said.

Mary realised that once she had left the *Dunkirk* for this other ship moored further out to sea, she would have no further contact with England. If she was going to let her father and Richard know what was happening, there was no time to lose. Charlie Spence was her only link with the outside world. She knew what he wanted — in fact, what he thought he had already earned — a night with Mary. The thought of putting her father's and Richard's minds at rest convinced her that the price was right for this favour. Spence had ambitions she could satisfy. All she had to do was choose the right moment.

Mary moved into action. First she had to get a pen, and some ink and paper — a tall order in itself. She would ask Catherine or Margaret to write the letter for her.

The next time Charlie came below-decks to check on his charges, Mary approached the bars and whispered, 'Charlie.'

'Ah, ha! 'Tis my pretty little Mary,' he said, sounding a little drunk.

'Charlie, I have an idea to put to you,' she said.

'The one I been waitin' for?' he asked.

'P'raps, Charlie,' Mary said, coaxing him along. 'I want to send a message to my family.'

'But, I thought you didn't know your letters,' he said. 'You been lyin', then?'

'No, no. Catherine will write it. I just want you to send it,' she whispered.

'Got any money?' he asked.

'Nay, not a farthing. I'm appealing to your good heart, Charlie,' Mary said, looking him straight in the eye.

'Well, you'm in luck, chitty. A heart I do have,' he said, with a sly smile. 'But I need a small payment, I do. At least one roll, girl, after all I done for you. Then it's a deal.'

The deal struck, Charlie offered Crispy a tot of rum to sneak into the captain's cabin and take a pen, and some ink and paper, which he delivered to Mary the following night. Wasting no time, Mary dictated her letter to Catherine, who assured Mary that she knew her letters as well as anyone else:

From Plymouth to my Beluved Father and Mother,
I have not writ afore seeing as how I had Bad Tydings,
thinkin as I was to be turned off.
But it pleased God to spare my Life and
now I writes to inform my lovin Family, I am to be
sent Beyond the Sees to Botanny Baye
for some sevin yers before I can cum Hoam. But I will
as I am a proud Broad
Give my luv to my darling Sisters.
Plees tell Richard to Wate for me as I will Never be forgittin him till we
Meete agayne wich I'm swerin we will One Day, to join up our Pennie.
Your,
Dauter Mary

After making Catherine promise that she had written everything correctly, Mary signed the letter with her mark, 'MB'. She then tied it in a packet with some old thread. Early the next morning, Mary gave the packet to Charlie at her cell door as arranged, telling him that she would be waiting for him when he brought back the receipt with a stamp for her to see. After Charlie had left the cell, Mary asked Catherine for some brandy, which Catherine earned by giving her favours to various turnkeys. (Even old Crispy always had some rum for her.) Mary intended to keep her promise, but wanted to fortify herself beforehand.

When Charlie came to see Mary that night and showed her the receipt, she was considerably inebriated. She asked him to point to the date and stamp. When he seemed to do so, she believed that he had carried out her instructions and despatched her letter. She shoved the piece of paper into her pocket, intending to get Catherine to check it the next day.

Then, composing herself as best she could, Mary followed Charlie as he unlocked her cell door and led the way to his cabin — a room lit by a single candle flickering on a wall bracket and furnished with a low-slung bunk, a washstand and a large hook for his keys.

'Now, then,' Charlie said, with obvious delight, as he locked the door, took off his coat and boots, unbuttoned his fly and climbed on to his bunk. 'You be my little honey tonight, 'cause my relief is mindin' the cells.'

'I have agreed, Charlie,' Mary slurred. 'An' you swear that letter went off?'

'An honest man to an honest woman — who 'as never done nothin' wrong in her life,' he cackled. 'I swear on my heart,' he said, placing his large hand over his stomach. 'Now, let's see what you've got to offer me 'neath your shift.'

'I do believe you, I s'pose,' Mary said, swaying as she kicked off her shoes. She started to lift up her skirts, but then collapsed on to the bed. 'The arrangement stands, you've earned your reward,' she mumbled.

It was just as well that Mary completed her transaction that night, for the next morning, not long after Charlie sneaked her back into the cell, a new group of male convicts arrived with new gaolers who were to take over guard duty from the Exeter turnkeys. Charlie left the *Dunkirk* within days, taking with him Mary's only link to the outside world.

Soon, Mary had plenty of other distractions, as the women convicts were taken on deck for carefully guarded exercise along with the newly arrived male convicts. The commander of the *Dunkirk* wanted his charges to be healthy enough to be transferred to the waiting transport. Overhearing her first Cornish accent for months, Mary saw a young, good-looking, rather hard-faced man with a jaunty black ponytail and the build of a boxer. He was deep in conversation with a smaller man who, judging from his accent, was from the east country, perhaps as far east as London.

'Cornwall!' she called out as they drew level. 'Where'bouts you from? I'm Cornish, too.'

'An' who might I be a-speakin' to, first?' the handsome Cornishman shot back guardedly.

'I'm a Broad, of Fowey. Mariners, fishermen,' she said proudly.

'Aye. I've heard of Broads,' he said, more friendly now. 'Your name, then?'

'Mary, Mary Broad,' she said.

'Well, Miss Mary Broad of Fowey, Will Bryant is this man. Fisherman, too, but from north of Launceston, up St Ives way — bit warmer on north coast, you know.' He bent his right knee in a mock curtsey.

'Like my father, "William",' Mary said warmly, essaying a quick dip of her hips in response.

'Nay. I'm "Will". Never "William",' Bryant said. 'But I know how to look after myself and my own.' After a pause during which he looked her up and down, he added: 'An' also any friends.'

Later, back below-decks, Mary gave some thought to her encounter with Will Bryant. She was struck by his energy, confidence and sense of humour. Here was a man who could look after himself, she thought. He could be quite a useful ally, especially as, being a fisherman, he would know something about boats. It could be handy, she decided, to gather such people around her. Perhaps they could steal a boat from the *Charlotte* and make a dash for freedom. She expected she might have something more to do with Will Bryant.

The next time they met during deck exercises, the 27-year-old fisherman told Mary he was an old hand, having been in gaol for over two years.

'What for?' Mary asked, as she walked beside him. 'What did you do?'

'A little somethin' I hear those folk in Fowey weren't strangers to, from time to time perhaps, as the tide serves,' he said cheekily.

'Smugglin'?' Mary asked in a low voice, hoping that Will didn't mean shipwrecking, the idea of which she had never felt comfortable with.

'That's what Fowey be known for, ain't it?' Bryant said provocatively. 'Nothin' to be ashamed of — one for all, as the sayin' goes, and all for one, eh?'

'Fowey 'as brought many catches home,' Mary said guardedly. 'When did they get you, and on what charge?'

''84,' Will said, his face clouding over. 'Convicted in the March assizes at Launceston, I was. But I weren't taken,' he added proudly. 'Some weasel ratted an' I was done by the revenue officers with some partiklar property I had hold of.'

'Smuggled goods, eh?' Mary sympathised. 'Well, I'm sorry you were got, Will.'

'No more'n I,' he shot back. 'But if they hadn'ta caught me, I wouldn't have met you now, would I, Mary?'

Inevitably, coming from the same part of the world and having much in common, Mary and Will became friends. Besides being impressed by Mary's knowledge of sailing and fishing, Will found himself attracted to her. Mary, who considered herself promised to Richard, was more interested in learning what she could from this old hand who, she could see, had developed many survival skills over the years.

On their next exercise walk around the deck, some days later, Will introduced Mary to the man with the east London accent whom he described as his 'shipmate' and 'the best carpenter or chippy on board the *Dunkirk*', the 30-year-old Jimmy 'Chips' Cox.

'Where ye be from, Chips?' she asked.

'Well, bein' born wit'in sound of the bells of St Mary-le-Bow, I'd 'ave ta say I'm Cockney,' he said proudly.

'You taken for smugglin' as well?' asked Mary, as they walked up and down the deck.

'Not I! May be fine for me china, Will, but too risky for Jimmy Cox, by 'alf! Only a little 'ousebreakin' for me, weren't it?' he replied. 'Weren't easy. 'Ad ter go up the apple an' pears to find that thread lace, didn't I? Oh, an' some very dandy cotton stockings — would 'ave looked 'andsome on your calves, Mary, they would.'

'I could do with 'em now,' Mary replied. 'When were that?'

''82, believe it or not. An' I's still waitin' for me punishment,' he said, shaking his head. 'Yeah, I'm a lifer an' I bin in longer than anyone I know. Fact is, I'm one of them as were goin' to America afore that bloody war. Fancy Carolina, I do; not so sure 'bout this 'ere Botany Bay.'

Over the next few exercise sessions, Jimmy Cox explained to Mary how he had initially been sentenced to hang in 1782, but during his long wait for his place on the Tyburn Tree he was reprieved, his sentence commuted to transportation for life to the Carolinas. He was despatched on the transport ship *Mercury*, which sailed for the colonies in early 1783, bound for South Carolina where he had been assigned to work with other convicts on the tobacco plantations of the British settlers. 'A few little 'iccups 'appened,' he said, 'which put paid to that plan of 'is Majesty.'

Jimmy explained that the convicts had mutinied and successfully seized the ship. Jimmy was one of the ringleaders, although the mutiny was organised by a fellow convict, Robert Sideway, also a clothing thief sentenced at the Old Bailey. Sideway had stolen a key to his cell from a turnkey and persuaded some of the soldiers on board to sell him their weapons and turn a blind eye to the uprising. With a loyal band of ringleaders, including Jimmy Cox, they rose and took over the *Mercury* off the coast of Devonshire, locking the captain and his mates in the cells.

Sideway ordered the helmsman to steer the ship back towards the coast, where he and his bold band planned to land and run for it. But the harbour authorities noticed that the *Mercury* was flying the wrong signals for a returning ship, realised that something was amiss, and mustered a party of constables to seize the ship. They arrested Sideway, Jimmy Cox and the other ringleaders, clapped them in irons and returned them to gaol. Jimmy had remained in gaol another four years until the decision was made to transport convicts to Botany Bay. 'I'm a professional tea-leaf, frew an' frew, but I knows me ropes — shippin' ropes, that is, not the hangin' rope.' Lowering his voice, he added: ''Nother time, if anybody wants ter start a risin', I'm the first in. I knows the ropes.'

Mary realised that she could have some useful partners in Will Bryant and Jimmy Cox. Although the exercise periods were shorter during the bitter month of February, Mary nevertheless got to know both men well enough by the end of the month to know she could rely on them. She hoped they would get on well with James Martyn, whom she also met occasionally during exercise periods on the main deck. In her mind, he had become her main confidant and ally. If ever there was an opportunity to escape, she was committed to acting with James. But when she introduced him to Bryant and Cox, they got on well. James said later that they were a tight-knit pair of mates who could be trusted.

Before first light on the morning of 12 March 1787, the turnkey Crispy came below-decks with some news. 'Show a leg, ladies — an' any gentlemen wot is out of his rightful quarters. You're movin' today — goin' on a journey, you are, an' you gotta go on board now.'

'What journey's that?' Catherine murmured, half-asleep. 'We're already on board, Crispy.'

'Oh, no, you're not — this is just a hulk. Now you're goin' on the real thing. The *Charlotte* awaits you,' Crispy said.

'When?' Margaret asked, coming to.

'After yer slops,' he said, 'so look smart.'

Within the hour they were put in a new form of leg-irons to be used on the voyage and herded on to the deck. They were then pushed down the gangplank and rowed across to the transport in longboats. From what Mary could see, it was huge. Catherine confirmed that the name on the stern was *Charlotte*, before they were dragged up the gangplank, across the main deck and down into their cells in the hold, where the sailors said they had to remain in their leg-irons. All this had taken place under the watchful eye of the master of the *Charlotte*, Thomas Gilbert.

As the female convicts got to know the sailors on the ship — and there was no shortage of approaches by the men — they learned that the *Charlotte*, at 335 tons, was a much bigger vessel than the *Dunkirk*. Yet she was almost as crowded for apart from the 20 female convicts who had just arrived, she was also taking 88 male convicts (among whom, Mary hoped, were James, Will and Jimmy), along with a number of marines and their wives, naval officers and sailors, all bound for Botany Bay. The ship would soon sail to Portsmouth, where it would join up with a number of other ships, the sailors explained. But from a convict's point of view it was a better ship than the *Dunkirk*, being only three years old. The three-masted barque had been built in a good yard on the Thames, her crew boasted. She was also a decent size, at 105 feet long and 28 feet wide.

The sailors were looking forward to enjoying themselves in the various ports the *Charlotte* called in at. She was on charter to the East India Company, and, after depositing his human cargo in New Holland, her skipper, Thomas Gilbert, planned to sail on to Canton, where he would collect tea for the profitable London market. If the cargo sold well, the sailors even hoped for a dividend.

Mary tried to make herself comfortable in the new cell she shared with Catherine and Margaret. There was no turning back now, she realised. But at least she had seen the last of the *Dunkirk* and of Charlie Spence.

Charlie wasn't to be so easily forgotten, however, as in mid-March, a week after they had arrived on the *Charlotte*, Mary realised that she had missed her time for the second month running. Usually steady on her feet on board ship, she had attributed feelings of giddiness to the fact that the *Charlotte* was moored further out to sea than the *Dunkirk*. But after discussions with Catherine, Margaret and some of the older women in the cell, she now suspected that she was pregnant — the payment she had made to Spence had backfired. It was a cruel twist of fate. She had been prepared to compromise herself to get a message to her father and Richard but had never dreamed of getting pregnant.

''Tis not the end of the world, chick,' Catherine said, as they sat in a corner of their dark cell. 'You may say 'tis the start of a new one.'

'Mayhap you'll get some perks,' Margaret chipped in. 'You know, extra slops for the little 'un.'

'An' you won't do the backbreakin' work we is all gonna do,' Catherine said. 'Why, you lazy sod — you probably got pregnant to get an easy ride!'

'Well. It's happened, an' I'll make the best of it,' Mary said. I am sure Richard would understand, she thought to herself, after all I only did it to tell him and my father what was happening to me.

On 16 March 1787, the *Charlotte* weighed anchor with a full cargo of 108 convicts. She sailed out of Plymouth and east along the Channel coast to Portsmouth for the rendezvous with the other transports. Mary tried to adjust to the new movement of the ship that was taking her further from her West Country home than she had ever been before.

The *Charlotte* soon proved to be a poor sailor, even on the short journey from Plymouth to Portsmouth. But, although pregnant, Mary didn't suffer from seasickness, unlike many of the convicts on board.

From discussions with the ship's crew, the convicts learned that the *Charlotte* was the last of the transports to arrive. The fleet was to be the biggest convict convoy up to that time, larger than any sent to the American colonies with about 1350 souls on board, 759 of whom were convicts. There were five other convict transports: the *Alexander* and the *Scarborough*, on which most of the men were imprisoned; the *Friendship*, which carried mainly women; and the *Prince of Wales* and the *Lady Penrhyn*. There were also two naval ships — HMS *Sirius*, the flagship, carrying the commodore, whom they later learned was named Arthur Phillip, and HMS *Supply* — and three store-ships carrying supplies: the *Fishburn*, the *Golden Grove* and the *Borrowdale*. Together they moored on the Motherbank off the Isle of Wight, opposite the little town of Cowes. Although Ryde was only several hundred yards away, and Mary could see the little church spires from the ship, there was no chance now of escaping overboard, especially as they were still in leg-irons.

The gossip that spread around the cells on board the *Charlotte* reported different people arriving throughout April to take up various positions. Mary saw some of these new arrivals. They included a handsome, red-coated marine captain, Watkin Tench, who began to lecture the convicts on a new code of discipline that he and others would be applying during the expedition to New Holland. He and his marines, he explained, 'had now established necessary regulations among you convicts and adopted such a system of defence to stop any mutiny in case you were ever seized by spirit of madness and desperation that hurried you on to attempt our destruction'. He warned them that 'any escape attempt will be punished with instant death'.

Tench also explained that he would be keeping a record of the voyage in a journal, which he hoped would become the official published account of the journey. He thanked the convicts for their 'humble, submissive and regular behaviour' so far, 'which was a testimony of the sobriety and decency of their conduct' as he had heard 'few complaints or lamentations among them'.

Mary and her cell-mates also saw the fleet surgeon, John White, arrive on board soon after Tench. Sailors who knew his work whispered warnings of how fanatical he was about cleanliness and good health. Mary was pleased to hear this, as during the months they had spent moored off Portsmouth she had heard there had been a great sickness among the convicts of a most dangerous kind. Sailors returning from shore leave reported that the local press were claiming the ships of the fleet were 'so very sickly as to bury 8 or 10 convicts every day out of the 759 on board the ships because of the malignant disease which raged with great violence on board the transports'. At least 16 men had already died on the *Alexander*, the newspapers reported, while on the *Lady Penrhyn* the convict Ann Wright died and was committed to the deep where, the papers said, 'corpses sew'd up in hammock floated alongside the Ships every day'.

Mary was relieved when, on Sunday, 1 April, Surgeon White banished all convicts to the main deck while he had their cells cleaned and whitewashed, and vinegar sprinkled between the decks. He ordered the convicts henceforth to keep their quarters clean. While on deck, Mary saw that Portsmouth was strongly fortified with guns at the ready on the high stone battlements that guarded the entrance to the port. Everywhere she looked, there were men-of-war, fighting frigates and naval ships, all of a size she had never before seen. One towering giant, the newly built warship and pride of the fighting fleet HMS *Victory*, looked like a floating castle.

'Ain't we gonna smell pretty,' Catherine said, as they were led back down to their cell.

'Well, 'tis better than it was,' Mary replied.

'As long as the sailors think so, Miss Broad,' Margaret added, 'as I do like my little luxuries from time to time.' Margaret was right, the sailors *were* helpful; Mary soon realised that just as the turnkeys on the *Dunkirk* had been corruptible, so would be the merchant sailors on the *Charlotte* because of their passion for the female convicts. In fact, the marines found it difficult to keep the sailors away from the women while the fleet waited to depart. According to a sailor named Sammy who befriended Mary and her cell-mates, on 19 April five convict women were found in the bunks of the second mate and four other seamen on the *Lady Penrhyn*. Apparently, this was to be expected during these idle weeks at anchor.

By the second week of April, Commodore Phillip had arrived in Portsmouth and had begun organising the ships for departure. First, however, he had to deal with the many disputes that had flared up during the long wait. One of these problems concerned the shortage of women's clothing. It wasn't until 8 May that sufficient supplies of stockings, drawers, worsted caps and shirts were finally delivered to the fleet.

By 1 May, when Mary turned 22 and was five months pregnant, the fleet had still not left. Apparently, they were waiting on a last group of convicts to arrive from Newgate Gaol, which, Mary recalled when she heard this, was the prison from which Jack Sheppard had so often escaped. But this lot, when they arrived, were put on board the *Prince of Wales* and the *Alexander*. Those on board the ships who faced many years of servitude in the distant colony of Botany Bay were full of envy when orders arrived from London to release two of the convicts, whose pardons had come through at the last minute. Catherine suggested that the pardons had been bought or that the papers had been falsified. Mary had no false hope that she would receive a similar last-minute reprieve.

Then, when at last it seemed they were ready, the marines themselves refused to sail with the ships unless they had three times their normal ration of grog guaranteed for three years. Once this was agreed to, the sailors demanded that they receive the back pay they were owed, plus an extra loading to cover them for the period the ships had sat idle. One of the women's main sources of news was a seaman by the name of Davy, who sometimes came below-decks to share his rum ration with Mary and the other women in the hope of lying with one of them. He explained that the sailors had gone on strike, and were refusing to go aloft and unfurl the sails until they were paid what they were owed. The captains of the fleet's ships, it was said, wanted to delay paying the sailors until they had sailed, in order to force them to use their wages to buy food and tobacco from the ships' canteens.

On 12 May, when Phillip had asked all the captains to weigh anchor and set sail, none of the sailors would man the ships, Davy reported. Instead, they sent a party to the commodore to present their grievances. The day was spent in negotiations between the Royal Navy, the merchant ship masters and their sailors before the dispute was settled. But several sailors walked off the job in disgust, which left some of the ships shorthanded until Tenerife, where the captains hoped to recruit replacement crew.

One night, over a bottle of rum, Davy announced that an additional ship was to have sailed with them, a Royal Navy expedition vessel, the *Bounty*, under the command of a Captain William Bligh — one of Captain James Cook's protégés — but the *Bounty* wasn't ready. The Admiralty had planned for Bligh to accompany the convict fleet to Botany Bay, from where he would continue in the *Bounty* to Tahiti in order to harvest breadfruit. The nourishing plants were to be taken by the *Bounty* to the British West Indies to provide a staple food for the sugar plantation workers and slaves. Phillip, however, had his own schedule and couldn't wait for Bligh. He promised to meet him in Rio de Janeiro en route; the *Bounty* should have caught the fleet by then, being faster than the transports.

Finally, on the night of 12 May, Phillip gave the long-awaited order to the 11 ships of the first convict fleet to set sail for Botany Bay at first light. Nothing short of a miracle could now stop Mary and her cell-mates from being banished to the far side of the world.

CHAPTER 3

Bound for Botany Bay

Despite the challenges of the voyage to Botany Bay, Mary
manages not only to stay healthy and deliver 'a fine baby girl' en
route, but also to learn from the mistakes of other would-be
escapees who try their luck along the way.

M ary was woken before dawn on 13 May 1787 by the sudden
movement of the *Charlotte*, along with the creaking and
groaning of her timbers as the wind filled the sails and she got
under way. With the other ten ships, she now left the Motherbank,
off Portsmouth, and headed out to sea.

'This is it,' Mary thought, as she lay in her bunk, uncomfortable
in the leg-irons the convicts were made to wear. 'Now we really are
leaving England — and God knows for how long.'

Nearly all of Mary's cell-mates were distraught, knowing that they would never see their families again. Many of them were on the water for the first time. They weren't used to the way their chains, buckets, boxes, drinking mugs and clothes slid backwards and forwards with the roll and pitch of the ship. Some quickly became seasick and reached frantically for their buckets. Others were frightened that the ship would crash into a rocky outcrop in the dark, spring a leak, and sink, leaving them floundering and drowning in the sea.

Mary braced herself against the increasing roll of the ship. She told the women to tie everything down, to stop things from sliding across the deck. Having sailed in the wildest weather, Mary wasn't frightened of rough seas and was never seasick. But while she had no fear of drowning, she didn't relish the long sea voyage that lay ahead. Her chances of returning to England — legally or otherwise — from the far side of the world were so slim as to be almost non-existent. Yet, she hung on to her dream of escaping and returning to Fowey. She touched the pouch where she kept her half of Richard's penny.

'Wot the hell's happenin', Mary?' Catherine groaned, between visits to her bucket. 'Wot's wrong with this furkin' ship?'

'Nothin', Cath. 'Tis only the normal roll of a ship at sea,' Mary reassured her.

'How do you know we won't roll over and sink, and end up in Davy Jones's locker?' Catherine moaned. 'Ships do sink.'

'Not in this sea. 'Tis nothin',' Mary said. '*Charlotte*'s a goodly vessel, so stop your complainin'. You can't do nothing 'bout it.

Keep your head up an' fix your eyes on the bulkhead. The sickness'll soon cease.'

'If she hit an' sink, we'll go down with 'er in these bloody chains,' said Margaret, rattling hers. 'No way we should save ourselves.'

'You can't swim — neither of you,' Mary said impatiently, 'so doan imagine the worst. None of us could survive in the water with irons on our legs.'

Not long after first light, as they got clear of the Isle of Wight, Mary saw one of the marines, the officer Tench, down on her deck peering into the cells. When a fellow officer asked him what brought him below, Mary overheard him say that he was strolling among the convicts to observe their sentiments for his book. 'And I must say,' he told his red-coated companion, 'a very few excepted, their countenances indicate a high degree of satisfaction, though in some the pang of being severed, perhaps for ever, from their native land, can obviously not be wholly suppressed.'

'I see,' the other marine said.

'In general, marks of distress are more perceptible among the men than the women,' Tench concluded. Although she couldn't have agreed less, Mary thought that Captain Tench certainly had a way with words.

Having also been reading the letters that convicts were permitted to send before departure, Mary heard Tench telling his brother officer that most convicts seemed 'distressed by the impracticability of returning home, the dread of the sickly passage, and the fearful prospect of a distant and barbarous country'.

'Not surprising at all,' the second marine said.

'No, and that's why most of the convicts' letters asked relatives to supply them with money and tobacco to make their lot an easier one.'

Mary was glad she sent her letter off before Tench or any other nosy officer could read it.

Not long after Tench's visit, Mary heard a rumour that their ship was sailing so slowly it couldn't keep up with the other transports. At first, Mary hoped that this would give them an excuse to turn back, but then another rumour went the rounds: a temporary navy escort ship, the *Hyena*, was now towing them, which accounted for the different motion of the *Charlotte* that she and the others had suddenly felt.

This towing, which lasted for the first three days and stabilised the motion of the *Charlotte*, enabled Mary and her friends to get their sea legs. Others were not so lucky and, according to one of the seamen who visited the women's cells, a marine by the name of Corporal Baker shot himself in the right foot while cleaning his musket above-decks and had to be attended to by Surgeon White.

On the third day, much to the relief of all the convicts, Commodore Phillip ordered the marines to remove the irons from the convicts so that they could 'strip their clothes off at night when they went to rest, be more at their ease during the day and be able to keep themselves clear'. For Mary, trying to cope with her pregnancy, this was a Godsend as it enabled her to change position. When a seaman removed her irons, Mary took heart, realising that her condition was already improving. She would now have a chance to move around the ship and might possibly be able to talk to Will Bryant again about the possibility of organising a boat at the first port of call in which to slip away. Vernon, a sailor who was now spending time with Catherine, said that Surgeon White had advised Commodore Phillip that the convicts would be healthier when they got to the land of the savages if they were taken out of their irons for the voyage.

'An' no doubt 'is lordship thought you could work harder,' Vernon quipped.

'I doan care 'bout the reasons,' Mary replied. 'It gives us more freedom to move.'

'Just don't try an' move too far, lassie,' he warned. 'You know what 'appen to escaped convicts, don't you?' He ran his finger across the back of his head. 'Turn they off, they do.'

'Oh, shut up with yer teasin',' Catherine said, pulling Vernon into her bunk.

Some days later, Sammy, the sailor who had formed an attachment to Margaret and supplied her with extra rations in return for her favours, told the women that two convicts on the *Scarborough* with sailing experience, Phillip Farrell and Thomas Griffiths, had already tried to escape. Once out of their irons on 18 May, they broke out of their cells and began freeing others in a desperate attempt to seize the ship. But they were overpowered by marines, who had been tipped off. Farrell and Griffiths were taken by boat to HMS *Sirius* for two dozen lashes each and clapped into double irons. Farrell had previously been a boatswain's mate on

73

HMS *Goliath*, while Griffiths had been master of a French privateer. The lesson wasn't lost on Mary; if she were to try anything, there would be no slip-up or flogging. She also recalled Jimmy Cox's story of his failed mutiny on the *Mercury* en route to America. Mary understood from this second failed mutiny attempt that it would be virtually impossible to escape from a ship as part of an organised mutiny. Nevertheless, to her relief as a mother-to-be, Mary heard that the humane commodore wasn't using the escape attempt to reinstate irons for the bulk of the convicts.

One morning Mary was woken by a Cornish voice saying, 'They tell me you're up the duff, you pixie.' On turning over, she saw the cheeky face of Will Bryant standing in her cell holding a bucket of water and a ladle, under the watchful eye of an armed, red-coated marine.

'What are you doin' here, Will?' she asked. 'I didn't know you were on *Charlotte*.'

'Doan change the subject, now. Who be the lucky father, or doan the likes of you normally know such things?' he said mischievously.

'Lay off, Will. 'Tain't your business. 'Twas an arrangement,' she said, getting to her feet.

'Well, you'd know. 'Bout arrangements, I mean, you bein' a veteran of the king's highway an' all.' He dipped the ladle into the bucket. 'Here, grab your mug. I'll give you a full ladle, one for baby pixie as well.'

Will explained that when the *Charlotte*'s captain, Thomas Gilbert, told the men they had to work for their rations, he had volunteered to cart water around the ship. 'So, you'll be seein' a bit of me, if you're lucky.'

'Not if I see you first,' Mary teased.

'Yer ole mate, James Martyn, is on board, I see, as is Chips Cox. They're doin' fine,' he said, and winked. 'And they're never short of water.'

During the second week at sea, Captain Tench announced that he needed to make note of all the convicts' and felons' names, and where and when they were sentenced, as there was no record of the crimes for which they were being transported, nor of their period of sentence. It seems that the officials from the Home Office had forgotten to deliver the full list of names and crimes to the ships before they had sailed. This news was received with great amusement by Mary's cell-mates, who joked about the stories they would make up.

Tench sat at a makeshift desk and interviewed each convict. When Mary's turn came, she found the handsome marine to be a kind man, and took a liking to him. In turn, he also put her at her ease.

'Now, where are you on this list?' he asked, producing the convict list he had compiled for the barque *Charlotte*.

'Please, sir, I doan know my letters.' The answer was a commonplace to him.

'Well, never mind, my girl. Tell me what it is they call you.'

She grinned at him. 'Well, Adm'ral, they call me Mary. Mary Broad.'

'Not that I am an admiral, as well you know, you sauce,' Tench smiled, searching through the names for 'Broad'.

'Sorry, sir,' she said diplomatically.

'Yet, your name is not on the inventory at all,' he said, sighing loudly. He dipped his quill into a white porcelain inkpot and scratched her name at the bottom of the list. He glanced at her swelling belly. 'But tell me, Mary, is it maid or ma'am I should be writing next your name?'

'Mary Broad will do,' she said.

'And your crime and sentence, Mary?' he asked, pen poised again.

'Armed robbery on the king's highway, Captain. Sentence seven years' transportation,' she said without flinching.

'God's truth!' he exclaimed. 'I thought you had a bit of bravado about you, but that's a crime-and-a-half. Seven years well earned, I'd say. Thank you, Mary Broad.'

Mary had decided to create a good impression with Tench and the other marines by telling the truth. She was pleased to hear that James Martyn, Will Bryant and Jimmy Cox had done the same. Many of the other convicts lied about their names and crimes, pretending they were in for minor offences and that their sentences had nearly expired. Catherine and Margaret both made up false names. But as the official records were to be sent to Botany Bay in a later vessel, Mary could see little point in being caught out and punished later.

The fleet, now well out to sea en route to Tenerife, was being tossed around in the high seas, and many of Mary's fellow convicts were by now desperately sick. Mary thanked her lucky stars that she was a good sailor, especially given that she was carrying a baby. By the end of the month, one sailor, William Mead of the *Scarborough*, as well as some of the convicts, had died of various fevers and been buried overboard. Mary saw these corpses from time to time as they were carried out in their hammocks, which now doubled as shrouds. There would be no point in getting sewn into one of those out in mid-ocean, she thought.

Determined not to lose her baby, Mary was distressed to hear that on 25 May a fellow convict, Elizabeth Evans, was so violently sick that she miscarried her child. The forlorn little body was committed to the deep. Mary feared that with the poor food and cramped conditions, her own child, if it were born alive, would be very frail and may not live. She was determined to stay as healthy as her situation allowed.

Scuttlebutt reported that on 28 May the notorious John Bennett, who had always vowed to escape, had broken out of the irons that he had been required to wear, and been caught moving about his transport, the *Friendship*. When caught, he was tied to a grating and flogged with 37 lashes under the orders of Marine Lieutenant Ralph Clark. The same day, Mary saw a corpse being carried up on deck in its shroud, and heard that Ishmael Coleman had died of a fever. Sailors had come down to sew his body into his hammock and take it on deck to be buried by the master, Thomas Gilbert.

On 31 May, Mary was heartened to hear of the first baby to be successfully delivered in the fleet, when Isabella Lawson, on the

Lady Penryhn, gave birth to a baby girl and both survived. Isabella's daughter was, in fact, the first progeny of the convicts who would survive the voyage to become a member of the new colony.

Male convicts on the *Charlotte* were certainly better behaved than those on the *Scarborough*, according to Catherine's lover Vernon, who told her that John Leary of Winchester, another highway robber, had been beaten senseless by four other convicts, who then cut open his left leg with a knife they had smuggled on board.

On 3 June, Mary felt the *Charlotte* cease its rolling motion and come to a halt. She could tell from the stillness of the boat that they must be close to shore; in fact, she soon heard the squawking sounds of seagulls and voices of the Spanish locals who had paddled out to the ship in bumboats used for selling fruit and vegetables to visiting vessels. Margaret's Sammy explained that they were at anchor in Tenerife, or Santa Cruz de Tenerife, in the Spanish Canary Islands to take on supplies of food and water. Sick and tired of salt beef, peas and oatmeal, Mary hoped for some fresh fruit. As it was oppressive below-decks, she was relieved to be allowed up on deck for some fresh air and exercise. As she walked around the deck, she studied the towering black volcanic mountain peak that rose from the forbidding-looking island into the clouds.

'Heard the latest news?' Will Bryant approached Mary during her walk a few days later and offered her some of his ration of salt beef.

'About what?' Mary replied. 'Are you now in charge of serving food as well as water?' she smiled, accepting the offered food.

'About John Powers,' Bryant said. 'From the *Alexander*. He's been caught.'

'Doin' what?' Mary asked.

'Escapin',' Will said. 'He got over the ship's side t'other night, pinched a boat an' rowed over to a Dutchman, an East Indiaman. The bastard Lowlanders wouldn't take 'im.'

'What then? Captured?' Mary asked.

'Nay. He escaped an' got to a cave on the island. A boatload of marines captured him later an' brought him back. Flogged at the gratin', 'course.'

'How many?' Mary asked.

'Thirty-six, double irons an' solitary.'

'God. When you choose your time, Will, you want to be sure of gettin' clear,' Mary whispered.

'Wadda yer sayin, girl?'

'If I wasn't in this condition,' said Mary, looking down at her belly, 'I would have been tempted meself.' She glanced over her shoulder. 'There's a spare boat tied up alongside right now, Will.'

'We fisherfolk know what can be done, but for Christ's sake, shut up,' Will said.

The next day, the sounds of anchors being hauled up and canvas unfurling told Mary they were leaving Tenerife. She wondered if she would have her baby before the next port, or if she could wait and have it in a sheltered harbour. Captain Tench, who was always writing notes for his book about their voyage, told Mary that they would be going to a country called Brazil, which was owned by the Portuguese. Perhaps the Portuguese would be more sympathetic towards fleeing convicts, Mary thought.

The fleet's progress slowed as the ships reached the doldrums near the equator. Mary sweated in the stuffy spaces of the cells below-decks, where there was no breeze to cool the convicts confined there. She became increasingly uncomfortable in the intense heat. Some of the sailors had gone swimming during the first day or two that they were becalmed, but sharks were spotted and they were forbidden to bathe in the sea.

By 15 June, however, fresh northerly winds drove the ships along their course again and before long they crossed the equator. Mary learned that this milestone was an excuse for the sailors to celebrate and pay homage to the mythical King Neptune. Vernon and Sammy were among those sailors who were ducked, lathered with tar grease and shaved. Vernon said that the *Charlotte* and the *Lady Penrhyn* almost collided when their helmsmen became distracted by the frivolities on board.

Not long after leaving the doldrums, word spread that the fleet had reached the Cape Verde Islands and that the commodore had ordered them to pull into Port Praya. Mary hoped that the *Charlotte* would be able to obtain some fresh fruit and vegetables on the island. Although the ships manoeuvred into position to drop anchor and fired the traditional salute off Port Praya, the surf was so great that HMS *Sirius* signalled them to abandon the landing. They would just have to go without fresh fruit and vegetables until they reached Brazil.

Conditions were rough for the next two to three weeks, with winds battering the ships in a series of storms. Vernon and Sammy kept Mary and the others up to date on events in the fleet. A convict was blown overboard from the deck of the *Alexander*; a convict on the *Charlotte*, Anne Read, drank mercury thinking it was water and was violently ill; and 60-year-old Mary Love fell down the companionway, breaking two of her ribs and bruising her entire body. Despite the bad conditions and regular punishment, the marines indulged in illicit drinking while on duty. Mary heard that, on the *Friendship*, Elizabeth Dudgeon, Elizabeth Pulley, Elizabeth Thackery and Sarah McCormack had been clapped into irons for repeatedly crawling into the bunks of some of the sailors on that ship. For their part, the sailors were flogged. Catherine and Margaret were lucky that their sailors came to them.

When Mary heard that Elizabeth Colley, on the *Lady Penrhyn*, had given birth to a stillborn child at the height of a storm, she prayed that she would be spared that ordeal. Surgeon John White then announced that the water ration would be reduced to three pints a day per person, as the supplies were rapidly being depleted. Occasionally, Mary scored a piece of fish when Vernon or Sammy caught one or collected the flying fish that landed on board.

'You count yourself lucky,' Vernon said one night. He had brought some rum to share with Catherine. 'We jus' passed a slaver under that new American flag. The stink! You could be worse off 'n here.'

'In what way is we better off?' Catherine sounded sceptical.

''Cause you're not shackled to the deck in irons, you get same food as us, an' you're in for seven years, not forever,' Vernon replied.

'Maybe, but we're imprisoned by our own folk, English against English,' Catherine said. 'They's savages, blacks. We're civilised.'

'Well, sup this an' drown your sorrows, woman,' Vernon said. ''Tis better than hangin'.'

By now the stench below-decks was becoming almost unbearable. The bilge water had risen such that the panels in the cabins and the buttons on the uniforms of the officers had been turned black by the noxious effluvia. When the hatches were taken off, the stench was so powerful it was impossible to stand over them. Mary constantly felt like retching. When Surgeon White realised that everyone on board was becoming sick, he ordered the bilge water to be pumped every day and allowed the convicts to go up on deck more often to get some fresh air. But it wasn't only the health of those on board the *Charlotte* that concerned Surgeon White. On 24 July, after the seas whipped up again, he was required on the *Prince of Wales* when a convict named Jane Bonner was injured. A jollyboat had broken loose on the main deck, slid down from its mounting and crushed her head against the bulwarks. The surgeon was unable to save her life.

At last, on 2 August, word passed around the convicts on the *Charlotte* that land birds had been sighted. Mary knew they couldn't be far from Brazil where, Tench had told her, they would be calling in at Rio de Janeiro. (Vernon told Catherine the name meant 'River of January'.) Mary anticipated there would be some trouble at this port. One of the convicts on the *Charlotte*, Thomas Barrett, had been making counterfeit quarter-dollars from old buckles and buttons and pewter spoons, which he intended to exchange for real money that he would use to buy his freedom. As a good seamstress, Mary had done sewing repairs of jackets for some of the marines on board and had obtained buttons for Barrett. He had promised to pay her with coins, which she could use to buy the fresh fruit that she now craved. Barrett had also bribed the cooks in the *Charlotte*'s galley; while pretending to help with the cooking, he was actually using the firebox to manufacture his counterfeit coins.

Barrett had finished his work by 4 August, when all the ships stood in to the harbour. The fleet had to wait until the following morning, however, when the wind failed. As soon as they dropped anchor, Portuguese traders could be heard coming alongside in small boats rowed by Negro slaves. On hearing that these traders were selling fruit, including oranges, Barrett decided to try out his new money. The transactions went smoothly until a suspicious trader, used to being cheated by foreigners, compared Barrett's coins with others given him by the ship's company and found them to be bogus. The fake coins were traced back to Barrett, who was subsequently dragged off to be punished.

As it turned out, Mary didn't need Barrett's help. On that first night in Rio, Will Bryant paid a visit to Mary's cell.

'Psst, Mary. You there?' the familiar Cornish voice said. 'Got somethin' for your babe-to-be.'

'Will. What is it? You're not takin' another risk?'

'Take this,' he said, pushing a bag through the bars. 'Somethin' I'm told you bin cravin'.'

'Oranges!' Mary exclaimed. 'Where did you get 'em, Will?'

'Providers don't matter, Pixie. 'Tis who gets it that's important,' he grinned. 'Now, doan go sellin' 'em, you hear? 'Tis for you an' your little 'un.' Will then disappeared into the darkness.

Mary heard later that the convicts didn't need money to buy fresh oranges because, once the black slaves in the trading boats heard that there were 'white slaves' in chains on board these visiting English ships, they threw the oranges on board for the convicts. Fresh fruit was necessary to keep the occupants of the ships of the fleet alive. Sixteen people had already been buried at sea since they had left England. Mary, eight months pregnant, was certainly glad of the sweet-tasting, nutritious fruit.

During her first exercise period on deck in Rio de Janeiro, Mary was struck by the beauty of the large harbour that lay before them. Behind the harbour were stunning mountains covered in green forest from which issued strange colourful birds of a type she had never before seen. At the southern entrance to the harbour was a mount that rose up like one of the Hurling Stones from Bodmin Moor, but which the locals called Sugarloaf, Vernon said. Forts were dotted along both the southern and northern sides of the harbour. Mary was surprised by the amount of shipping the place attracted, given that it was so far from England.

Although too pregnant to seriously consider escaping, Mary was sorely tempted when she heard that six trouble makers of her cell-mates from the *Charlotte* were to be exchanged with six from the *Friendship*. Mary thought that she might somehow have used the movement of people to and from the ships as a cover for concealing herself on board one of the local boats used for the transfer, and then use the money Barrett had given her to pay the boatman to drop her off at a Portuguese ship in the harbour. But being so heavy with child, it was out of the question. The six women who left the *Charlotte* were Margaret Stuart, Fanny Anderson, Mary Phillips, Hannah Smith, Elizabeth Cool and Ann Coombs; while the six new arrivals from the *Friendship* were Susannah Gough, Hannah Green, Francis Hart, Elizabeth Harvy, Mary Watkings and Ann Baighly.

One of the merchant crew did actually jump ship, becoming the first to leave the fleet. Vernon described to Mary and her friends how Henry Hill had fled the *Lady Penrhyn* and concealed himself ashore so that Commodore Phillip had to hire, in his place, a Portuguese soldier who had come on board begging for a passage from the colony. He, in turn, had to be concealed when, just prior to the departure of the fleet, the port authorities rowed out to the ships to search for three men who had deserted from the army that day. Mary took it all in, being determined to learn from others' experiences.

By 4 September the ships had taken on their supplies and were ready to depart. The hoped-for meeting with the *Bounty* and Captain Bligh hadn't materialised. Watkin Tench was phlegmatic about it with Mary, whom he met on deck during an exercise period when she asked him about their next port of call. 'Well, it's Cape Town, and we had hoped to have *Bounty* as our 12th ship,' he said, looking down the Bay of Guanabara. 'But, mind you, there were no plans for either expedition to wait for the other.' The concept of sailing in company was purely for mutual support, he explained. Bligh would make his own way to Tahiti, though it was possible that the two might meet in Cape Town. 'Anything is possible with the British Navy,' Tench said with a smile.

By the end of the first week in September the fleet weighed anchor, set sail and, with favourable winds, set forth for the Cape. Many of Mary's cell-mates were terribly frightened as it seemed that they were now bound for the end of the earth, especially given the terrifying tales they had heard in England about the savages of Africa. For her part, having not delivered in Rio de Janeiro, Mary was now praying that the passage to the African port wouldn't be a stormy one.

Although the weather was indeed favourable for the early period of the voyage from Rio de Janeiro, as the fleet headed into the South Atlantic towards the roaring forties it became increasingly stormy, and by the second week the ships were being battered by violent thunder and lightning. For days, heavy squalls threw rain and shafts of wind at the ships, tossing them around in the turbulent and confused seas. It was the worst weather they had struck on the voyage.

Most of the convicts below-decks on the *Charlotte* were worried that the ship might break up or take in too much water. Mary, however, had more than the fate of the ship to worry about: on 8 September, as she was being tossed around below-decks, her waters broke and she went into labour. At the height of the storm, Catherine Fryer and Margaret Shepherd, her partners in crime, helped to deliver the baby. Catherine caught the newborn as she slid into the world.

'Quick, check the face,' Mary panted, remembering the story of the caul on her own face at birth. 'Is it clear? Can 'e breathe?'

'Can now,' Catherine replied, smacking the baby's bottom. 'An' there's naught hidin' the pretty little face.'

'What is it?' Mary asked. 'Boy or girl? Tell us.'

''Tis 'nother little Mary Broad, just like her mam,' Catherine said, handing her the baby.

Mary examined her tiny daughter's body. 'Yeah, she's got everything a little girl needs. What a little angel, an' to bring to this awful world.'

'Well, she's here,' Margaret said, mopping at Mary's brow. 'Despite the rough an' tumble o' this topsy-turvy ship. Did well to come in such a stormy sea.'

'She be a fighter, then.' Mary put the baby to her breast. 'Which is what us women mus' be in this world of ourn. A fighter on our ship *Charlotte*, which took her safely through the storms. An' that's what I'll call the waif. Charlotte.'

Catherine and Margaret wiped the vernix from the baby's back and rubbed it on Mary's face and their own before tossing the placenta into a bucket. It had been a challenging ordeal. There had been as many stillborns as normal births on the fleet and Mary was relieved not to have lost her baby. Fortunately, everything was as it should be; the baby was small and presented perfectly. She also felt good about naming her after the ship *Charlotte*, which was also close to the name of the baby's father, Charlie.

By the time Surgeon White came below-decks to examine Mary and the baby, they were both resting as peacefully as a mother and newborn could on a ship being tossed about in a storm. Impressed with Mary's performance, he authorised extra rations to help her feed her baby. As Mary watched Charlotte suckling at her breast, she felt an even greater resolve to escape from her enforced exile from England and return to those people she loved in Fowey. She decided that she would give the baby the surname 'Spence', after her father. Charlie had been a help to her both in Exeter and on the *Dunkirk* hulk in Plymouth. Now, with the baby, she was even more conscious of how vulnerable she was, and was grateful that Will Bryant appeared to have taken a shine to her. She would need a supporter now more than ever.

Throughout September, with the howling winds of the roaring forties driving them ever forward, the ships battled through difficult seas and foul weather towards the misty Cape of Good Hope. The further south they sailed, the colder and wetter it became. The sea broke into the ship through the seams, pouring down the hatchways and the companionways, drenching everyone on board — seamen, marines and convicts alike. Mary managed to keep Charlotte dry and warm, as Catherine and Margaret scrounged extra bedding, blankets and clothing from their sailors, along with the extra rations the breastfeeding mother now needed.

Single man though he was, Will also helped, sneaking extra rations into Mary's cell on his water round.

'Here, let's see the young 'un,' he said on his first visit. 'Let's hope it took after its mother!'

'Enough lip from you, Will Bryant,' Mary said, pulling the blanket back from Charlotte's face. 'Here.'

'Beautiful — just like her mam. Even the same piercin' eyes,' he teased. 'What name did she take?'

'Charlotte.'

'After the ship, I trust, an' not the Queen we left behind,' he said.

'That same ship which carried us safely through the storm the night she was born,' Mary said.

'And let's hope it don't break up afore we get to the Cape,' he laughed. 'Quick, now. Somethin' for you both.' Will thrust into Mary's hands a piece of salted beef that disappeared quickly beneath the baby Charlotte's blanket.

The high seas continued to throw the little square-riggers around day after day, and not long after Mary brought a new life into the world, another was lost. William Brown, a fellow convict, fell overboard on 19 September from the bowsprit while bringing in the washing. Captain Thomas Gilbert hove to the ship while a boat was lowered, but Brown had disappeared. *Charlotte* had been travelling with a fair wind at six knots, Vernon told Mary, and Brown had fallen directly under the ship, which had passed over the top of him. ''E was lucky, Cap'n even put boat over side,' Vernon said. 'Yer know the old seaman's sayin', "Man overboard stays overboard", doan yer?'

By 23 September, the fleet reached the halfway point to the Cape on her voyage across the South Atlantic. They were sailing below 40 degrees south and the seas had become mountainous, engulfing the ships. Sail was shortened as the following sea broke over the poops; and, for the first time since leaving England, the topgallant masts were struck to reduce their top hamper. Lightning, thunder and hail hounded the fleet as it battled through the confused seas. On 25 September, some of the ships were rolled until their main decks were in the water. Below-decks on the *Charlotte*, the female convicts screamed at every shudder and howled with fear as bucket-loads of water splashed into their cells, and bedding, clothing and buckets were hurled from port to starboard, and back again.

It was all that Commodore Phillip and his fellow officers could do to keep the fleet together.

The gales played beautifully into the hands of the bravest convicts on the *Alexander*, who exploited the confusion by slowly amassing weapons from sailors and marines who were off their guard and trying to keep the ship afloat. By the time the fleet reached Cape Town, these would-be mutineers were ready. They were led by John Powers, the convict who had escaped briefly by boat at Tenerife. This time, Powers had sworn that he would succeed in taking over the *Alexander*; he knew this port of call was his last chance. Powers and his gang were armed with knives, swords, pistols, iron bars, belaying pins and rope, and looked set to take the ship. Powers had also paid off at least four sailors who had promised to join his gang, as well as two marines who would let the convicts on to the main deck. It seemed that nothing could go wrong. When the mutineers got control of the *Alexander*, they intended to sail off to freedom.

In his haste to recruit rebels, however, Powers failed to anticipate the deception of his shipmates and on 6 October, the day before the planned mutiny, an anonymous convict who had been brought into his confidence squealed. When he was escorted by a disbelieving marine to the master of the *Alexander*, Captain Duncan Sinclair, the traitor betrayed not only Powers but also the identities of those convicts, sailors and marines who had joined the mutiny party. Sinclair rowed across to consult with Commodore Phillip on board the *Sirius*, and the commander immediately ordered Powers to be put into heavy irons and stapled to the deck, while the other convicts were put in lighter irons and the treacherous sailors and marines were transferred to other ships. The anonymous squealer was transferred to the *Scarborough*, where he was taken below and given protection for his own safety.

By the time that Vernon told Mary and her friends the story, it had been embellished somewhat, to the point where Powers had actually been in command of the *Alexander* before he had been captured. But, even so, Mary was further convinced that convicts couldn't take over a ship. One other convict on the *Alexander*, Sam Bird, had also been tempted to take part in the mutiny. But had decided against it, however, doubting that Powers could take the whole ship, or that he could sail it back to Rio de Janeiro on his own. He decided he would to bide his time for a better opportunity.

On 10 October the fleet reached the calm waters of Table Bay, Cape Town, capital of the Dutch Cape colony, where the fleet was to be watered and repaired while the commodore organised fresh supplies — including livestock for the colony. When Mary came up on deck for the first time, she noticed immediately the gigantic flat-topped mountain that loomed above the little port town. She winced in horror when she caught sight of the bloody bodies of Dutch convicts and prisoners broken on the torture wheels, and of the corpses hanging from the gallows in a sad row along a wharf. This was no place for a convict to be caught trying to escape, she thought.

'An' we reckon we have the lying hard,' the kindly voice of James Martyn broke into her reverie.

'James! I'm so glad to see you,' Mary said, giving the fatherly Irishman a hug. 'We never seem to be on the same exercise shift.'

'Ah, you're like my own daughter to me. Don't you forget what I said in Exeter, mind; there'll be a fatherly eye on you. An 'specially now you have a little bairn.' He patted the head of the tiny infant wrapped in Mary's shawl.

'Well, James, you know the sort of help I'm wishing for,' she whispered, nodding towards the shore.

'To be sure, Mary, an' I'm warned of the risks. I'll be here as you need me — like a father helping his beloved daughter return to her man.' He then lowered his voice. 'You can count on me — us two Exeter residents should always stick together — but you'd better not try anything here. God help us, but we're far, far better off with the English and the Scottish than with any Lowlander. Never have I seen so many gallows and punishments in any town.'

'What do they do to us poor folk, James?' Mary asked.

'I hear that to punish a thief they tie him to a wheel, cut off his right hand now, an' fix it by a nail to the side of the wheel. Then they lift the wheel up, oh, ten feet or so, an' leave the poor bastard to perish. Sure, an' it's a long time to die.'

'Then the sooner we're out of here, the better,' Mary said, holding Charlotte close to her breast. 'The savages of Botany Bay surely can't be worse.'

'I don't know about that, my girl. In London I heard some tales of cannibals in the South Seas.'

The fleet had by now run out of bread, vegetables and fruit, and everyone was looking forward to some fresh supplies. Thirty people on the *Charlotte* alone were sick with some kind of fever and dysentery. But day after day, fresh supplies failed to arrive. Rumour had it that the Dutch authorities wouldn't give the fleet any food supplies because they didn't have enough for themselves.

''Tain't the true reason,' Will confided to Mary when he brought some oatmeal to her cell. 'The Dutchmen here hate us English.'

'Why's that, Will? I remember me old dad, who sometimes received Dutch goods from smugglers, told me old King William was part-Dutch.'

'Too many wars, lass, an' too much blood spilt, even in this place, the Cape. We sent 'em fleeing out of the Americas, an' likely we'll send 'em fleeing out of the Cape, too, given time.'

'So, the Dutch ships should be more sympathetic to convicts on the run?' Mary asked.

'Maybe, but remember Tenerife an' John Powers. Never trust a Dutchy!'

On the 11th day in port, boats arrived from shore with supplies of fresh bread and other foodstuffs. Fruit and vegetables were then distributed among the ships, which event was followed soon after by an outbreak of diarrhoea. The weather stayed fine, enabling the ships' companies to dry out. Soon the rigging was covered in clothing. Many of the convicts were put to work doing cleaning and painting jobs, or repair work for the skilled.

For nearly four weeks, as the fleet lay at rest, many foreign ships came and went, providing Mary and her fellow convicts with a tantalising glimpse of freedom from that other world. Then, one afternoon during her walk on deck, Captain Tench told Mary that the fleet was due to leave as soon as the last of the livestock was loaded.

'You see, Mary Broad — as I understand you would be called, rather than plain "Miss" or the respectable "Ma'am" — we are creating a truly biblical Noah's Ark.'

'Meaning, kind Captain?' she asked.

'Because we are re-creating life all over again, exactly as Noah did after the Great Flood. Two of every species, male and female, so that they may reproduce for the new colony. Exactly as you have,' he said, glancing at baby Charlotte.

'Does that include us convicts?' Mary asked cheekily, ''cause I un'erstand there're far more men than we women.'

94

Tench smiled. 'I'm afraid you are quite right, Mary. That is something we didn't calculate a-right. Yet, I believe you shall not be short of suitors as a result. And you'll surely be treated better than these wretched Dutch convicts. For, as you can see, Mary, sadly these Dutchmen punish as severely here as do those in their East Indies colonies.'

'Is that colony by Botany Bay?' Mary asked casually.

'The cartographers place the East Indies — the Spice Islands — including Timor immediately north of the upper promontory of New Holland. Or, rather, New South Wales, as we now must call it,' replied Tench pedantically. 'Yet, too far to be of any assistance to our colony of Botany Bay.'

Just before the fleet sailed, four convict women were brought across to the *Charlotte* from the *Friendship*, which needed more space created in order to transport livestock. Elizabeth Dudgeon, Elizabeth Pugh, Elizabeth Thackery and Susannah Holmes, whom Lieutenant Ralph Clark said were the *Friendship's* worst troublemakers, were rowed over. Then, when the last of the livestock was loaded on 12 November, the ships sailed out of Cape Town.

This last leg towards the unknown colony of New South Wales was feared most by those below-decks. They had been told this was the longest section of the voyage, and that the fleet was sailing into unknown waters, as no English ship had previously taken this route. Once in Botany Bay — should they arrive in Botany Bay, that is — they would likely remain there for the rest of their lives. All that was there were savages, like the ones Vernon said had clubbed

Captain James Cook to death several years earlier in Hawaii. Cape Town was the last town, the last harbour, of the world.

Mary refused to be depressed by their circumstances. Although she had no firm plan as yet, she believed that there would be visiting ships in Botany Bay — as there had been in the other colonies of Brazil and the Cape — and that she might slip away on a foreign vessel. Perhaps a Dutchman from the East Indies colony that Tench had mentioned.

This last part of the voyage couldn't have started worse. The fleet sailed into such unfavourable winds that it was blown off course and southwards; it took a week before it could return to its easterly track. Then the fleet was split up, depriving the ships of their safety in numbers. Because the progress of the fleet had been greatly delayed, Commodore Phillip had decided to split the convoy into three divisions. The fastest vessel, HMS *Supply*, was sent on ahead to establish a camp; it was followed by a second division of the *Friendship*, the *Scarborough* and the *Alexander*; while the slowest ships, the *Charlotte*, the *Lady Penrhyn*, the *Prince of Wales*, and the three store-ships, the *Golden Grove*, the *Borrowdale* and the *Fishburn*, comprised a third division under the flagship, HMS *Sirius*.

For the next eight weeks the ships tossed and swooped in the high following seas as the westerly winds drove them eastward through the forties latitudes. They passed through the worst storms of the voyage, with great seas crashing on to the decks and pouring below, wetting everything and everyone. As the hatches had to be closed, the air was trapped below-decks and the stench became foul. The temperature fell steadily in the higher latitudes of the Southern Ocean. It was all that Mary could do to keep baby Charlotte warm and dry. Seaman Jorgan Jorgenson of the *Prince of Wales* fell overboard and was lost; in these seas, there was no possibility of heaving to and lowering a boat.

The voyage had become hellish. Officers, sailors, marines and convicts alike wanted only to get to the new land. The commodore was most anxious, as the livestock had begun to perish for want of hay and feed. And yet, by 24 December, their progress had been good enough to celebrate Christmas. Sheep were killed for a special issue of mutton, and everyone, convicts included, was given a double ration of rum.

On Christmas Day, Will Bryant appeared on his water round when Mary was feeding Charlotte in her cell. He was half-drunk on the ship's rum. With a wild laugh, he said: 'Here's a Christmas special for the virgin Mary.' He thrust at her a battered pewter mug brimming with the fiery spirit. 'Madonna an' child, in 'er manger, that I, as a true Cornish Catholic, have worshipped from the day I set eyes on her,' he teased.

'For Gawd's sake, Will, this be a convict ship, not a cowshed nor stable. But thank ye for the rum.'

'And thank ye for the Christmas kiss,' he said, lurching forward and planting a cheeky kiss on her defenceless lips.

Since she was still breastfeeding, Mary gave the mug to Catherine and Margaret to share, and persuaded Will to return to his water round, as best he could. Vernon and Sammy defied the stormy weather and snuck into the women's cell to lie with their women.

*   *   *

After a further two weeks, during which the storm-bound ships rounded the southern capes of Van Diemen's Land, they began at last to head north towards the coast of New South Wales. Mary, ever the mariner's daughter, felt the new winds pushing the ship, which Vernon said were a Godsend for vessels heading north off this coast. Soon the fleet was back in a known part of the world. From the first week in January, a low coastline with mountains beyond was sighted on a regular basis, so that by 14 January the leading ships had reached latitude 34 degrees south. This was known from Captain James Cook's charts to be the latitude of Botany Bay. All the ships ultimately collected off the headlands, and the anticipation of a longed-for landing increased hour after hour. Yet, even now, winds blew against them for four more days. Finally, on 18 January 1788, a favourable southwesterly wind propelled the first of the fleet of little ships towards the coast and into the quiet harbour of Botany Bay itself, where Cook had landed 18 years earlier.

By 20 January, all 11 ships had dropped anchor. The fleet had made it. Mary's ship, the *Charlotte*, lay motionless and strangely quiet.

The silence was soon broken by the menacing cries of the scores of savages who ran up and down both of the rocky headlands. They gesticulated at the ships and waved their spears in a threatening manner, shouting '*Warra, warra, warra*' as they had done at Cook's party 18 years previously. The marines prepared their muskets — after all, there had been many stories about savages and cannibalism. For those officers, marines or sailors who had fought in the American war, these savages, prancing about in war paint, looked as fearsome as the American Indians had been.

If some of those below-decks on the *Charlotte* didn't hear the bloodcurdling yells, everyone heard the drumming anchor cable snaking out into the water. Charlotte began to cry at the unaccustomed sound, and Mary put her to her breast to comfort her.

'So,' Mary thought, watching her dishevelled friends chattering among themselves, 'despite having to be towed at the first, our stinking old *Charlotte*'s made it to Botany Bay.' The long and difficult journey to the far side of the world from Richard and her poor father had taken over eight months.

A stillness descended as the first boats bravely left the ship for the shore. Even the savages had stopped screaming. All Mary could hear was the screech of seagulls; their cries were different from the gulls she was used to in Cornwall, yet they were unmistakably gulls.

Catherine and Margaret took a seat either side of Mary and leaned against the darkened bulkhead.

'Well,' Catherine said, spitting on to the deck. 'Now what, chittie?'

'Pr'aps our marines are rowing ashore to kill them savages,' Margaret said, only half-joking.

'I doan think they'd spend their powder so soon,' Mary replied, moving Charlotte to a more comfortable position. 'They'd save it to stop us escapin'.'

'God, girl, you're not still thinkin' 'bout that, are you?' said Catherine.

'If an old wreck like *Charlotte* can sail here in eight months, a well-trimmed boat with a clean bottom could get home in half that time,' she whispered.

'An' your babe?' Margaret asked. 'What of the babe?' She leaned towards the young mother. 'Let it go, Mary Broad. Let it go. I'm plain sorry we got you into this, that day on the moor — sorry as plain can be. But you listen, lass. We're in this 'ere Botany to stay, as our sentence of transportation beyond the seas for seven years may as well be for the term of our natural lives.'

CHAPTER 4

Abandoned in a land of savages

*After waiting for some time before being allowed ashore
in the land of savages, Mary accepts Will Bryant's
offer of a marriage of convenience and begins gathering
a crew of useful sailors around her to assist
her escape.*

After the weeks of cold, wet and stormy passage from Cape
Town, all Mary and her cell-mates wanted to do after they
arrived at Botany Bay was to get off the ship and on to firm ground
— savages or no savages. Mary had now been behind bars for more
than two years and yearned to walk around freely. As she said to

Catherine, 'My poor liddle babe, Charlotte, is been alive four months but ne're been outside a gaol.'

'Doan 'ee worry, Mary Broad,' her friend reassured her. 'We'll git outta 'ere soon enough.'

But just as obstacle after obstacle had plagued their departure from Portsmouth, their disembarkation was delayed in Botany Bay. The main problem was the natives. There had been a lot of talk among the sailors about the Botany Bay blacks, some of it based on second-hand reports from Cook's voyage of 1770. It was said that he had been forced to fire over their heads in order to keep them back. Yet, one of the sailors on HMS *Sirius*, Peter Hibbs, who claimed he had been to Botany Bay with Cook on that earlier trip, said the savages had attacked Cook. Hibbs, who was becoming a bit of a hero below-decks, had been boasting about his knowledge of these savages ever since the fleet left Portsmouth. He told fantastic stories about the white face paint some of the natives wore, and of the white, skeleton-like markings they painted on their black skin. He also claimed to have seen them practise cannibalism.

Not long after the ships dropped anchor, some of the convicts on various duties saw their first savages on the shore. Will, on his water rounds, came below-decks with the news. 'Jus' seen them savages, or Indians actually,' he reported. 'Well, that's what the marines call 'em, though Cap'n Tench sez these are blacker 'n them 'e fought in America. Leastways, they look hideous — utterly black, rude an' painted all over with white paint.'

'Do they look dangerous, Will?' Mary looked up from feeding Charlotte. 'Or is they puttin' on a show, like when we dress up the frightening 'Obby 'Oss back 'ome?'

'Doan look like they 'ere for dancin', Mary. They pointin' spears 'long the beach the blue-jackets are landin' at, an' them red-coats is all carryin' muskets.'

'Oh. Well, time will tell us all. If us treat 'em right, they may let us pass,' Mary said hopefully. 'Especially a woman with baby, 'cause they'd have plenty of women with children, too.'

Despite the threats, which Mary believed the marines could deal with, she yearned to walk about on solid ground, dry her clothes, and get away from the stench of the stale bilge water that wafted up from below. The heat was more intense than she had ever known, making conditions muggy and unpleasant. However, all the convicts were to be kept on board while Commodore Phillip looked for a suitable base ashore. Then a rumour circulated that the commodore had decided they wouldn't even stay at Botany Bay. Coming below later that day, Vernon told Mary, Catherine and Margaret that he had overheard Captain Tench say that Captain Cook's charts for Botany Bay were incorrect in the land detail, and that there was no fresh water around the bay. The whole scheme might be abandoned, it was suggested. Some on board were saying they might have to sail northwards to Batavia in the Dutch East Indies for supplies, and then make their way back to England. Others claimed that the fleet would sail direct to Cape Horn and return home through Drake's Passage. But no one knew for sure.

At least the savages weren't killing the new arrivals. When some naval and marine officers had gone ashore, Vernon said, the savages had retreated inland from the beach, and accepted the presents of beads and looking glasses that were left for them on the sand. But whether they were staying or not, men had to go ashore very soon to get fresh grass for the livestock that had survived the journey.

Vernon told the women later that another naval officer, Lieutenant King, who had arrived ahead of the fleet on HMS *Supply* to look for a site for a settlement, had reported that the savages were no threat. They were quite naked and looked miserable, King had said. They used primitive canoes, and carried no weapons apart from a spear each. Their hair smelled strongly of fish, and most of them wore beards. Some had a fishbone through their nostril, which made them appear even more repulsive. They were all missing a tooth in the centre of the upper jaw, and had raised scars from cuts across their backs, chests and arms. The convict James Ruse, from the *Scarborough*, who had been ashore on a watering party, told Vernon that the savages lived in simple little wigwams made out of tree bark that were not at all weatherproof.

With great merriment, Vernon recounted how King had offered the savages wine, though they had spat it out. They asked King if he and his strangely attired party — the officers in wigs, breeches and shoes — were, in fact, men. After King had ordered a sailor to unbutton his fly and present his manhood, the savages offered a group of their women to King and his men.

'But 'igh an' mighty Lieutenant King, 'e sez, "No, thank you very much, we won't 'ave none o' that, thank you".' Vernon laughed. 'Stupid bastard! An' you know what 'e does then?'

'Tell,' Mary said.

''E gets 'old of a neckerchief, 'e does, an' 'e ties it 'round the cunt o' one of them wimmen!' Vernon grinned. 'Who's 'e think 'e is, ter knock back their wimmen?'

''Ceptin' for you, Able Seaman Vernon, not everyone wants female favours all the time,' Mary said. 'An' them women savages were fortunate. They'd 've got the pox, likely as not.'

On 21 January, a party set off in three rigged longboats to search for a better location for the convict settlement. Phillip, his second-in-command, Captain John Hunter, and a party of officers and men headed northwards to explore a likely bay that had been reported, but not investigated, by Captain James Cook.

'You there, Mary?' Will called, when he appeared at her cell the next day. 'I'm off.'

'Off? Escapin'?' the startled Mary asked. 'Not without us, Will. Please!'

'Nay, nay, lass. Not yet. Goin' ashore with the marines.'

'Oh. How's that, then?'

'They heard about us fishermen, ain't they?' he laughed. 'They be askin' of volunteers who know fishin' an' boats. I'll see what I can get for you an' your babe.'

'Doan you take no risks, Will,' Mary said. 'Could be very 'andy, this, for later. See which boat handles the best for a small party. You know.'

'Aye. I get your meanin'. 'Tis a chance, true.'

Will handled the boat well in the open waters of the none-too-sheltered bay, and located some productive fishing spots. Under the supervision of Major Robert Ross and a party of marines, he was able to take a good haul of fish using a purse-seine net cast from the beach, as he had done many times before in Cornish coves, demonstrating his great usefulness to the colony. On the low scrubby beaches the savages crowded forward to watch. They were astonished at the number of fish caught in the net, and gave great shouts of admiration. But, no sooner were the fish out of the water than the savages began to lay hold of them as if they had a right to them, at which Major Ross restrained them. Instead, he had the catch transferred to one of the boats and then handed out small portions to everyone, including the savages, which satisfied them for the moment. But as Major Ross proclaimed, 'We're not gonna last long 'ere if we have to share everythin' with these bloody savages. I don't like our chances. It don't look like good farmin' country around 'ere.'

In case the savages were dissatisfied with their share of the catch, Captain Tench stepped forward to help Ross demonstrate the power of the muskets. He placed one of the savages' shields upright in the sand and indicated for the owner to throw his spear at it. The spear knocked over the shield, but didn't pierce it. Tench then stood the shield up again and shot a hole clean through the centre, at which display of firepower the savages shouted with admiration and then rushed forward to inspect the damage. As news of such feats spread, more and more savages came down to the shore to watch the British fishing and beginning the preparations for a settlement. They seemed most interested in trying on the hats and jackets of the officers, offering to trade their spears in return.

Four days after the first ships had entered Botany Bay, Phillip and the scouting party returned and announced that they would all move north to the harbour Captain Cook named Port Jackson. It had a good freshwater stream and offered better shelter than Botany Bay. Will Bryant and his fishing party came back on board, while Lieutenant King, James Ruse and other convicts working on the settlement site packed up their tools. As Will said to Mary when he sneaked her a small fish he had caught in the bay, 'We doan know whether we be comin' or goin', lass! Chippy Cox says Jackson's Bay will be his third destination, havin' started with America.'

'Well, I doan like the sound of this bay here. 'Tain't no hills, 'tain't no shelter. Us'll need shelter an' good trees for buildin'.'

'*Us?*' Will said. 'Doan you get ideas in yer pixie 'ead 'cause I called you Madonna.' But Mary, inadvertently or not, had planted the seed of a thought in Will's head. If they were to share quarters, they could certainly be of help to each other.

On the following day, as they were preparing to sail out through the heads, a shout went up on deck. People began running about the *Charlotte* in a great commotion. Mary wondered if they were being attacked by the savages, and Catherine and Margaret agreed that this was most likely. Then they heard that two unknown sails had been sighted across the entrance to the bay. The fleet might be under attack. It could have represented a chance for some of the convicts to slip away, if there was a battle between the unknown ships and the British. When it was discovered that the ships were French, the possibility of escape seemed even more likely to some, given that Britain and France were traditional enemies. At the same time, of course, they realised that if the French had come to fight the English for possession of New South Wales they might sink ships like the *Charlotte* and many convicts might die, trapped below-decks, especially those in chains.

Not taking any chances, Phillip launched a boat from the flagship that carried the English colours to a beach Cook had named Sutherland Point. There the flag was hoisted to show the French that the English had first claim on the place. Then, before anything could happen, the French ships were blown off course and away from the mouth of the bay. The winds then turned around, preventing the English fleet from sailing out through the heads. Once again, parties were sent ashore to cut grass for the surviving stock.

The next day, the orders were given for the fleet to sail through the heads and north to Port Jackson. Phillip and King went ahead on the *Supply* brig with 40 convicts, including James Ruse from the *Scarborough* and Henry Kable from the *Friendship*, to clear a site for a settlement. The winds were worse than the day before, however, and the *Supply* was the only ship able to leave Botany Bay. The other ten vessels had to drop anchor and wait until the winds changed. Mary wondered when she would ever get off her hot and stuffy, stinking ship.

It wasn't until the next day, 26 January, seven days after the fleet had first entered Botany Bay, that the winds were favourable and the *Charlotte* and the other nine ships were able to set sail for Port Jackson. Once again the French ships reappeared, coming close enough for a boat to row across. The two vessels, under the command of a navigator named Captain La Perouse, were the *Boussole* (meaning 'compass') and the *Astrolabe* ('quadrant'). The ships didn't wish to challenge the British, the Frenchman said; they were on a voyage of discovery and exploration, and were simply looking for a safe harbour in which to rest.

Some of the transports were caught by backwinds as they passed slowly through the narrow heads and out to sea; there were shouts as Vernon, Sammy and the other sailors worked their ships to prevent collisions. Then Mary felt a jolt, and shudders ran through the *Charlotte* and the *Friendship* as they ran on board each other. There was a splintering render from the stern, as a portion of the carved gallery in the transom was torn away from the *Charlotte*. Before long, however, the ships had negotiated the mouth and were heading north along the coast where they reached the grand and wide entrance to the harbour of Port Jackson.

Once inside the harbour, those on board could see or hear the hundreds of savages lining the headlands. The ships soon reached a little cove where they saw the *Supply* already made fast, with bow and stern lines tied to trees that grew right down to the water's edge. After mooring the other ships as securely as possible, the marines fired off four arms of volleys to celebrate their safe arrival at journey's end — shots that Mary and her friends could hear in their cell below-decks.

Soon after, darkness fell and the fleet spent its first night aboard in Port Jackson. There was a strange atmosphere of suspended motion. They had finally arrived at their final destination after an eight-month voyage, but were unable to go ashore. That evening, after their usual slops, Mary, the watchful mother who was acutely aware of potentially threatening noises, couldn't get to sleep because of the call of a bird that seemed to be laughing at them all, even as the last light faded.

The next morning, Sunday, 27 January, Mary was woken early by the same sound. She fell asleep again briefly, only to be woken once more by a bird calling out, in a mournful manner, '*Ark, ark, ark, arrr.*' The sound reminded her a little of a churchyard raven. 'I have much to learn, yet already I know the last and first sounds of the day,' she thought. ''Tis as good as a church clock.'

Soon, parties of men began going ashore armed with axes to cut down trees to make room for the new village. The women stayed on board and spent the day collecting their belongings together and getting ready to be transferred from the ship, which had been their home for so long, to the shore. Some of them cut their hair, or tried to clean up as best they could in the circumstances, mending torn clothing and repairing their shoes. For Mary, Catherine and Margaret, it was also a day of rest; they knew they would soon have to start work and they were all weakened by their journey. Catherine and Margaret were upset, too, about saying goodbye to Vernon and Sammy, who had been a great help and comfort to the women during the voyage. The sounds of axes chopping trees and their crashing to the ground could be heard throughout the day, and by evening enough ground had been cleared for a few tents to be pitched, enabling some of the officers to sleep ashore that night.

'Mary, we'll meet ashore,' Will said quietly as he handed out the water on his last water round. 'I'm gone today fishin', an' they keepin' us on shore this night. Doan you sail off in the ship as a stowaway back to Fowey, now,' he said with a laugh. ''Less that be your plan?'

'As if. With the babe cryin' out all the time, Will,' Mary replied. 'I've got another idea.'

'We'll talk 'bout that on shore. Maybe we can work together, one for all and all for one,' he added with a wink before disappearing up the companionway. Mary thought of the three friends gone ashore that day with all the male convicts from the fleet: Will, James 'Paddy' Martyn and Jimmy 'Chips' Cox. She realised that she had started pulling together a boat's crew; strength in numbers, she mused, as she put Charlotte to sleep in her bunk. The men ashore were bedded in large tents inside a makeshift palisade; only the women convicts and their minders remained on board. Mary wondered if any of the men had thought to try and get back to Botany Bay and sail away with the enemy French ships.

With the men gone, the women on board spread out into the abandoned cells to await their turn to go ashore. Time passed unbearably slowly in the airless space between decks. Next to go ashore were the livestock, which were considered more important than the women. The horses, cattle and sheep were hoisted overboard from the yardarms and into longboats alongside, then rowed ashore. The smaller animals — goats, pigs and poultry — were carried by hand. Ashore, the livestock had all the grass they needed.

From the start, as he was a fisherman, Bryant was given charge of one of the ships' boats. On his first day on the harbour he managed to net a good catch. Once again, it was shared with the savages in an attempt to keep the peace. On the fourth day in Port Jackson, enough ground was cleared for Commodore Phillip's house to be constructed using a frame brought out from England. Yet still the women were kept on board. At eventide, Vernon explained to Catherine that the officers knew there would be trouble unless separate quarters were built to keep them apart from the men. 'Not that I be worried,' he said, cuddling up to her. 'You want your sailor, don't you, Cath?'

'Aw, shut it, Vern,' Mary heard Catherine reply, already saddened by their impending separation.

Stories filtered back to the *Charlotte*, through Vernon and Sammy, about the problems ashore. The savages were now demanding most of the fish caught, and the marines, sailors and convicts had reported that the ground was so hard and full of rocks that the building and farming tools taken ashore were already breaking.

By her fourth day in Port Jackson, Mary was becoming increasingly impatient to go ashore. She didn't want to lose touch with Will Bryant. A makeshift hospital had already been set up, and sick women as well as men had been taken ashore. She wasn't worried by the savages, who hadn't hurt anyone as yet, but she feared that if she stayed on the ship much longer she or baby Charlotte might fall ill from the stench of the bilge water. Yet, still no word came of when they could step ashore. The following day, the last day of January, the heat was finally broken by a thunderstorm that belted down violently, attacking the little tents that lined the shore. The lightning broke branches off trees and caused havoc in the little settlement, where some of the livestock were struck dead by falling branches. Little work could be done throughout that day. The next day, conditions on board the *Charlotte* were even worse than previously; Mary felt that she was suffocating.

Although no women had yet left the ship, Vernon and other sailors who returned to the *Charlotte* from time to time announced that six women from the *Lady Penrhyn* were to leave Port Jackson and establish a colony on an island Cook had named Norfolk. The women would be part of a group that included nine convict men, which was to start a settlement under Lieutenant King. The women selected included Elizabeth Lee, Elizabeth Hipsley, Elizabeth Colly, Olivia Gasgoine and the pretty Ann Inett, to whom, it was suspected by some, King had taken a fancy. Mary was relieved that she hadn't been included in this group, for if it would be difficult to return to England from Port Jackson, it would be nigh on impossible from Norfolk Island.

While she endured the wait aboard the *Charlotte*, Mary thought about Will Bryant's fear that she would stow away. The

Charlotte was continuing to China, where she would take on a cargo of tea at Canton for the British East India Company and then return to England. Although it was tempting to try and stow away, with one or two of the sailors protecting her, she knew that it would be difficult with a child. The babe might cry out at any time. Neither Catherine nor Margaret wanted to risk putting to sea again, but Vernon and Sammy, who seemed amenable to helping Mary, would have been punished severely if they were found to have helped a convict. Mary decided she would have to find another way.

Mary heard on the convict grapevine that, finally, a convict had succeeded in escaping. It was good news. Peter Paris, a Frenchman who had been taken ashore from the *Scarborough* to work, had walked south through the forests to Botany Bay, where the French ships lay at rest. The French officers had taken pity on one of their countrymen and hidden him on board. Several English convicts who escaped and tried to get aboard were turned away, despite the two ships being in need of extra hands.

By 4 February, relations between the savages and the British began to deteriorate when the natives objected to the number of fish the British were catching with their nets. The situation was made worse when drunken marines made approaches to the native women, the female convicts being unavailable.

Finally, on 6 February, 12 days after the fleet arrived in Port Jackson, Mary heard that they were to be taken ashore. Before being let out of their cells, however, they were searched by Captain Tench and two marines to ensure that nothing was stolen from the ship.

'You shall be pleased to hear, Mary Broad, that we have experienced as good a fortune as Noah,' Tench said, as he escorted her out of the cell and up the companionway to the main deck.

'How's that, sir?' Mary replied, shifting Charlotte on her hip.

'We have landed all our species, two by two, so that now they may go forth and multiply, as I hope you will.'

'They need to, sir, if they going to feed us,' she replied. 'But I cannot, unless there is enough food for an extra mouth.'

'Indeed, that food production is what we are all praying for. We do have many mouths to feed already,' he agreed. 'Meanwhile, your young friend Bryant must continue to catch his fish.' Tench helped her over the ship's side and down into the longboat.

Mary looked around at Port Jackson as she, Catherine, Margaret and others were rowed ashore. The horseshoe-shaped cove was smaller than it had appeared from the ship, the strange-looking trees taller. To the east there was a wooded peninsula, and to the west a rocky point. In the clearing either side of the flowing stream were a large number of huts and tents, with pens for the livestock. When Mary took her first steps on the shore, she staggered. Her legs felt like jelly. The ground seemed to be moving with the same motion as the ship. She hadn't walked on land for over a year now, and found it hard to adjust. Captain Tench allowed her a few moments to sit down.

'This often happens, even to us marines after months at sea,' he said. 'It's a matter of balance — in the ears, they say. It'll come back to you.'

'I'm sure it will, sir,' Mary replied. 'I have felt this after long fishing trips in Cornwall.'

When she had regained her balance, Mary was shown with the other female convicts to their tents. The settlement was a hive of activity. Teams of male convicts were busy pitching tents, digging vegetable gardens, constructing huts, building a landing wharf and cutting down trees, all under the watchful eyes of armed marines. Mary didn't see Will Bryant and supposed that he was off fishing in the boat. 'His luck,' she thought. Her thoughts turned to her father working on his boat back in Fowey. No doubt he was on his own with her sisters by now. As for Richard, they could use his farming skills here, she thought, but he couldn't be further away from this far side of the world.

No sooner had Mary and the women been taken to an area in the clearing that had been set aside for the women's tents when there was a cloudburst, and a storm was unleashed that drenched the settlement and turned what had been busy activity into pandemonium. When the storm broke, it seemed to unleash the emotions and lust of the men and women both, who had been kept apart for nearly two weeks. There followed a night of debauchery and riot that proved unstoppable. The thunder, lightning and rain were more violent than any of them had ever seen. At around midnight, a severe flash of lightning struck a large tree in the centre of the camp under which some pens had been constructed to hold the sheep and pigs. The tree split from top to bottom, killing five sheep and a pig.

The physical orgy that erupted was fuelled by grog, as the

sailors had been issued with extra rations for having delivered their human cargo halfway around the world. Everyone expressed their relief that, after more than eight months at sea, they had made a safe landing. Mary stood at the entry to her tent and surveyed the scene. Men were chasing women and lying with them where they caught them; people were singing, drinking, swearing; while all the time the tempest roared around them.

'Doan miss this, Pixie,' said Will, arriving at Mary's tent. 'Here, take a sup.' He thrust a mug of rum into her hands.

'Well, Charlotte's out to it in the tent. I jus' fed her, so I shall, my Cornish companion,' Mary said mischievously, caught up in the mood of the revelry.

'There room for me?' Will asked. 'I knows Cath an' Marg'ret are with their sailors. Fond farewells.'

'In you come, Will,' Mary said. She certainly owed him a favour or two. Aye. It was a long way from Fowey, and Richard would understand that she needed protection. Better to have Will looking after her than be ravished by a drunken sailor or marine. Will took Mary's mug, planted a full-blooded kiss on her lips, took another swig of rum and passed the mug back to her.

As the thunder and lightning exploded around them, Mary pulled Will towards her and encouraged him to unleash the passion that had been building in him since he had first met his 'Madonna'. Mary, also, was comforted by their lovemaking.

The storm blew itself out during the night. When the raucous laughing bird woke Mary the next morning, she shook Will awake in time for him to return to the men's tents before the marines were up. She smiled as she thought of the pleasure he had given her. Now that their relationship had taken this new turn, she realised that she wanted the protection that Will could provide her, even if only temporarily, until they could escape and return to England, she to her father and Richard. The relationship could meet both their needs, as well as give them some much-needed comfort.

With everyone now ashore, the marine officers ordered that they all gather in an area that had been set aside as a central parade ground. All the souls who had sailed on the First Fleet were crammed into the area, while Commodore Phillip and his fellow officers assembled at a table on which were some documents. With the British flag flying above the table, and a small marine band playing marches as the marines moved into position on either side of the table, it was obvious that Phillip had an announcement of some significance to make.

Mary, who was standing with Catherine and Margaret between the two lines of marines and directly in front of the table, had a clear view of the proceedings. Commodore Phillip, who was henceforth to be known as Governor Phillip, announced that he was now the representative of the King as governor of the colony of New South Wales. Accordingly, he had the authority to rule the new settlement that they would build on this site. He named it Sydney Cove. Mary thought of the half penny she wore in the small calico bag against her breast, which bore the head — or, rather, half-head — of that same King, George III, given her by her beloved Richard back in Cornwall.

Phillip's commission was read out by Judge Advocate David Collins. Fortunately, Mary thought, Phillip seemed a humane man who, so far, had treated the convicts fairly. Governor Phillip told the convicts that if they behaved well and worked hard, he would treat them well; if they did not, they would be punished accordingly, he said. Anyone who stole food or tried to escape would, when caught, be hanged. Mary doubted that any convicts would be hanged, as the settlement needed all the labour it could get, and so wasn't deterred. The troops then fired three volleys. Following the ceremony, the convicts were ordered back to their sleeping areas and told to complete the pitching of all tents, which Mary and the others managed to do by nightfall with the help of the marines and seamen.

Mary's decision to link up with Will was vindicated within days, when the marines began drinking and molesting the women they had watched on the ships at close quarters for so long. True to his word, Governor Phillip arrested one of these men, Private Thomas Brinage, who was tried by a military court, found guilty of beating a woman who had refused his advances, and given 200 lashes. 'Thank God, I have Will,' Mary thought. Other frustrated marines, unable to get women of their own, were flogged for fighting among themselves.

Once all the tents had been erected, Mary was told to work in the vegetable garden along with Susanna Holmes, who had been on the *Friendship*. She told Mary that she had taken up with Henry Kable to protect her from the drunken marines.

'Much safer to keep with one man,' Susanna said, sinking her spade into the ground. 'And you?'

'Well, I have a man back 'ome I want to keep meself for,' Mary said, finishing off a hole with her hands. 'When it comes to marrying, that is.'

'You may never see 'im agin,' Susanna said. 'But for here and now, it'd help you get by if you had a man. Otherwise, you doan know if you'll make it back at all, least not on yer lonesome.'

'You're right. What happens here is like another world. We have to be practical and think of our survival,' Mary agreed. 'It'd be like a marriage of convenience, as the old wives used to call it back in Fowey.'

On Sunday, 10 February, Governor Phillip called a meeting at which the judge advocate and chaplain to the settlement, Reverend Richard Johnson, announced that any couples who wanted to get married were to do so that day. Governor Phillip wanted the settlers to start producing children for the future, as Captain Tench had predicted, and so offered married couples a hut of their own, rather than a tent, plus other comforts and privileges not available to single convicts.

Will fronted Mary. 'Shall we do it, Pixie?' he asked.

'I thought we 'ad, Will,' Mary replied, grinning as she moved Charlotte to her other hip. There was a new bounce in her voice; she knew exactly what Will meant.

'Build a hut, I mean,' Will blurted. 'Do you want to?'

'Well, we mus' marry first, Master Bryant.'

'Right,' Will nodded, sounding unsure.

'So?' Mary teased.

'So? So what?' he asked impatiently.

'So, you mus' ask me to marry you,' Mary laughed.

'Aye, of course, lass,' Will said. 'Well, if we marry, no doubt you'll have more chance of making it back to England. An' we can hide tools in the hut.'

'So, is thee proposin'?' Mary asked, cocking her head to one side.

'Well, yes. At least for while we are here in this far-flung land, we can be man and wife,' he said. 'But who knows what we'll do if we leave 'ere? I haven't heard any banns being read, for a start.'

'Aye, Will, 'tis a good idea.' If their marriage was a temporary arrangement, as Will indicated, this would leave her free to marry Richard when she returned to England. 'But, Will, you mus' vow to stand with me, an' help me leave this place,' she insisted. 'I've got this idea I been hatchin'.'

'I will, lass. I'd like to hear your idea. You've been hintin' 'bout it long enough. We'll talk on it in our hut.' He paused. ''Tis "yes", then?'

'Aye, Will, 'tis "yes". An' I thank thee for the askin',' she added formally.

Mary and Will, along with Susanna Holmes and Henry Kable and three other couples, stood by the banks of the Tank Stream as it was now called on the shores of Port Jackson to be married by the Reverend Johnson. The good reverend performed the traditional ceremony, though his voice was occasionally drowned out by the sound of the laughing bird. He then pulled out a gold ring that he had brought along to create some semblance of the real ceremony as performed back in England, to consecrate the unions. He handed the ring to Mary and Will, instructing them to place it on each other's third finger on the left hand. He then retrieved the ring and performed the same ritual with each of the other couples in turn.

Mary was sure that she and Will stood a far better chance of escaping from Sydney Cove now that they had joined forces. Their combined knowledge of the sea and fishing would stand them in good stead, she believed. And they would have the privacy of their own hut in which to plot their escape. Mary had come up with an idea about how they might succeed. She felt ready now to share it with Will.

CHAPTER 5

Preparations for escape

*Now married to a competent fisherman, Mary has
the basic relationship she needs to start pulling together the
crew and equipment needed for her daring escape voyage
in the governor's cutter.*

M ary and Will moved into a rude two-roomed hut that Will
constructed near the rocky point on the western side of the
settlement. There was a bedroom for them all, and a kitchen. By
comparison with the cells in which she had been confined for so
long, it seemed to Mary a luxury to have both space and privacy. She
would use the hut as a base for preparing and executing their escape.

'So, love. Tell us 'bout this idea of yourn,' Will said, just after
they had moved in. 'An' I'll tell 'ee mine.'

'Right.' Mary sat beside him on the log they were using as a seat, cradling Charlotte in her lap. 'No way us'll go inland. Doan know where it goes to, and there's them savages. All moves to take a ship have failed, as we saw on our voyage, Will. The first one by Falmouth on *Scarborough* with them two, Farrell and Griffiths, to last one on *Alexander* with Powers at the Cape.' She poured him a mug of water, water taken from the Tank Stream that ran through the settlement.

'Aye. Can't trust no one not to squeal.' Will took the mug and drank from it greedily.

''Tis true. An' 'tain't practical to slip away on *Charlotte* for China. But there's no need to take a ship. Us both knows we could sail through these waters in a ship's boat, longboat maybe, with sail an' oars. Doan need a deck — jus' like father's fishing boat.'

'True. Same as us smugglers use. But, which way, lass?'

'Northward, Will, along the coast. You felt the winds comin' up from south of this country, didn't yer? Sail when us can, row when us can't. To them Hollanders' colonies, the East Indies–Timor. Our little Cap'n Tenchie told me 'bout 'em. They lie directly north of New Holland. An' there's no love lost between Dutch and English — in fact, I hear they hate English government.'

'Aye, aye. Maybe. But shall they welcome us?'

'Doan know, Will. But if they hate the English government they should help convicts escaping from that hated government. So would be sure to 'elp us. We'll say we were shipwrecked. What do yer think, eh?'

124

Will thought about the scheme while Mary began cooking their meal.

'But what was your idea, Will?' she asked.

'Same as yourn, likely. 'Cept I'd take a cutter, rigged an' ready — bugger any longboat. You know the saying, "Might as well be hanged for a sheep as a lamb." Cutter'll sail faster an' closer on the wind.'

'Governor's cutter, you mean?'

'Aye. None less,' Will nodded.

'God, that's brave. But that's six-oared, Will. Us'll have to row betimes. You'd need to man the sails and I'd be on tiller. Where'll us get six more men?'

'Well, there's me mate, Chips. An' there's yourn Irish, Paddy Martyn.' He counted on his fingers. 'That's three with me,' he said. 'How's Paddy?'

'James? Known him since Exeter assizes. 'E's true, an' he wants shot of all this. Knows his letters. Keep writin' a diary, too. Might be handy.'

'If'n he comes, then, what with Charlotte an' all, an' yes, you take the helm. Reckon us'll find five more.'

'One of us'll have to navigate, Will. Us doan know the coast. Tenchie says 'tis many weeks' sail north of Port Jackson.'

'We'll never get a navigator. Jest 'ave to take the risks, Mary. Risks an' dangers. Won't be fishin' off Fowey overnight. Doan have a chart an' compass, anyway. Where you goin' to get them? Ask your "Tenchie"?' Will scoffed. 'Nay, forget that.'

'Will, look at me,' Mary said. 'Us mustn't rush this an' get caught. Us'll be flogged or turned off. You heard what the governor said 'bout escapin'. We wait till we find a navigator. Doan' have to be a captain.'

'Who, then?' Will said impatiently. 'There ain't no navigators in Sydney Cove, 'cepting the officers.'

'Governor said there'll be 'nother fleet comin' soon from England. May be able to buy a boat compass with some rum, if we can get some from any of our mates in the marines, like Tench. I could say it was for medicinal purposes. Mus' be patient, Will. We only get one chance. Take us a while to store supplies, anyway.'

'At this rate by time we 'ave got away my sentence would 'ave expired,' Will replied.

The next day, Will invited James Martyn and Jimmy Cox to the hut for a meal.

'Are you in, Chips?' Will asked, after outlining the plan.

'I'd do anything for me freedom, and I'd give all the tea in China to get out of this place,' Jimmy replied, twisting the earring he wore in his right ear. 'I'm a bloody lifer, I am, an' I vowed when that mutiny failed on *Mercury* I'd get away again, an' this is it. I know we'll do it,' he said excitedly. 'And being a chippy, I can repair the cutter along the way, long as I can borrow some tools from His Majesty's store. Do you want me to sign a pledge of secrecy?'

'No, Chips. We go back too far for that. Just shake on it,' Will said and extended his hand, which Jimmy shook enthusiastically.

'And you, Paddy. Want to take the risk, or stay here?' Will asked.

'You remember me talking about something like this, James, back in Exeter?' Mary asked.

'Well, I said then I'd help ye, Mary, as father would help daughter, and ye could be my daughter with them grey eyes same as mine, so I stand by my word.' He stroked his greying hair. 'Fact is, I can keep the cutter's records with my diary writin',' he said.

'That makes four of us, the old gang from the *Dunkirk* and *Charlotte*,' Will said. He held out his right hand, with the palm upwards. 'Let's all place hands on each others' together — as we say in Cornwall: one for all and all for one.' The pact was sealed. The core members of the escape crew were now committed.

No sooner had their escape plans been agreed than Will seemed to go cold on the idea of his and Mary remaining married. Perhaps, Mary thought, the talk of life after Port Jackson made him want to be a free man in every sense of the word. Almost overnight, he turned from being cheerful and affectionate to moody and remote. When, on the Sunday following the meeting with Jimmy Cox and James Martyn, Mary and Will returned to the hut with Charlotte after an open-air church service, Will declared: 'Ours weren't a true marriage last week, Mary. Now we got our plan in place, I jest thought I'd let yer know.'

'Why not? 'Cause you had no fancy ring to give me?' she chided.

'Weren't no banns read out. Three weeks the banns mus' be read. I know my church,' he said.

'Well, Mr Bryant, seein' as there be no church, an' no parish, an' I been ashore here less'n a fortnight— why, that don't figure,' Mary said. She finished changing Charlotte's swaddling. 'We got the hut, didn't we?'

Will collected his nets and left the hut without saying anything further.

A day or so later, Will burst into the hut with some news. A party of naval officers had just returned from an excursion up the harbour with four convict women who had tried to escape but became lost. Exhausted, hungry, and frightened of the savages, he said, they had been pleased to give themselves up, especially as a fifth woman had gone missing in the forest and couldn't be found. Later, when Mary met the women, they described how difficult it was to find food, especially not having a gun with which to shoot local game such as the jumping marsupial that Captain Cook had named the kangaroo, which was apparently good eating. Mary was further convinced that it would be unwise to attempt to escape inland. She also vowed to find out what plants were edible, and to stock up on supplies, which she could hide beneath a loose floorboard in their hut.

It was difficult to put aside any of their food supplies, as the fledgling colony was struggling to feed itself. Earlier that month, Mary had watched the brig *Supply* with its contingent of female convicts set sail for remote Norfolk Island. In Port Jackson, hungry convicts had started stealing from each other, despite receiving up to 150 lashes if caught. One convict who stole some biscuit was confined for a week on a small island off Sydney Cove known as Pinchgut, with only bread and water to sustain him. One day, while returning to the hut from her work in the vegetable garden, Mary saw John Bennett and a woman, both from the *Friendship*, tied to a cart and flogged for stealing food. Having been flogged for escaping his irons on the voyage, Bennett was now a serial offender. It was as the governor had promised.

Both Mary and Will resolved to stay out of trouble. Will continued to take the boat out each day with a fishing party, impressing the supervising officers whenever he netted a big catch. Apart from locating the best fishing spots for different conditions, the experienced smuggler from the rugged coast of Cornwall also taught himself the layout of the harbour, so that he would know it well by night. He located quiet coves that provided safe shelter or suitable hiding places, and studied the currents and winds that moved the boat up and down the harbour in different conditions. He got to know where the savages lived. Whenever he encountered them, he would give them a handful of fish. He hoped that they would recognise him by his distinctive ponytail and recall his generosity if ever he was in a potentially dangerous situation with them.

Will was excited when he discovered a fellow sailor who could help with the rowing. If this one worked out, they would only need three more.

'Found 'nother seaman with strong arms for rowin',' he announced to Mary upon returning to the hut one night. 'Could be our fifth of the nine escapers we need.'

'What ship, an' what's his name, Will?' Mary asked, turning from her cooking.

'Bird, or "Birdy", they call him. From *Alexander*. A good seaman, 'tis said. He was sent to my boat today, and was very 'andy on the water.' Will placed two fish on the table.

'An' trustworthy, Will? We doan know 'im, as wasn't on *Charlotte* like rest of us.' Mary began to fillet the fish.

'Reckon so. One o' Powers' cronies from Cape Town. He's desperate to clear out.'

'What's he in for, this Birdy?' Mary asked.

'Thievin' hemp bags an' saltpetre. But he broke into a bloody warehouse in Lunnon. Done it with his brother,' Will said, impressed with the man's daring.

'So, that makes him part of our family, you reckon?' Mary asked, dropping the fish into the pot.

'I'll watch 'im an' see,' Will said. 'Then I'll bring 'im to meet you.'

Well, Mary thought, as she returned to work in the vegetable garden the next morning with Charlotte strapped to her back. If Will's right, that gives us a gang of five skilled crew including myself at the helm: fisherman Will Bryant, carpenter Jimmy Cox, record-keeper James Martyn and now seaman Birdy. Turning over the soil, and planting and tending seedlings, Mary took heart. Having a keen interest in growing herbs, she soon began getting results that pleased the officers in charge of the gardens and gave her ideas about what she could grow for the journey. She had to get it right, as a convict had just died from eating some strange berries that grew around the harbour, while one of the cooks from the *Prince of Wales* ate something that made him dizzy and he fell into the water and drowned.

'Here he is, Mary,' Will said, as he arrived at the vegetable patch with a good-looking man of 29 years with a bushy beard. 'Birdy.'

'Sam Bird, it is, ma'am,' the newcomer said politely, removing his weather-beaten cap. 'It's just Will here calls me "Birdy". Others, you know, ma'am, they call me "Squawk", after losin' me job as a labourer in Wandsworth. Worst I get is "Bird-brain", but you can use whichever you like. Mind you, I do have another name or two. You might have heard some call me John Simms, but I stopped a-usin' that one.' He spoke well and colourfully.

'I'll call you "Birdy",' Mary said. 'Will told me you know boats.'

'Aye, that I do, backwards, ma'am. That is, I knows boats backwards, not saying I sail 'em backwards,' he replied, with an endearing laugh.

'An' you're his starboard hand in the fishing?' she asked.

'Right or left, port or starboard, all the same to me, ma'am. I do what Will says, ma'am, an' I'll do what you says, ma'am, anytime, anything, I will,' he said with a grin.

'Why you here, Birdy?' Mary asked.

'Borrowing, ma'am. Borrowing a few hempen bags of goods — nothin', really, only five bobs' worth, if that,' he said. 'Oh, an' a little saltpetre for making powder — gunpowder, that is, ma'am, not your baking powder. Nothing, really.'

Mary laughed. She had taken a liking to this Sam Bird. 'Well, I hopes to see more of you, Master Birdy.'

'At yer service, ma'am,' he said, stroking his beard. 'Count me in as crew, and you can cut me throat if I ever talk of it afore we go.'

Mary hoped they would survive long enough to make good their preparations, as by 27 February, one month after they had dropped anchor in Sydney Cove, the first starving convicts were caught stealing bread and pork from the public supply and were sentenced to death. Mary knew their ringleader, Thomas Barrett; another serial offender, he had forged coins in Rio. She also knew Barrett's partner, Joseph Hall, both of whom had been on the *Charlotte*, but she didn't know Henry Lavell or John Ryan, who had come out on the *Friendship*. It was the first hanging in the colony on the newly created gallows, a tree between the male and female camps, and all the convicts were required to attend. The marine officers marched the convicts to the place of execution, where the Reverend Richard Johnson read out the prayers before tying a scarf over Barrett's eyes and putting the noose around his neck. Barrett then mounted the ladder. As she watched the proceedings, Mary pictured the highwayman Jack Sheppard being rescued at the last minute from the gallows, but even as she did so the ladder was removed and Barrett was launched into the next world with an agonised groan. The crowd of onlookers gasped. It was the blackest moment so far for the fledgling colony. As if moved by the collective fear of all the convicts present, Governor Phillip postponed the executions of the remaining convicts until the following day.

Overnight, however, the convicts organised a petition to which Mary added her 'MB' mark and which Will also signed. The petition was sent to the governor, begging him to pardon the remaining three thieves. Despite their apprehension, all the convicts gathered again at the hanging tree the following afternoon. Again, the doomed men were marched up to the noose, where once again Reverend Johnson read a prayer. But just before the noose was placed over the head of Henry Lavell, Judge Advocate David Collins arrived to deliver a pardon from the governor on the condition that Lavell and Hall were banished to live on a remote island and Ryan received 300 lashes.

The following day, 29 February, a further four convicts were caught stealing wine and flour: two black West Indians, John Williams (also known as 'Black Jack') and Daniel Gordon, and two English convicts, James (or Robert) Freeman and William Shearman. Once again, the proceedings progressed as far as each of the four having a noose around his neck before their sentences were reprieved. Freeman was reprieved to become the settlement's full-time hangman, while the others were to be exiled from the settlement. The governor, however, soon regretted releasing 'Black Jack', who escaped as a stowaway in April 1790 on the *Supply*, then after being caught and punished he escaped again in 1792 on the *Atlantic*, and yet again he was caught and punished.

By early March, an increasing number of people were falling sick with dysentery. Mary experimented with local herbal remedies and managed to ward off the disease that soon ran right through the settlement, weakening the workforce. The building of huts and barracks by the convicts and marines slowed as the men fell sick. It was all that Chief Surgeon John White and his team of assistant surgeons, working out of the tiny hospital, could do to keep up with the numbers of people requiring treatment.

During the second week of March, Mary learned that two convicts had escaped the settlement, but not the savages. William Allen (of the *Alexander*) and Alexander MacDonald had been killed by savages, who then hung the men's clothes in a tree in a triumphant gesture of victory. Despite such events, convicts continued to attempt to escape. On 12 March, two convict women eloped from the settlement with their beds and baggage, chancing their luck in the bush. They were never seen again. It was supposed that they would have died at the hands of the savages. It was hardly safer in the settlement. On 16 March, six convicts were attacked while cutting rushes in a bay just to the east of the village; one had his collarbone broken by a spear before the men had been able to frighten off the savages.

Mary was more convinced than ever that the only way out of New South Wales was by sea. Some convicts believed that there were other settlements in New South Wales, and that China could be reached by going inland, over some blue mountains that could be seen in the distance to the west; however, both Mary and Will thought this was unlikely, since the *Charlotte* was planning to sail *north* to China. There was a lot of discussion among the convicts about China, the next destination of the three ships that had been chartered by the British East India Company. Vernon and Sammy, on board the *Charlotte*, were now taking their leave of Catherine and Margaret, as the three vessels were ready to set sail.

On 27 March, the *Charlotte* sailed out of Sydney Cove, in convoy with the *Scarborough* and the *Lady Penrhyn*, bound for China. Mary dismissed any thoughts that she might have stowed away on board one of the vessels. It would be far preferable for them to have their own boat, she knew. Her father's words came back to her: 'There's nothin' like a boat to give you all the freedom you want, Mary. That's the good thing about a boat.'

Arm in arm with Catherine and Margaret, who had had to kiss their sweethearts goodbye, Mary watched the departing ships. 'That's it, friends,' she said wistfully. 'Our last link with home an' England gone.'

'An' our men, Mary,' Catherine said bitterly. 'Our men gone, too. 'Tis fine for you with your man still here, but we must fend for ourselves.'

'Doan you take on so,' said Mary. 'There be more men than women in Sydney Cove.'

'True. But not as good or as generous as our *Charlotte*'s. Oh, time will heal, I s'pose.'

'Well, why did you not try and stow away on board, if you felt so strong?' Mary asked. 'Yer men loved yer enough.'

'Never wanna go out to that frighten sea again. I hate it more than anythin',' Catherine said.

'I'd rather die here than get on another ship,' Margaret agreed.

'You'll find men 'ere, girls,' Mary said.

*   *   *

On 2 May the enterprising convict John Bennett was caught stealing food from the commissary. En route to Botany Bay, he had slipped out of his irons and was flogged; and in February he had been flogged for stealing. Now, this spirited convict was hanged with no question of reprieve. An example to all, Bennett's body was left to swing from the gallows for days.

Mary's concerns that the settlement might run out of food were justified. No one seemed to be growing anything, she complained to Will. There were no farmers — like her beloved Richard Thomas, she thought — to show others what to do. Some convicts felt they would fare better in the forest, but there was little food for the British in the bushland around Port Jackson. Two or three of the escaped convicts were found dead; the head of one was found on its own beside a cave. But by 14 July, even the chance of escaping on board ship was lost, when the last of the commercial ships chartered by the navy left — the *Alexander*, the *Prince of Wales*, the *Friendship* and the *Borrowdale* — leaving a very empty expanse of water off Sydney Cove. Where once there had been 11 square-riggers, a floating village, now there were only the small store-ship, the *Fishburn,* and the flagship, *Sirius*, as a final link to England and home.

Mary, tending her vegetable patch as usual one day in October, was relieved to see the *Sirius* set sail on a voyage to Cape Town to get badly needed supplies. The *Fishburn* departed the following month, in company with the *Golden Grove*, which had returned from supplying Norfolk Island. Now the only seagoing vessel in the harbour was the governor's cutter itself. It seemed so conspicuous, but Mary knew this wasn't the time to make their escape. They must continue to prepare properly for the voyage that would restore them to freedom.

When the governor announced stricter rationing until the *Sirius* returned, as the settlement was low on most food supplies, it became increasingly difficult for Mary to store food for the journey; there wasn't even enough for their daily needs. She was grateful that she was still able to breastfeed Charlotte, but that would change in time. The situation worsened when a number of the cattle, which provided beef and milk to the colony, got loose and disappeared into the forest. Apart from the low food supplies, planning for their escape was going well and they hoped to leave as soon as they could recruit a navigator from the next fleet. However, Mary's grand plan then suffered a serious setback on 4 February 1789. Worried about the lack of food for their own table, Will stole some fish from his catch for their private use.

'Why, what are you thinkin' of, Will?' Mary said, as he dropped the fish on the table. 'We're obeying the law, now. Remember?'

'Just fishes, Mary. God knows, we need food badly, an' there be plenty in the sea!' he said.

'Nobody saw you?' Mary asked, as she wrapped and hid the fish.

'Only Paget, the new man with us. He do look a bit rat-ish, come to think of it,' Will said. 'An' he took none 'imself.'

'Paget from *Scarborough*?' Mary asked. 'I doan trust him. 'E's got shifty eyes.'

Paget did, in fact, alert the marines. They arrived soon after to search the hut, while Will, Mary and little Charlotte waited outside holding their breath. Fortunately, the marines found the two fish before they uncovered the supplies for the voyage, which were concealed under the floor and in the roof of the hut. Will was sentenced to 100 lashes, taken off the fishing boat and, along with Mary and Charlotte, expelled from the hut that was the base for planning their escape. It was a serious, painful setback. Will received his sentence over a period of time, so that just as the torn skin on his back began to heal, he would be subjected to a further round of lashings. In despair at his folly, and in great physical pain, Will's temperament became increasingly moody and sullen.

None of the convicts blamed Will for stealing; they were all hungry. His crime hadn't been a heinous one like stealing from the government store, which seven marines had been doing for some weeks. Mary gave Governor Phillip his due. When the marines were found to be stealing, six of the seven were hanged at once in front of a startled assembly of the community, in the same fashion as convicts had been hanged.

But as food was becoming increasingly scarce, Mary looked for another solution. She decided to learn all she could about local food sources, the plants the savages survived on. She started to make friends with the savages she met around the settlement. One such was a man named Arabanoo, whom the governor had captured and wanted to teach English, so that Arabanoo could serve as an interpreter. Mary seized her chance to learn some local words from this tall, gentle savage with his disarming smile and ready laugh. Now free to wander around the settlement, Arabanoo would visit Mary in her vegetable garden. In exchange for something to eat, he would teach her words that could come in handy during their escape voyage. Unable to write them down, like Arabanoo himself, she learned them by heart. In time, when she knew enough words, she would take walks with Arabanoo during which he would point out those plants that were edible. Over the next few months, Mary came to know plants that could substitute for spinach, leeks and parsnips in the English diet, as well as various edible berries, fruits and seeds.

'Well, we're not going to starve once we get going, Will,' she announced one evening on returning to the tent they now called home.

'Why's that, Pixie?' he asked, sounding more like his old self.

'I now know about ten plants that the savages eat which grow along our route.'

'How do you know we can eat 'em?' he asked. 'We're not savages.'

'Of course we can. We have the same stomachs inside, whether our skins are black or white,' she said. 'Anyway, we won't get enough food from this starving place, so count yourself lucky that Arabanoo has been teaching me.'

'He's in the governor's pocket. Are you sure we can trust him?' Will said.

'You organise the cutter, Will, and leave the supplies to me,' she said, as she began to prepare their evening meal.

Will had no need to worry for long about the trustworthiness of Mary's local mentor. On 18 May, Arabanoo died of smallpox, a disease that had been brought to the country by the English and which killed hundreds of the savages over a period of a few months.

Although HMS *Sirius* returned to Sydney Cove in May with extra food supplies, Mary knew they wouldn't last long and were no substitute for farmers growing crops or meat locally. Even Major Ross, who was in charge of the marines, was critical of Governor Phillip. The colony was doomed to failure, he argued. They should all pack up and go home before the supplies ran out. Then, in July, when the last thing Mary and Will needed was another mouth to feed, Mary discovered the biggest setback of all — she was pregnant again.

'What the hell? 'Ow come, lass?' Will asked.

'Reckon you mus' know that, Master Bryant!' Mary replied. 'You an' that son you been talkin' 'bout.'

'But Jesus, not now! I thought you'm knew when we could an' when we couldn't.'

''Tis one thing for me to say, an' 'tis 'nother for you to leave well alone.'

'Nay, nay, you mus' be strong, woman. 'Tis down to you,' he said.

'Well, we both mus' be strong,' Mary said. 'An' maybe a deal stronger. There'll be two little 'uns to feed now.'

'Christ! Means we can't leave afore nine, ten month or more,' Will said.

'True. But by then the next fleet will 'ave come and we should have our navigator.'

'How do yer know that?' he said.

'Have faith. I know in my bones. So, have patience.' Mary patted her stomach and then said softly, 'Will, this is yours.'

'Yeah, I s'pose it is,' he said, calmer now.

'Come over here,' Mary said, and took his hand as he sat down beside her. 'Now, us'll finish that rum from the store,' she added. He nodded. After the last drop was gone, they fell into bed and lay with each other as passionately as they had that first night in the storm soon after their arrival in Sydney Cove.

Slowed down by Will's loss of position as the colony's head fisherman and by Mary's advancing pregnancy, the would-be escapees bided their time until Governor Phillip realised how badly needed were Will's fishing skills. He was reinstated as head fisherman, and the little family returned to their hut. The supplies brought by the *Sirius* lasted until November, when Governor Phillip was forced to cut the food ration by one-third. With so little food in the colony, Will was ordered to catch as many fish as possible to prevent the settlers from starving. The governor also captured two more savages and shackled them up near Government House, in hopes of teaching them English so that they would replace Arabanoo as interpreters. But the new savages, Bennelong and Colebe, weren't as compliant as Arabanoo had been and regularly escaped. Mary managed to meet Colebe's wife, Da-ring-ha, from whom she learned a little more about edible local plants.

By the new year, January 1790, two years after the First Fleet arrived in Sydney Cove, the colony's spirits had hit an all-time low. For 24 months they had been waiting for relief ships, but none had come. They felt they had been abandoned in this land of savages. Even the savages themselves were still dying in increasing numbers, mostly from smallpox, so the whole community was shrinking, both white and black. In March, Mary was relieved when she and Will weren't chosen to be relocated to Norfolk Island. Governor Phillip put 200 convicts on board the two naval ships, the *Sirius* and the *Supply*, and despatched Captain John Hunter and the commander of the marines, Major Robert Ross, to take them to Norfolk Island where he hoped that Lieutenant King would be better able to feed them. Although Governor Phillip and his farmers had still not grown any substantial crops around Sydney Cove, King's farmers had been more successful on Norfolk. Mary was thankful that Will was a skilled fisherman, or they might have been sent out into the Pacific from which there could be no escape.

Had Mary not been about to have her baby, Will said, this would have been the ideal time to go. 'There be no ship in the harbour, lass, not one. Governor 'as nothin' to chase us in. Only seagoing vessel is the cutter. Why, I could take it this night — if only you weren't fat with child!'

'Sure, Will. But who navigates? An' no compass, an' no chart. An' we need more men to pull six oars.'

'Aye, aye,' he conceded reluctantly. ''Tis true, 'tis true, all you say. But 'tis right frustratin'.'

A few days later, while the naval ships were still away, Mary gave birth to a baby boy, again with the help of Catherine and Margaret. Compared with Charlotte's birth at the height of a fierce storm at sea, it was an easy birth.

'Look, Will,' she said, lifting the baby towards his father when he returned to the hut from fishing. 'What do you say?'

'Boy or girl?' Will asked, seeming reluctant to take the bundle.

''Tis a boy. 'Tis another Master Bryant!' Mary said. 'Come, man, take 'im. 'E doan bite!'

'A boy-child, eh?' Will took the tiny bundle to the door to get a better look in the evening light.

''Tis a terrible place to be born, child,' Will said. He looked at the squeezed-shut eyes. 'Doan fret, now. Us'll mind you well enough. An' get you from this place soon as can — won't we, Mary?'

'Aye, course, Will. By three month us'll be ready, an' surely a ship'll come by then. Mus' have a compass to steer by, Will. Here.' She took back the baby.

'What name do we call him by, Mary?'

'Emanuel,' she said. 'Means "the chosen one".'

'Chosen? For what?' Will asked.

'Freedom,' Mary said. 'The babe'll bring us luck.'

'Aye, we'em need that. Fine by me,' Will said. He picked up the axe and went to chop wood for the fire.

It was just as well that Mary and Will hadn't escaped up the coast in early 1790, as within weeks Captain Ball returned from Norfolk Island on the *Supply* with the terrible news that the *Sirius* had been wrecked on a reef, stranding hundreds of people on the island. The *Supply* then headed straight up the coast to Batavia, in the Dutch East Indies, to bring back more supplies. Lieutenant King would go on to England to advise the government that the colony needed the greatest assistance, as it was on the verge of collapse. Captain Ball, on his speedy *Supply*, would have easily caught the cutter with its crew of escaped convicts. Mary and Will had no doubt that their punishment would have been death, and breathed a sigh of relief. When Governor Phillip announced a further severe ration cut, Will's fishing assumed even greater importance, although by now the sailors, marines and convicts alike all detested fish.

'Do you see, Will?' Mary said in the privacy of their hut as she fed Emanuel. Charlotte played at her feet with a rag doll. 'If Captain Cook an' Captain Ball can fetch these winds to that Dutchmen's colony, why, so can us.'

'Aye. Yet we mus' mind the time carefully, when no other vessel is sailin'. No doubt 'tis the closest habitation.'

'We'll go soon, Will. Only need a navigator an' two or three more crew,' Mary said.

To Mary, it seemed that the young colony had suffered all it could suffer. Shipwreck, storms, searing heat, failed crops, and attacks by savages, combined with intense isolation and loneliness. Any more problems, she thought, and the settlement would collapse. With the marine commander, Major Ross, and other marines marooned on Norfolk Island, where martial law had been imposed, the convicts in Sydney Cove might have arranged a successful rising. Yet, where would they go? What could they do? The best possible chance for survival lay in everyone, convicts included, working together. A rumour circulated that the governor had sent a letter to London on the *Supply* requesting a replacement for himself. If true, it was depressing news. Phillip was a good and kindly man; the colony relied on him. It wasn't surprising that he wanted to leave before the place collapsed. Will told Mary that he had overheard Captain Tench telling another marine that he believed it was only a matter of time before they all starved.

Finally, on 3 June 1790, when many people in the colony had given up hope, the watch at the heads signalled to Port Jackson that a ship had been sighted coming northwards up the coast. The settlers in Sydney Cove downed their tools and flocked to the water's edge. Hundreds of people waited with bated breath, including Mary and Will, James Martyn, Jimmy Cox and Sam Bird. The vessel was the *Lady Juliana* under the command of Captain Thomas Edgar. After she anchored off Sydney Cove, her captain came ashore and explained that she was the first to arrive of the four ships of the Second Fleet, three transports full of convicts and one small store-ship. Sadly for the colony waiting for food and fresh workers, the *Lady Juliana* carried only 221 convicted prostitutes and 11 children. The arrival of the transport rumoured to be nothing more than a floating brothel may have helped with the shortage of women in the colony, but it would make the food shortages worse, especially as a store-ship, the *Guardian*, sent previously from England and intended for Sydney Cove, had been wrecked en route when she hit an iceberg south of Cape Town the previous December.

'P'raps now 'tis a good time for a rebellion,' Will said that evening, 'if what them *Juliana* sailors says is true.'

''Bout?' Mary asked, as she prepared the family's meagre supper of fish stew.

'Them mad Frenchies 'ave organised a bloody revolution and clapped King Louis in gaol — that's what 'tis about, lass!' Will said.

'Nay? When was that?' Mary asked, stirring the stew.

'Aye, last year. I think 'twas July. 'Tis what they sayin'. The mob mutinied and took over.'

'No, is that true?' Mary asked. 'It sounds too hard to believe.'

'Well, it's 'xactly as the parli'ments did with our'n King Charles, nigh on 150 year ago,' Will replied. 'What with Americans rebelling against our king, and now this French mob takin' over France, these are revolutionary times.'

Will stared out of the open door of the hut. It was warm for May, just like May at home. But it wasn't home. Mary was still considering the astonishing news from the world they had left behind.

'Wonder if parli'ment'd lock our King 'Mad Farmer George' in Newgate Knocker?' Will said.

'Nay, man,' Mary said. 'England 'as a parli'ment. 'Tis the diff'rence. My old dad used to say since that Cromwell chopped off Charlie's head, parli'ment has always ruled the king.' She put her hand to her bodice and touched the pouch she concealed there; her thoughts flew to Richard, all those miles away.

'Just as well,' Will said. 'The bastard is mad.'

The *Lady Juliana* was soon joined by the other three ships of the Second Fleet. The store-ship *Justinian*, with food, seeds, tools and other supplies, received a joyous welcome by the settlement. Then a familiar vessel from the First Fleet once again anchored off the Cove; the *Scarborough* was making her second visit, carrying male convicts. Two more transports arrived in company, the *Neptune* and the *Surprise,* with both male and female convicts. However, many of these convicts — those who had survived a dreadful passage in which some 260 had died out of an original 1000 that had embarked in the Pool of London — were sick and dying. The private shipowners and their masters had placed the convicts on reduced and poor-quality rations in order to make a greater profit from the venture. Mary was reminded of the stories of the slavers, which William Wilberforce had spread about the harbours and towns of the country. Some of these sick convicts died in their tents at Sydney Cove. It appeared that many of these new arrivals would be in no condition for some time to help the settlement grow more food; the colony would be reliant upon the stores brought by the *Justinian*. Best to be away from the stricken settlement as soon as possible, Mary thought. She prayed that one of these hundreds of reluctant settlers could navigate.

Within days of the last vessel arriving, Will had the news for which they had been waiting.

'Mary, lass. We found 'im,' he said, rushing into the hut.

'Found who, Will?' Mary asked. She was feeding Emanuel, who had been fretful.

'A navigator! Sez 'e shipped as second mate in the Carib trade.'

'Oh! Oh, wonderful, Will!' Mary cried. 'What's 'e call 'imself?'

'Moreton. William Moreton. Of *Neptune* transport.'

'Good, good. 'Tis possible 'e may be jus' the man. But, Will, now, doan you say nothin' till we both talk to 'im.'

'Aye. I'll find a reason to bring 'im by,' Will said.

The next evening, Will brought a 32-year-old mariner to the hut. Tall and thin with a dark complexion, he had a tattoo on both upper arms of square-rigged sailing ships on which he had served.

'Evenin', Mother,' William Moreton said. He was proud-looking, with a moustache that reminded Mary of the driver of the coach that she and her companions had robbed near Plymouth. He had spent time in Newcastle in the north of England and spoke with a northern accent.

'Will, here, tells me ye may be needin' a navigator, like.'

'Already told you, has he?' Mary said, giving Will a dark look. 'Well, Master Moreton, p'raps we do an' p'raps we doan. What's your'n partik'lar trade, now?'

'Call me Bill, Mother. Most does, although my pet name at sea is always Master Moreton,' he said. 'Signed on second mate in the sugar trade from the Caribbean for some years. Back an' forwards to London. Master stood the eight-to-12, mate stood the four-to-eight an' ran the deck, and second — me — took the 12-to-four an' the navigation.'

'Then 'ow come you're here, Master Bill? What brung you down so?'

He grinned, looking embarrassed. 'Shall we say, a little mistake in the paperwork?' His grin disappeared. 'Seven years! If I had me time again …' he added bitterly.

'You steered a ship on to the rocks?' Mary asked in alarm, imagining him misreading a navigational chart.

'Nay, nay, Mother. I mean ship's papers. Cargo manifest.'

'Oh! Forgery!' said a relieved Will.

'Aye. Yet, nay. Judge called it false pretences,' Bill explained. He shrugged. 'Leastways, here I find myself, in Botany Bay.'

''Tis called Sydney Cove, now. 'Twas Port Jackson, but governor wants his promotion so named it after some government bigwig back 'ome,' said Will. 'Botany Bay's to the south, ten mile or so.'

Mary looked Bill straight in the eye. 'We doan intend to stay in neither spot long, Master Bill.'

'Aye, Will were tellin' me, like.' He paused, taking in the mean and rude hut in which these two lived, their two children asleep on the straw bed. 'Happen I don't intend to stay either. I didn't take to the crew of *Neptune*, the way I was treated. Starved us, they did. I'd like to get me own back. I never treated me own crew that bad. Not fitting.' He nodded towards the children. 'What of them?'

'They mine. They come,' replied Mary. 'Me an' Will are fisherfolk. Cornish. I'll mind 'em well.'

Bill nodded. 'Right ye are. Ye must keep 'em quiet, though, Mother, afore we go and if we sail by night. We'll need a compass, an' one of Cook's charts of his 1770 voyage. Or a Dutchman's chart. Either'll do, with the Spice Islands. A quadrant, chronometer an' mathematic tables will be right handy, too, but I doubt ye'll lay hands on them. Usually locked away in the cabin. It'd be difficult to pinch off of me old ship *Neptune*, I can tell ya. Try for a quadrant an' declination tables, if ye can. That'll give us the latitude.'

'Aye. 'Tis as we thought. But "Spice Islands"?' Mary asked.

'East Indies. Dutch colonies. Spice Islands–Timor. Same place, different names, like.'

'We're in luck, Will,' Mary said. 'An' so is you, Master Bill of the North Countree. Maybe you won't be so long in Sydney Cove as you thought.'

With Bill Moreton navigating, Mary and Will now had a crew of four, two short of what they needed to row a six-oared cutter, as Will would be bow lookout and handle the sails, and Mary would steer at the tiller much of the time. But within weeks of the arrival of the Second Fleet, Will had tracked down a pair of shipmates who had been together since 1787. Willy Allen, a seaman, and Nathaniel Lilly, a Jewish craftsman, had met on the *Lion* hulk moored in

Portsmouth Harbour, and then sailed out on the *Scarborough* on its second trip to New South Wales.

'What be your trade, Willy?' Mary asked the baldheaded Allen on meeting the two men for the first time late one night. Will had enticed them to brave the night guard and come to his and Mary's hut by the promise of a tot of illicit rum.

'Bein' now 50 year, an' bein' at sea most of that time, you might say I was bred to the sea — that you might say, Mary,' Willy replied. Another convict from the north of England, he hailed from Kingston-upon-Hull, a fishing town and harbour on the banks of the broad Humber Estuary, where middle England's water emptied into the North Sea. ''Sfact, they call me Silly Willy Seadog, they do, as I been silly enough to have been on and off of merchantmen all me life.' He giggled. ''Sfact, I'd be there still, an' wishin' I were, too, if it weren't for 'elpin' meself to a few ladies' kerchiefs while on leave in Norwich Town. Jest borrowed 'em, I did, for me girls in different ports. Harmless, really.' He licked his lips. 'Sooner I get back to sea the better, Mary. After the way they treated Nat and me on that *Scarborough*, starvin' us an' so many dyin' an' all, 'tweren't a merchant ship, 'twere a hell ship. I want to get out of this Port Jackson fast.'

'Aye, 'tis true, Mary,' said the dark skinned Nat Lilly in a slow, flat Suffolk accent. 'In my 35 years I never seen menfolk treated so bad. I'd like to come along,' he said. 'Jus' want away from here back to my family. I'm a weaver by trade, no seaman, I. Yet, I'm strong, an' handy for repairin' an' fixin'. Mebbe boat sails, nets an' clothin'. I'll come, if you'll take me.'

'What they get you for?' asked Mary. Will poured another measure of rum into their mugs.

'Jewellery thief. You know, silver spoons, a silver fob watch. I want to see my dear wife an' our two kids. In London, they be now.'

'You're missin' 'em, can tell,' said Mary, thinking of her father and Richard. Were they still alive, she wondered? Could Richard possibly still be waiting?

When Willy and Nat left the hut, Mary counted off the men on her hands: Will would handle sails, Bill Moreton would navigate, and they had five rowers — James Martyn, Jimmy Cox, Sam Bird, Willy Allen and Nat Lilly. They had only one more rower to recruit for the cutter, and they could go.

Willy and Nat might have read Mary's mind. They suggested a shipmate of theirs from the *Scarborough* whom they had come to trust. 'Long John' Butcher, a 47-year-old tenant farmer, had hunted for a living in the past and knew how to handle all manner of muskets. Butcher, they said, was strong and could help in gathering food along the way. Mary and Will agreed to meet him.

'I'm keen, I am,' the red-headed Worcestershireman said. He towered above Mary. 'Find me a musket or blunderbuss. I can shoot well and straight, an' set traps.'

''Tis what we wants, 'cause we mus' eat as we go an' wherever we land. We'av mouths to feed, nine an' two young 'uns,' Mary said. 'So we need some 'un to shoot the game, kangaroos and all.'

''Tis how I'm here,' John Butcher said, with some pride. 'Catchin' three pigs on the run, an' settin' for rabbit, an' squire's deer, too. Only I got caught, red-'anded with a haunch of venison hangin' at the hearth.' He stroked flat his springy red hair. 'Aye, I miss the Vale.'

Mary and Will now had enough crew and a wide range of skills to man and sail the cutter. All they needed were the instruments and tables for Bill Moreton, which they hoped to buy, barter or steal from the next visiting ship. Then, in September 1790, when Mary and Will were finalising their preparations, a gang of five convicts stole a longboat moored down the Parramatta River, below the farm at Rose Hill, and escaped.

'Won't get far,' Will said that evening, warming himself before the fire. The nights still felt chilly and dank by the cove, and a hearth fire gave them warmth and comfort. 'I seen that boat. 'Tain't a good 'un. She'll ship a deal of water. She ain't tight. Likely they'll perish.'

'Makes your governor's boat the better choice, Will,' Mary said.

'Aye, Pixie. Yet, 'tis harder for us. Ev'ry leather neck'd marine an' 'is mistress shall watch the remaining boats like 'awks to see they doan get thieved.'

'Likely, Will, yet 'tis an omen for us. I feel it.' She pulled Will to her and held him tightly in her arms. Although she had born two children, Mary's body was lean and strong from the demands of simply surviving each day in the colony. Will returned her embrace.

'Damn, Mary, doan anything pull you down?'

'I recall that old Cornish saying: "If it were meant to be, then you mus' sit back an' wait an' see".'

'Not waitin' to see nothin'', my girl. Us'll leave, an' bloody soon,' Will said.

'Patience. Us'll leave at the right time. Master Bill Moreton told us, mus' have a compass, chart an' all. Nothin'll stop us then.' She smiled at Will.

They heard that the escapees only got as far as a bay to the north named Port Stephens before their boat was wrecked. The men disappeared, apparently inland to face the savages. Mary grimaced. That could still be her escape party's fate. They wouldn't be able to call into harbours on the way. Will was right: they had to leave soon, for the general security in the colony was improving. The kernel of a new militia, called the New South Wales Corps, had arrived with the Second Fleet ships, and she didn't like the look of their commanding officer, Captain John Macarthur. The savages were also getting worse and had even attacked the kindly governor himself; in September he had been speared in the shoulder when he was visiting a bay near the heads, a spot he named Manly. The longer we're here, the bolder the savages become, Mary thought.

Then suddenly, in October, the feasibility of Mary's original plan was confirmed. A long sea voyage could be — had been — done in an open boat. The *Supply* returned from the Dutch colonial port of Batavia, minus a few of her crew struck down by the deadly fever there, with startling news. There had been a mutiny at sea, on the *Bounty* (which sailed just after their convict fleet) on its breadfruit expedition to Tahiti. The news spread like a cold throughout the colony; the *Supply* sailors told and retold the story in return for tots of rum and brandy. The *Bounty* had been seized at night after leaving Tahiti in the South Pacific Ocean by some one-third of her crew led by one of the officers, a Fletcher Christian. Captain Bligh and as many loyal crew as could fit into the ship's cutter were cast adrift, near the island of Tonga. The *Bounty* turned about and sailed eastwards for an unknown destination, leaving the cutter overloaded almost to her gunwales, and was seen no more. And how did the sailors know of all this? Because Bligh, incredibly, had navigated the boat 4000 miles much through uncharted seas to Timor. He had lost just one man when they went ashore during the voyage, who was killed by the savages in the Cannibal Isles, present-day Fiji.

The settlement buzzed with the tale. 'So, we can do it, too,' Mary said to Will. 'This is the best news, don't you think? It's like a sign, a light shining on the path ahead for us.'

'Sooner the better, Pixie,' Will replied. 'I can sail as good as that naval-trained, wig-wearing bluecoat. Just let me get goin', eh?'

In December the last piece of the jigsaw puzzle fell into place. A Dutch barque, the *Waaksamheyd* ('good lookout'), arrived in Port Jackson from the Dutch Indies; it had been chartered by Captain Ball of the *Supply* to bring supplies of beef, pork, flour, sugar and rice to the colony. Apart from the visit by La Perouse nearly three years previously, she was the first foreign vessel to visit the colony. Yet, still there was bad blood between the two nations. The settlers heard that the honourable British East India Company had begun to compete with the Dutch East India Company for the valuable spice trade, which displeased the Dutch. Mary persuaded Will to row out to the *Waaksamheyd* during one of his fishing trips and meet its captain.

Will bided his time, waiting for the right moment. On a day when he could do so unobserved, he rowed across to the ship, got permission to come on board, and introduced himself to the captain, Detmer Smit. Liking the look of the forthright Will Bryant, Captain Smit showed him into his mess and invited him to take a seat.

'To what do I owe the honour of your visit?' Smit asked.

'This,' Will said, handing the captain a bottle of good-quality Indian rum that he had taken from a marine's tent.

'Very nice. I don't mind if I do,' Captain Smit said, 'now that I'm safely in port. Will you drink a glass with me, Mr Bryant?'

'Thank you, sir. I will.'

When the rum was poured, Captain Smit said 'Skol' and drained his glass in one draught. 'Ah! Now, what can I do for you, friend?'

'Well, Captain, as the head fisherman in the colony, I'm offering to supply you with the best fish during your stay here, as good fish in this harbour are difficult to find.'

'I see,' Smit said, but with little enthusiasm. 'I suppose my crew would benefit from your catch, and it is a kind offer.'

'I have also brought you some gifts made by the savages here,' Will said, taking from a canvas bag a boomerang, and carved wooden replicas of a lizard and a male figure.

'Wonderful objects,' Smit said, studying them. 'But why such generosity, Mr Bryant, from an Englishman, when we Dutch and you English have so often fought over ports like Cape Town and other trading posts?' He poured them each another glass of rum. 'Even now, we Dutch don't like your government helping the British East India Company to invade our traditional trading ports.'

'Well, you see, I am no friend of the British government,' Will said, leaning forward. 'And I think they have no right to push into Dutch territory.'

'Well, we agree on that, Englishman. I have no love for the British. As it is, they are invading this island we call New Holland without our permission, even though we discovered it first. So, anything I can do to undermine them, I do,' Smit said. 'But surely, there must be some way I can repay your generosity now?'

Finally, feeling he had won Smit's confidence, Will said, 'Well, Captain, I wish to buy a chart from you, should you have a spare, of the east coast of New Holland. Perhaps you have Cook's chart?'

'A spare chart, eh?' Smit said. 'Well, you're in luck, Mr Bryant, as I *do* have a spare. I got a new issue in Batavia last month. But I would need more than rum, and artwork from the savages, in return.'

'What about this, then?' Will said, producing a small bag full of coins that he had earned by selling fish illegally. He placed it on the table.

'More like it, Mr Bryant. I must say, I am interested. But, pray tell me, why does a fisherman need a chart of the east coast of New Holland?'

Swearing him to secrecy, and shaking hands on the matter, Will, emboldened by the rum, told the Dutch captain of the convicts' plan to escape in the governor's cutter and journey northward to the Dutch East Indies.

'You are a brave man,' Smit said. 'That will hurt the British governor here, and all his fancy, self-inflated officers, will it not? I like your audacity, and if the money is enough you shall have your chart.'

'Thank you, Captain,' Will said, clinking his glass with Captain Smit's 'Skol'.

'But, man, you'll need more than a chart,' Smit said. 'If you have enough coins, you can buy my second compass — that's essential — and I can sell you a spare quadrant, too. What do you say?'

'Yes, Captain. That is what we need,' Will said. 'Do you also have mathematical tables and a sextant?'

'That is pushing your luck, Mr Bryant,' Smit said. We cannot spare such necessary navigational instruments.' He refilled their glasses. 'But show me your coin and we can conclude this arrangement, which I swear will be between just the two of us. I pray that you will succeed and embarrass this haughty little settlement set up to insult our Dutch claims to New Holland, made over a century ago on the west coast.'

Will emptied the bag of coins on to the table. After counting them, Smit fetched a chart, which Will approved, a standard compass and a quadrant, and handed them to Will. The arrangement completed, Smit shook Will's hand and wished him a successful journey. He chuckled to himself at the thought of the small band of convicts escaping from the authorities on the Dutch island continent which the British dared to call New South Wales.

The captain, by now rather drunk, escorted Will to where his boat was secured. They shook hands yet again, then Will climbed down the rope ladder into the boat and pushed off into the night. Smiling as he rowed back to shore, Will rejoiced that they now had everything they needed. He had done well, as he still had in his pocket a stolen marine's watch that he had been prepared to trade also if necessary, although he also hoped to keep this as a time-keeper for the escape voyage. He had kept back a few coins for their voyage, or in case he needed to bribe a soldier to leave his musket, powder and balls lying about unattended long enough for them to be stolen.

As it turned out, Will managed to relieve a couple of the less-experienced, newly arrived members of the New South Wales Corps of their arms and ammunition when, late one Saturday night soon after Will had visited the Dutch ship, the soldiers were distracted at the end of their guard duty. When a couple of convict wenches lured the soldiers into their beds with the promise of rum, Will discreetly relieved them of their arms.

By Christmas, their preparations were complete and Mary and Will could set a date for their escape. They planned to leave in a matter of weeks, immediately after the Dutch ship left. But as the date approached, Will's mood changed and he became ill at ease. Now that they had everything they needed, he seemed to be losing his nerve. The tension and secrecy had finally got to him, and he started to become reckless in talking about the planned escape. When he was overheard by a marine discussing fleeing the colony, a watch was kept on his and Mary's hut. Then, one night, he got drunk while fishing and overturned the governor's cutter, the very boat he and Mary had planned to use for their escape. Being thrown into the water made him come to his senses; furthermore, as he had to repair the damaged cutter, the accident gave him the opportunity to fit it out secretly for the voyage. The accident also allayed the suspicions of the marines, who thought the boat was now too damaged to make any sort of sea voyage.

Once the repairs were finished, there was no reason to delay their escape any longer. Mary told Will not to tell the rest of the crew until the last minute. They all had women who wouldn't want them to leave and might betray them, especially Jimmy Cox whose lover, Sarah Young, begged him not to go. Then, suddenly, it looked as if they should get ready to sail at a moment's notice, for on 22 March the last naval ship, the *Supply*, sailed again for Norfolk Island. It would be gone for over a week. Now there were no ships in the harbour apart from the *Waaksamheyd*, which some of the marines had claimed was leaving soon. This was all they were waiting for. Mary quietly went ahead with getting her stores in order.

Then, at 6 am on 28 March 1791, when Will was out fishing, they got their best chance when the *Waaksamheyd* upped anchor and sailed out of the heads bound for Batavia. The harbour was now empty but for the cutter. No ships could follow or chase them. This was it.

Will hurried back to the hut early. 'See, the Dutch ship's gone, Pixie. This is it, lass, wouldn't you say?' he said excitedly.

'I know it is, Will. 'Tis the time!' Mary agreed.

'That's it, then. Us'll leave this night!' he said.

'Aye, Will. 'Tis no ship in Port Jackson, an' *Supply* will be some time at Norfolk. Sooner we go, the better. We doan know when the next ship is comin', only hearsay. 'Tis the best chance now.'

'Aye, Mary, so you say. The time be good, no ships, an' the moon's late risin'. Right, lass, 'tis tonight. I'll tell the crew one by one during the day, but as late as possible. I'll tell 'em to meet at the boat after everyone's candles are out at 10 pm. They don't have much to pack. Us'll go directly after sunset.'

After a light meal, Mary gave Emanuel a small amount of the sleeping herb that Arabanoo had shown her. She told an old Cornish fairytale to three-year-old Charlotte to make her sleepy, before giving her a larger dose. 'Doan need them cryin' or whimperin' in the night air, Will.' She then wrapped Emanuel in a sling, which she placed across her chest. Then they waited.

When the kookaburras had laughed their last laugh for the day, and the last candles had been blown out and all was silent, Mary and Will looked at each other and nodded. They listened again for the crunch of a marine's boot on the path that wound past their hut, but the coast was clear. Mary stepped forward and embraced Will, who returned the hug with a loud sigh. The moment they had been waiting for since their first meeting had finally arrived.

Will, feeling his way in the dark, lifted the corner of the wattle roof and took down the supplies they had hoarded, along with some recently dried fish which they packed into cloth bags. Mary lifted the loose floorboard and removed the preserved foods she had hidden there some months before. Will then hoisted the sleeping Charlotte around his neck in a hammock. After giving Mary another silent nod, Will opened the door and surveyed the darkened settlement. There wasn't a sound apart from an eerie night owl. Mary thought of the owl that had broken the silence during the highway robbery that had changed her life. It was another time, another world. This, she thought, is a good omen; it's the call of a bird from my home, and a wise old one at that. Then Will beckoned with his head and she followed, with Emanuel slung across her chest, closing the door silently behind her.

They moved quietly, working their way slowly around the perimeter of the settlement from their hut by the rocks on the western slope. Fearful of discovery, they breathed quietly and shallowly. Both children slept deeply. They waded across the Tank Stream above the bridge, and back down to the harbour by the pathway to Bennelong Point. In the shadows near where the governor's cutter was moored alongside a jetty, the other men, with lighter loads, were already waiting. All was quiet, all was normal, in the sleeping settlement. They were keen to get aboard, lest any overzealous sentry should challenge them. Jimmy Cox had dropped a handsaw somewhere between his hut and Bennelong Point, but he dared not go back and look for it. Mary, too, had let slip a five-pound bag of flour, which had spilled over the path.

They all seemed to be there. Mary did a headcount: there was James Martyn, Jimmy Cox, Sam Bird, Bill Moreton, Willy Allen, Nat Lilly and John Butcher. Will nodded. The suspense reminded him of his smuggling forays along the Cornish coast, and it felt good to be at it again, defying the English authorities. One by one they slipped aboard the empty cutter, taking their prearranged places on the 30-foot vessel, each stepping gently a-midships so that the boat wouldn't rock and announce their presence. Suddenly, they heard the clang of metal hitting rock.

They all froze. By the light of the moon, Mary saw a single sentry walking slowly along the path above the shoreline on the last round of the night watch. His scarlet uniform looked black against the white cross-buckles; his musket was sloped at his shoulder. He halted, turned and disappeared at a leisurely pace into the darkness, up the easy slope towards the governor's house. They breathed again and blessed the children for not crying out. The stores and provisions were stowed temporarily beneath the thwarts, and the oars were unshipped and eased between the tholes.

At about 11 pm, Will Bryant at the stern, with Mary beside him and the navigator Bill Moreton at the bow, slipped the mooring lines. A-midships, Willy Allen pushed the boat away from the rough jetty with his hands, his face split wide by an ecstatic grin so that his teeth flashed in the moonlight.

'Back-water, 'an'somely,' hissed Will. The cutter moved quietly out from Bennelong Point, a slight chuckle of water coming from around the rudder, the six oars dipping pools in the still water. 'Easy.' They stopped rowing. Will put the tiller down and the bow swung across the blackness of Bennelong Point; the shore seemed darker, and the harbour lighter, from the boat. 'Row,' came the quiet order. The blades bit the water, propelling the cutter forward, away from the point, away from Sydney Cove, out into Port Jackson towards the heads and the open sea.

CHAPTER 6

In the wake of Captain Bligh

Within five weeks of Mary and her party of desperate escapees
putting to sea in their cutter, they run short of food and water
and the boat begins to leak. They cannot put into shore for fear
of being speared by the natives, who make threatening gestures at
them from the beach. Mary decides to take extreme measures.

By just after midnight on that late March night in 1791, Mary's hand-picked convict crew had rowed and sailed the governor's cutter quietly down the long length of Port Jackson. 'So far, so good,' she thought to herself. As they had pulled quietly away from Bennelong Point, Mary had been struck by the changes that had taken place around the foreshore since she first came ashore three years before. Not only did the governor now have a fair house and office of his own on the eastern side of the cove, and the marines an imposing barracks on the western ridge, but there were further cottages and huts all around the bay on either side of the Tank Stream. A network of tracks linked them together and led out of the settlement to the farms; even to the gallows on the hill — Mary's last chilling sight of the founding colony of New South Wales and a reminder of their fate if they were caught.

They rowed steadily towards the dark heads silhouetted in the moonlight. Once away from the settlement, past the rush-cutters' bay, Mary had changed positions with Will and the lugsail was raised to take advantage of the wind, a light land breeze flowing from the colder land to the warmer sea. With an experienced hand on the tiller and her children still deeply asleep beside her, she surveyed the crew, sitting on the thwarts in a small euphoria of joy and amazement at this initial taste of freedom and independence from authority. Will and Bill Moreton gave quiet instructions for the safe stowing of the stores, victuals, and the precious water barrel. The compass, chart and quadrant were secured in the transom locker aft, the only compartment in the boat protected from spray and water. Mary could see that her original confidant from Exeter Gaol, James Martyn, now 40, was already scribbling notes in the store-book he had pilfered as his diary. He had just one more year to serve. Up forward on the bow she could see her husband, Will Bryant, 31, whistling happily as he coiled the mooring lines. Although his sentence had actually now expired, he was ecstatic to be leaving the starving colony in his own boat in a bid to return to England. Immediately forward of Will was his mucker, Jimmy Cox; the 34-year-old carpenter had been transported for life. Mary felt good about this core group, all of whom had been together since they met on the *Dunkirk* hulk. Then there was Sam 'Birdy' Bird. The 32-year-old bearded mariner, with one-and-a-half years to serve, had been born to the sea and was now in his element.

Further aft in the cutter were the trio she and Will had recruited from the Second Fleet of transports: the 33-year-old mate Bill Moreton, now to be called Master Moreton as a mark of respect, with five-and-a-half years to serve, was the most qualified seaman on board — without him, Mary knew, they couldn't have sailed; Willy Allen, aged 51, had also been transported for life; his friend, the weaver Nat Lilly, 36 (also transported for life), was desperate to see his wife and two children again. Finally, the towering 48-year-old farmer of the Worcestershire vales, 'Long John' Butcher, had four-and-a-half years of his sentence remaining. Mary, a month short of her 26th birthday, drew in her breath proudly. 'Yes,' she thought. 'I always reckoned that if Jack Sheppard could do it, I could, too.' She rejoiced in the thought that, with the help of Will Bryant and the other hardy souls on board, she had escaped from a penal colony on the far side of the world.

She nudged the cutter to starboard to avoid the shallow water and rocks near the long cove trending north to Manly. It had taken time, but she and Will had done well. The range of skills on board was better than she could have dreamed of. But, their talents apart, these desperate souls were strongly united by their shared determination to escape the ill-fated Sydney Cove prison camp which, when they left, looked doomed to failure through either starvation or disease. She also hoped that these hardened convicts would be better behaved with a mother and two small children in the cutter than they might otherwise have been. Up forward, Will looked as happy as Mary felt.

Mary congratulated herself and Will on choosing the right boat. At 30 feet, the cutter was big enough, yet still handy; its three thwarts were wide enough for two men to sit, pulling an oar each. The lugsail would give them good driving force, while the two foresails gave them steerage. She didn't mind that it was an open boat, having grown up on one in Cornwall. She recalled her father's advice: 'There's nothing like a boat, Mary, to give you freedom. Once you leave the shore, you can take control of your own destiny.' And now, she thought, I'm heading back to him, should he still be alive, and, possibly, to Richard. She tried to picture Richard's face as she stared through the heads and out into the Pacific, and strained to recall his voice. Would he have kept his promise to wait for her, she wondered? She suspected that, once free, Will Bryant would have other plans. He had never considered their marriage to be valid in law.

A-midships, Master Moreton pointed out the Southern Cross to Nat Lilly. Will had said that the Hollanders' chart showed an imperfectly marked, but great and treacherous reef along the east coast of New South Wales, for half its length at least. This was just one of many obstacles that lay between them and Timor. It was only the beginning of a very dangerous journey, Mary knew, but still, it looked like they might have a chance of making it.

Although Mary had wanted to take more food and drink for the escape crew, they had been unable, in the food-strapped colony, to hoard or steal as much as they needed. All they had managed to take with them was a hundredweight of flour, the same amount of rice, 14 pounds of pork, a good supply of preserved foods and dried fish she had hoarded and eight gallons of water. But she was confident of finding edible plants along the way, thanks to Arabanoo. Like all experienced sailors she knew that the longer they could stay at sea the better, as going ashore risked smashing the boat, like the Parramatta escapees, or being speared by savages. Also Mary had insisted on taking at least two buckets (which doubled up for baling) into which the nine adult crew could defecate, and she recommended the men urinate over the gunwales. Also on board were two muskets and some ammunition, which Will hoped would protect them from the savages, as well as a wide assortment of tools and utensils for repairing the cutter, cutting down trees, setting up camp and preparing meals, and a sewing kit she had obtained from Catherine Fryer. There had been many tears shed as she had explained to Catherine and Margaret, just hours before she was due to leave with Will and the children, that she was at last about to make her bid for freedom.

* * *

The cutter passed through the looming headlands at the mouth of the harbour and turned to the north, following the trend of the coast. Squawking seagulls, louder than any in Fowey Harbour, greeted them in great numbers, hovering around the boat in the hope that some fish scraps might be thrown overboard. 'No other sails anywhere,' an exhilarated Will called back from the bow. 'Take a look out across that water, now. 'Tis empty, I say!'

Master Moreton trimmed the mainsail, easing the sheet from the cleat, and the cutter increased speed.

''Twill be a while before *Supply* returns from yon Norfolk Island,' he said. 'It's a fair passage, there 'n' back.'

''Tis grand, for sure,' said James Martyn, looking east across the Pacific Ocean. ''Tis grand to see a horizon once more.'

Willy Allen smiled with delight and slapped his thigh. To celebrate being back at sea, he started singing an old sea shanty.

Nat Lilly spoke. 'I's so pleased to be away, but is a mortal expanse of water, an' the boat not over-large, I's thinking.' He gripped the gunwale with both hands, looking eastwards alongside James.

'Look t'other way, lad,' advised Master Moreton. 'Keep your eyes to the shore. Happen ye'll feel better at that.'

'We're away, Pixie!' called Will again. 'By God, we're away!'

'An' them bastards 'ave no ship,' said Jimmy Cox, 'nor no sea-boat.'

'Do you set a course, Master Moreton?' Mary asked.

Bill Moreton nodded. 'Aye. It's time to set a course, sea watches, an' the like. Pass me that compass, will ye, girl? I'll set it to this thwart with line.' Moreton passed a thin line about the brass case of the Dutch compass, securing it to the aft-most thwart for each helmsman to see. 'Ye all mind it, now. Don't knock it. The chart, Mary.' He studied the Dutch chart, still labelled 'Nuewe Holland'; sparse though its entries were, it showed Cook's careful and exact plotting of the New South Wales coastline from south of Botany Bay northwards to Cape York.

'Make it 0-3-5 degrees for the present, Mary. We'll assume little or no deviation. Leastways, till we find otherwise.'

James Martyn recorded their passage in his journal. Will and Bill Moreton slipped into a shared command of the cutter, the one as a fisherman and ex-smuggler most experienced in small-boat work, the other as navigator and deep-sea sailor. They agreed a change of watch every four hours using Will's stolen watch for timekeeping, although the experienced sailors on board could also approximate the time readily. By early morning on 29 March they were sailing past a series of small yellow-sand beaches, each divided from its neighbour by cliffs, towards a peninsula that Moreton said must be Barrenjoey Head.

'Put that in your journal, Paddy,' he said to James. 'It's so distinctive, like, it must be the headland that this same cutter came to some weeks back. I recall some sailors mentionin' it.'

'Aye, aye, sir,' James joked.

These first few hours at sea were ones of exhilaration for most of those on board. Mary and Will were all smiles. Mary put the baby Emanuel to her breast for another feed and chatted to Charlotte, now three-and-a-half years old, who had woken up. 'Are we nearly there, Mama?' she asked, the first of many times.

'Not yet, sweetheart. But you can play with Emanuel while we're waiting,' she replied.

Jimmy Cox also had a grin from ear to ear, though he was angry with himself for dropping the handsaw, which he might need for boat repairs. Some of the crew, of course, were seasick. Nat suffered grievously, but said little. 'Sip some water, lad,' advised Bill Moreton. 'It seems to help, it does.'

The cutter continued the northerly course that would take it past Broken Bay, the wide entrance to the recently named River Hawkesbury. A southeasterly wind took over from the land breeze, and by midday of their first day at sea, with the strong southerly continuing, they were abreast of the bay.

'What be this latitude, according to the chart, Master Moreton?' Mary called out. She had just completed yet another change of Emanuel's swaddling.

'It's marked as 33 degrees 35 minutes, lass,' he replied. 'Mind, we don't know as how accurate these Hollanders were in the copying of James Cook's observations,' he added.

'An' what be the latitude of Timor?' Mary asked.

'Ah, now I see what ye're after. Ten degrees, more or less. It's a lengthy island, like, is Timor. A difference in latitude of some 23-and-a-half degrees. Let me see now. I make that near enough 1500 mile from here, at latitude 33 sailing up north to latitude ten degrees, to Cape York, which I think is the figure ye want. But we've our westing to make as well, mind, as well as various departures, course deviations, landings for water an' victuals, all the tacks, leeway.'

'So, how far to the Dutch colony, Master Moreton, if you can reckon that?' Mary asked.

He studied the chart a long while. 'A fair distance for sure. In sum, near enough 3250 mile. Maybe a trifle more. Mostly in sight of land, but the last 1200 miles will be at sea, outta sight of land,' he said, looking up from his chart.

'Well, at least that's far less than our First Fleet voyage, which was took more than eight months, weren't it?' she said.

'Oh, lot shorter,' Moreton agreed.

'But, 'tis a distance. 'Tis a *great* distance. I recall Cap'n Tench sayin' the same,' Mary said. 'Well, Master Moreton. If Lieutenant Bligh done it, we'll do it, I say.'

'Aye, indeed! An' we'll be coastin' for the best part,' Moreton added. 'With the compass, we'll skim the great bays an' save distance.' He paused, thinking ahead to their trials. 'Rocks, reefs an' nigger-heads, like, will be our main danger. Few 're charted, an' they'll be many. We must keep a right good lookout, day 'n' night, an' keep a goodly distance seaward of all capes an' headlands.'

''Tis warm enough, tho',' said James. 'Sure, I never thought I'd be glad of the terrible heat of this country, but 'tis plain 'tis better off we are warm than cold.'

Moreton nodded. 'We've precious few clothes. Nat, there, may be serving his needle and thread afore too long.'

*   *   *

The cutter was sailing well in the steady southeasterly wind, swooping and rolling slightly in the low easterly swell. Will set bait on to a line and trailed it astern, with good results.

For three days they sailed without a stop, putting an initial good distance between themselves and the authorities at Sydney Cove. But water was now running low; they must land soon and replenish the water barrel. A little river, some two degrees latitude north of Port Jackson, was abeam.

'What say you, Master Moreton?' Will called from the bow. 'Seems safe enough for us. Maybe a few 'falls — nothin' we can't manage, though.'

'Aye, it looks promisin'. Cook marked it as a river entrance. No name, mind. But the head he named Nobby's.'

''Tis them savages we mus' mind,' John Butcher said, fingering the musket he'd been issued as one of the two guards of the cutter, along with Jimmy Cox.

'Nay, can't see none. Yet, will you keep that musket handy, John, in case?'

And so they sailed northward before entering the mouth of a fair-sized river, where they beached the boat on the southern shore of what was to become Newcastle harbour.

On going inland a little way to gather firewood with James Martyn, Bill Moreton, the Novocastrian of the party, almost immediately discovered some surface coal. 'This'd be right useful to the governor, now,' he commented. He squatted to examine the black seam. 'Seems good coal, like.' He dug with a branch end. 'As good as any I saw along the Tyne. Rich an' dark, like the Sultan of

Araby.' He stood and looked upriver. 'May be there's brass to be made here,' he mused, ever on the lookout for an easy pound.

'Well, now, Master Moreton. Why should we not take the cutter back an' show His Lordship?' James mocked. 'Sure, an' he'll grant us a pardon. An' maybe promote you to adm'ral — Adm'ral of the Sydney Cove Fleet! To hell with the governor, let's find some kindling.'

That night, after a meal of fish and damper, Will asked John Butcher, Willy Allen and Nat Lilly to take the watches; they should keep the fire burning and a good lookout for savages, he said.

The next day, along the free-flowing river, the escaped convicts found fresh water, plenty of biting fish, and some kangaroos, wombats and possums. John Butcher dropped a small kangaroo with a musket ball, sending its companions bounding away. They all agreed to rest awhile on shore, confident that the *Supply* wouldn't have returned to Sydney Cove yet. Even if it had, as the colony's last ship, it couldn't be spared to search for them. They stayed two nights and a day in this spot, resting and catching fish and game. In between feeding Emanuel and playing with Charlotte on the sand, Mary spotted one of the cabbage trees that Arabanoo had told her about and, with the help of the men, cut off the edible parts. She also found some warrigal spinach on the inland side of the sand dunes and picked enough of the wild vegetable for a few days' supply.

On the morning of the second day, John Butcher shouted in alarm. 'Here they come! Savages! Savages!' He reached for his musket. A small group of tall naked Aborigines, perhaps half a dozen, loped easily along the riverbank towards the convicts' camp fire, their spears trailing at their sides.

'Wait awhile, John,' Mary said. 'They not be many and doan 'ave no war paint, see?' She opened her arms towards them. '*Gni-a Wy-an-na. Go-mul, Al-lo-wah*,' she said, using the Port Jackson words Arabanoo had taught her, meaning: 'I am a friendly mother, stay and sit down'

'*Go-mul, Go-mul*,' one of the savages said, repeating the words for friendship and smiling gently. He came closer to Mary and patted Emanuel on the head.

'*Pat-ta-baw-me*,' Mary asked, inviting them to eat.

'*Beall, Beall*,' they declined.

'Quick, Will, give 'em some clothes if they doan want food,' Mary said. 'Have you got anything you don't want, James?'

Will gave the visitors a worn and greasy waistcoat, now past its prime, which he had been using as a pillow on the boat. James offered a pair of torn breeches. All the men stood nodding and smiling, to show that they were friendly. This seemed to please the Aborigines. One of them put on the waistcoat, with some help from Will, and another the breeches, with a great deal of help from James and Willy. They pointed and laughed. Then they beckoned towards an outcrop of rocks lying half on the bank and half in the river, saying: '*Yen-ma-nia, Mah-n, Mah-n*.'

'What they after now?' Will asked suspiciously.

'I think that means come and see fish,' said Mary, making a swimming motion with her hands and repeating the word for fish, '*Mah-n, Mah-n*'. The Aborigines nodded vigorously. 'Follow them,' she recommended. The native men led them to a hidden fishing hole. Mary thanked them with their word for good, '*Bood-jer-re*'.

'Fish! An' 'undreds of the tasty little buggers,' Will called excitedly. 'Us'll stock up an' dry 'em.'

When the escape crew put back to sea on Friday, 1 April, they felt refreshed and cheered by their first experience of camping ashore. They continued north in a moderate–strong southeasterly wind, so that by the evening of Sunday, 3 April, they had reached as far north as the entrance Cook had named as Port Stephens, where the earlier band of convicts escaping in a stolen longboat had foundered. A leaky seam in the cutter's hull had been found to be the cause of constant bilge water, and it had been decided to beach as soon as possible and caulk.

'Aye, it's Port Stephens,' confirmed Bill Moreton. 'Cook marks it a fine harbour.'

'We'll risk it,' decided Will at the tiller, and brought the helm up. 'Trim the mainsail, Nat. Wearin' now.'

'Ready by that musket, John?' asked Moreton.

They landed safely in a broad, deep sheltered bay that seemed deserted. They ran the boat up a gentle beach, removed the stores and equipment and placed them on the sand, rolled the cutter on to her side, and wedged her with stones jammed under the keel. Will, Jimmy, Willy and Bill Moreton began the repairs, using skeins of unravelled rope for oakum stiffened by beeswax and resin heated in a pot on the fire they had made on arrival. The other men began to set up camp and collect firewood for a night on shore, as they had in the Newcastle harbour. But Mary didn't like the place. Something about it made her feel uneasy, and not just the fact that the Parramatta escapees had crashed their boat here. The big black birds, like the raven, with their mournful '*Ark, ark, ark, arrr*' cry, circled above, appearing to Mary as a bad omen.

'We'em not stayin', are we, Will?' she asked her husband.

'Looks quiet, lass. Cutter's not finished yet, an' now we'em here, may stay as go.'

''Tis diff'rent from that coal river. There be danger here,' she warned.

Will sighed. 'Us'll see what Master Moreton says.'

Suddenly a group of angry savages appeared out of the forest.

'We'll have to go,' Mary said, leaping to her feet. 'I know it in my bones. See that white paint? They're covered with war paint.' Holding Emanuel in her arms, she walked slowly towards the savages, who were waving their spears menacingly.

'*Gni-a Wy-an-na. Go-mul, Al-lo-wah*,' Mary said, confirming she was a mother coming in friendship and inviting them to stay and sit down.

But the savages shouted words Mary had never heard before, and she did not like the menacing tone in which they were being shouted.

'*Gni-a Wy-an-na. Go-mul, Al-lo-wah*,' she tried again.

But it was no use; they did not understand a word. The savages advanced threateningly towards the group of convicts, their spears raised and pointed. John Butcher raised the loaded musket.

'They doan understand you, Mary,' Bill Moreton called out. 'Come back, now. Likely a different tribe to the Port Jackson savages and may talk another tongue an' all, like the Indians in the West Indies. Come back right slowly, lass. Don't run. Stow the boat, Will. John? D'ye see that savage to your left?'

The savages continued to chant something that sounded like a version of '*Warra, warra, warra*' which the southern tribes used as a warning. They pointed with their spears towards the sea, and stamped their bare feet on the tussock grass. The stores and equipment were tossed hurriedly into the boat, which was run back down the shallow beach. Mary handed the children to Will as they all clambered in.

''Tis as I said.' Mary's face was pale.

'Push off, Nat,' Will called. 'Oars. Pull, you bastards! Pull!'

Satisfied, the gesticulating savages stood on the beach and watched them go.

The next morning, Monday, 4 April, they went ashore in another part of the expansive Port Stephens waterway. Another group of savages advanced towards them; again, their language was unfamiliar to Mary.

'We need water, Will,' said Bill Moreton. 'Likely, if we give 'em a gift, as we did at that river, they'll back off. Likely, too, they'll be more friendly in the light of day. What's the word for water, Mary?'

'*Ba-do*,' she said 'but it won't work this far from Port Jackson.'

'We can but try,' Will agreed.

So, Will and Bill Moreton approached the savages together, calling out '*Ba-do*' and holding out items of clothing to indicate that they meant no harm. But the natives, not understanding or trusting them, continued to advance in a frightening manner. The jumpy John Butcher and Jimmy Cox fired off their muskets without warning. Although the savages were startled for a moment, the warning shots were of little use, as the savages had apparently not encountered muskets before and continued to advance towards and to threaten the escapees.

''Tis no good, Master Moreton. I'm away. They too many for us.' Will turned, and the two retreated back to the boat. Willy and Nat had the cutter ready by the water's edge and, after Will and Moreton stepped aboard, they pushed her off and scrambled in after them.

'Mus' complete them repairs afore long,' Jimmy said.

'We'em try an island,' Will suggested. 'Should be free o' them savages.'

They rowed ten miles up the bay, and landed on a small sandy island. In relative safety they then prepared the boat for sea.

'Let's us stay here,' Mary said. ''Tis Godsent. There be no haste. We need rest an' sleep.'

'Aye, 'tis true,' said Jimmy. 'Needs time for the beeswax an' resin to seal the caulkin'.'

Will and Moreton looked at each other. 'Agreed,' said Will. 'But us'll keep watches the while. Doan trust them savages.'

*   *   *

After two days on the island, during which the escapees celebrated their first full week at sea, they repaired the cutter and used it to visit various beaches and to collect water, cabbage trees, more warrigal spinach, and some wattle seeds in pods that Mary wanted to try. Then, on Wednesday, 6 April, suitably rested, they got ready to put to sea again. They did this in the nick of time, as the word had got around. Dugout canoes loaded to their gunwales with savages started arriving and surrounded the island. However, before any trouble broke out, a good southwesterly breeze enabled the crew to set the sail and slip through the growing flotilla of native canoes. They sailed down the bay to the narrow mouth and the relative safety of the open sea.

As the cutter headed away from the beach, it passed a few curious dolphins surfing the waves on their way inshore. The crew steered northwards, but the wind veered to a fierce westerly, driving them out of sight of land. They were now much further out to sea than they had intended, and were dependent on Bill Moreton to return them safely to within sight of shore. Some of the crew, including John Butcher and Nat Lilly, became frightened. They knew little of the ways of the sea, having been included among the escapees for their other talents. Mary tried to soothe their fears by explaining that she had been out of sight of land many times while fishing off Cornwall, and in far rougher and much colder seas.

The wind backed into the southwest overnight, and Bill Moreton worked a compass course for the next headland, which they steered towards. By the evening of Thursday, 7 April, Will happily called out, 'Land!'

'See, friends,' a relieved Moreton said. 'Cook's observations are correct. A log would be handy, mind, to work out distance.' He calculated that they had sailed as far north as Cape Hawke at latitude 32 degrees south and were making good progress. They would continue to do so, if only they could stop wasting time on land, he said.

They remained within sight of the shore for some time, but found that they would be unable to land even if they ran out of supplies. A heavy and terrible surf crashed on to the long, sweeping beaches along that stretch of the coast. They must keep a goodly distance from that surf, Bill Moreton and Will agreed. 'We'd make better speed as well,' Will said. 'Water may be low, is it?'

'Us'll be on rations again,' replied Mary. ''Tis no hardship, 'ceptin' for the little 'uns. We're used to hard rations at Sydney Cove.'

Some days later they spotted Mount Warning, at latitude 29 degrees south, which Cook had marked clearly on the chart as the most easterly point on the coast of New South Wales. Then Moreton announced that they had passed Point Danger, at latitude 28 degrees south. They could now sail more to the northwest as they followed the coastline. Moreton had only a rough guide to their exact position, but it was enough. After they passed Glass House Bay, at latitude 27 degrees south, they were looking out for the big headland of Sandy Cape, marked prominently on Cook's chart at latitude 25 degrees south. But it was the hazards of unknown and unmarked rocks and tides and reefs that Moreton most feared, along with the rough surf that broke along the interminable beaches.

During this long, unbroken stint at sea, Moreton announced: 'By my reckonin', the compass is working well and the chart we are using has proved accurate since escapin' Port Jackson.' The news cheered them up for a time. But day after day, as the hot sun beat down on them and the salt water splashed into the boat, wetting their clothing and stinging their sunburned faces, they had to keep pulling their weight — altering the sail, baling the cutter, rowing where they could, and keeping each others' spirits up. Mary handed out smaller and smaller portions of the meagre rations. Thankfully, Will's line kept them in fish.

But even after Mary announced that they now had to replenish their water supply, Will, who was on the bow look-out, couldn't find a harbour or a creek. Mary wished that she had put in her plea earlier, when, five weeks after leaving Port Jackson, she confirmed that they had almost run out of both water and food, and wood for cooking on the little makeshift stove. Although she had no shortage of milk for Emanuel, she was short of water for her thirsty daughter, who refused the offer of breast milk. Charlotte had become bored with playing at the stern with the same old coils of rope, and tired of filling up the barrel with bits and pieces of scrap, and wanted new toys to play with. By now they were just past Cape Capricorn and were abreast of Keppel Bay at 23 degrees south, where the surf was crashing hard against the shore.

'Daren't land in that surf,' Will said. 'Might be alright for 'em porpoises,' he pointed to the dolphins that were surfing the breakers, 'but we'em lose the boat for sure. Us'll die then.' Bill Moreton nodded in agreement.

'Nothin' else but me an' Jimmy'll swim it with the small puncheon,' Will said.

'Likely ye'll find water by the cliff face,' Moreton told them. 'There's a gully.'

John Butcher nodded. 'Aye, 'tis very likely a watercourse, I'm thinkin'.'

'We'll heave to now.' Moreton turned the bow of the cutter into the wind while Sam Bird lowered the mainsail. Willy Allen backed the foresail and Moreton put the helm down. The boat steadied, just out of the pull and surge of the swell.

'Right, Chips?' Will challenged Jimmy Cox. Jimmy nodded, his face set. They removed their worn shirts and slipped overboard with the puncheon. Turning their backs to the cutter they struck out for the shore, through the surf for the beach, with the rest of the crew waiting in the cutter which was hove to.

No sooner had the two swimmers broken through the surf and scrambled on to the beach than an angry group of savages appeared, shaking their spears at the white men. Their chests were painted with the telltale white war paint. Exchanging a quick look, Will and Jimmy wasted no time: they turned and waded back into the sea, breasted the first waves, and then swam back to the boat.

No words were spoken as the others hauled them back on board. Mary was reminded of the qualities in Will Bryant that had attracted her to him back on the *Dunkirk*. 'Us'll wait,' she said flatly. 'You can take some milk from my tit, if you'm parched. Emanuel won't mind — there's plenty of it.'

Some days later, off Cape Townshend at latitude 22 degrees south, Will and Jimmy stripped off and again swam ashore. This time there were no savages; yet, search as they might, they were unable to find any fresh water. For a second time, they swam back to the boat empty-handed. But the cutter was now leaking badly through the earlier repairs made to the seams. They were baling constantly. They must land for repairs, or sink.

Will stood in the bow, straining his eyes shoreward. Suddenly he called out, 'There be a break between them islands. We'll chance the channel. There'll be a lee inside an' a landin'. Leastways, a beach of sorts.'

Moreton agreed. 'It looks like we've reached the Whitsunday Islands on Cook's chart, about 20 degrees south, and we've now got as far north as that great reef Cook mentioned which will be on our east like a barrier between us and the Pacific and stretching for miles. You can see the passage ahead. Must have been some time in June when he sailed through here,' he added, thinking of the date on the religious calendar that Cook must have taken as his inspiration for the name.

Mary, who was at the helm, obediently turned the boat towards the channel Will had spotted. Sam handled the mainsheet and Willy worked the foresail.

Steering carefully, with Will watching for any reefs, Mary took the cutter into a large, wide, partly sheltered bay. 'There!

On t'other side,' Will cried with relief. 'A river mouth, estuary. Us'll land there.'

On the opposite shore was the mouth of a large river, towards which they steered. They were greeted by squawking, multicoloured birds, which none of them recognised. After beaching the boat, Will, Jimmy and Nat set about repairing it with beeswax and resin. The other crew members found fresh water from the river, but couldn't find any shellfish or other fish, though young Charlotte cleverly caught some small crabs. Exhausted, they rested there for two days searching without luck for food, apart from some mauve berries that Mary gathered from the dinella bush.

'Mus' be more crab or lobster 'ereabouts,' said Willy. 'Stands ter reason. Estuary, 'n' all. You can get little Charlotte loose on 'em,' he laughed.

'We might try upriver a way,' Will said. ''Tis shallower there for crab.'

They rowed further inland, against a strengthening breeze, past muddy banks and heavy mangrove swamps. The air became humid and moist.

'Reminds me of the Caribbean rivers,' Bill Moreton said. 'There weren't much to eat there. This doan look promisin', Will. These mangroves are difficult to navigate an' the mud is uncommonly deep.'

'We'll not waste time,' Will decided. 'This wind'll serve us well. Raise the mainsail, Birdy. Us'll get to sea again.'

*   *   *

So they put to sea and sailed further north until, once again, they were short of food and on light rations and the boat was leaking badly. But Will continued to resist going ashore, always concerned that the cutter might crash on unseen rocks or that savages might appear out of the forest. He wanted to get through the Whitsunday Passage, which Moreton had shown him on the chart, as quickly as possible; the place looked dangerous, he thought.

'Surf's too heavy to land,' he said, pointing at the white beach on the mainland.

'Well, how do we stop the leak, Capt'n Bryant?' Jimmy Cox asked sarcastically. ''Cause I need to do some repairs. Our balin' can't keep up with the water pourin' in now.'

'That's right,' panted Nat, looking up from his baling. 'We gotta stop this leakin'.'

'We're not keepin' pace, Capt'n Bryant. It's pourin' in,' Willy added. 'And me arms is achin' somethin' terrible.'

From her perch at the tiller, Mary could see the water level was indeed rising in the bottom of the boat, both from the leak and from the waves that sloshed over the side. The sea sometimes broke over the gunwales like a small surf on a beach. If they sank, they'd be lost, she realised. *She* could swim, as could Will, Jimmy and Willy, but not many of the others could, she thought. They were more than a hundred yards from shore. Suddenly she remembered what her father used to say: 'Don't get rid of the valuable fish you've caught if your boat starts shipping water. Throw out your heavy clothing — that's easy to replace.'

'Will, let's get some o' that heavy wet clothing over the side,' Mary suggested. 'It's too hot for these tropics, anyway, and it'll lighten the cutter.'

'Good idea, Pixie,' he called back to her, relieved to have a solution. 'Get rid of the ballast. Everybody throw any clothing you don't need over the side — that'll lighten her.'

Mary's plan worked for a while. By the next day, however, despite frantic baling overnight by the exhausted crew taking it in shifts, the boat was so full of water it was hardly moving. Everything inside was floating around, with some things over the side and in the sea. Emanuel and Charlotte were terrified. Mary spoke up again. 'Will, I doan care if there are savages on shore, we have to sail into the next open bay before the end of the day.'

'I can't see any bay,' Will replied, still reluctant to risk landing again.

'Looks like somethin' up ahead,' Bill Moreton said. 'Ten points to port, see?' He pointed to a beach on the mainland some way past the northern tip of the last of the Whitsunday Islands and just south of Cape Upstart.

'Alright, then,' said Will. 'Hard aport, Mary. Hard aport.'

As they rode the surf into the beach, Will realised there was no place to land. He ordered Jimmy Cox and Sam Bird to throw out a grappling hook to hold the cutter in position overnight. Unfortunately, it broke at about 2 am and they were driven into the surf, where they all expected the boat to break up.

'We're done for now,' John Butcher moaned. 'Best we say goodbye to our maker.'

'Yeah, I'm gettin' all my things and swimmin' for it,' Willy, the old seadog, said. 'I've been in high seas in a small boat before, but this is the worst.'

'The hull can't hold anymore water,' Nat said. 'We pract'ly under the sea. It's pourin' over the starboard gunwales. We should have repaired it days ago. It's no use.'

Listening to the men panicking, Mary remembered her father telling her that there are two types of people in a storm: those who'll sink, and those who'll swim. 'You've got to stop the sinkers from sinking the boat,' he'd told her.

'I knew I should'na taken the risk,' John Butcher howled. 'I cannot swim to save me life.'

'Damn fool, Bryant!' Sam Bird shouted. 'You should have beached for repairs long ago. Now it's too late — can't do nothin'.'

Watching the cutter listing to starboard, Mary snapped. 'Shut up, for Christ's sake!' she screamed. 'All of you, throw any ballast over — jackets, boots, everything — and grab a container and bale for your life. If she goes down, we're all done. Anybody who swims for it alone will get speared and eaten by the savages. It's all for one and one for all!' she shouted.

'Aye, aye, ma'am,' John Butcher said sarcastically. 'How would you know?'

'Shut up, you stupid bastard. Have some faith in the cutter!' she snapped back. She could see that Will was flat out trying to catch some wind in the sail to steady and drive the boat. No one could see what she could see from back aft. She suddenly recalled how her father had once corrected his boat when it was shipping water off Fowey, and she screamed an order that no one could ignore: 'Everybody on starboard, move across to port, *now*! Shift your weight and bale, you lazy bastards!'

'What'll they do, woman?' John Butcher protested, as all the others changed sides. 'It can't be saved! Look at the waterfall coming over gunwales,' he moaned. 'She's so full, she'll keel over anyway.'

Mary leaped forward and wrenched him off his thwart by the scruff of his neck, so that his great weight fell on to the port side. 'I've been in boats all me life!' she bellowed. 'Now stay portside and bale, you fat bastard! We've corrected the list, but we've got about five minutes to save her.'

CHAPTER 7

Sailing to freedom

Mary and the crew of the cutter continue to face dangers en route to the Dutch East Indies, including a flotilla of warlike savages who stand between them and freedom.

Within seconds of the men transferring their weight to port to balance the boat, and throwing everything they could overboard, the cutter was buoyant once more and upright. A further five minutes of frenzied baling lifted the overburdened and leaking cutter so that her gunwales were well above the waterline. The immediate danger had passed. Mary had acted in the nick of time.

'Thanks be to God,' said James Martyn. 'I was thinkin' then we'd all be swimmin', swimmin' for our lives. We're all here, still, though I saw an oar go by the board.'

'Aye, 'tis fortunate we are,' Mary said. 'Mus' work together an' have faith in the seamen among us. Keep balin' the while.'

'I'll do me best to fashion 'nother oar, I will,' Jimmy Cox said. 'But be 'ard without me wood saw an' all.'

With the help of the moonlight they found a safe way ashore and made a run for the best beach they had seen for many days. Bill Moreton believed they had now reached latitude 19 degrees south and were in Upstart Bay. Although they were wet through, they got a fire going with dry wood found on the shore and slept for the remainder of the night. Woken the next day by the screech of cockatoos, Mary and Charlotte gathered some desperately needed fresh water, shellfish, crabs and oysters. 'Look, Mama, another one,' Charlotte said, holding up a wriggling crab she had pulled out of a hole. 'Can I put it in the bucket myself with its friends?'

Fortunately, there was food to be had here. John Butcher shot a kangaroo and some possums, which he skinned and cooked over the fire. Mary also found some midjin berries, and the crew sat down to a feed of the round white fruit. They spent two days and two nights on the beach, recovering from their exhaustion. Then, on the third day, the savages arrived in large numbers, encircling the convicts' camp on the water's edge. With their spears pointing they crept closer.

'I'll try 'em with my Port Jackson words,' Mary said.

'Yon words of greeting won't aid thee here, Mary,' John Butcher said. He fired his musket at the savages, and Jimmy Cox fired a second shot. Although neither ball found a mark, the noise and smoke issuing from the unfamiliar weapons confused the savages, which gave the crew time to run the boat into the low surf and hastily get aboard.

'Aye, they appear to be more bold, like, the further north we sail,' said Bill Moreton. 'Must be careful. We doan want to get clubbed to death on a beach, like the maker of this chart, poor old Captain Cook, do we?'

'Maybe is cannibals!' shouted Nat Lilly.

'Woan ever know, less us speak to 'em,' Mary said.

'Any case, 'tis past time we left,' said Will. 'Back-water larboard. Easy! Together, now.'

By this stage of the journey, everyone on board the cutter was feeling its effects, and tempers were becoming frayed. John Butcher's resentment at Mary for shouting at him during their near-capsize continued to fester as the days wore on. Nat Lilly distrusted and feared the sea, and the presence of Mary's children exacerbated his longing to see his own children. Willy Allen, whose joking had begun to irritate his companions, had by now become largely silent.

The strain had also got to the core members of the crew. Will was physically and mentally exhausted. Jimmy Cox resented the hold that Mary had over his great mate from the *Dunkirk*, as well as Will's earlier refusal to land so that they could repair the cutter. Even James Martyn had lost heart and rarely wrote in his diary. It all seemed the same now, he said. He had no idea where they were and he couldn't see the use of writing it all down. Sam Bird had withdrawn into himself. And the navigator, Master

Moreton, was frustrated at not being able to take proper sightings for lack of navigational tools.

It was all that Mary could do to keep this group of disgruntled men focused on their goal of reaching the Dutch East Indies. Their situation wasn't helped by the bad weather that daily battered the little cutter, which was shipping heavy seas continually. Baling was constant, everyone, apart from the children, taking their turn.

Once again, the cutter sprang a leak, and this time they all agreed to land for repairs as soon as they sighted a suitable beach. 'Maybe this wide bay that James Cook charted will serve,' Bill Moreton suggested. 'The great captain called it Halifax Bay.' The surf prevented their landing close by the entrance, so they rowed two or three leagues deeper into the bay. To their great surprise, they saw that two mean huts had been constructed on the shore.

'Mayhap were built by sailors,' Will said.

'Or pirates,' thought Moreton.

'Or savages,' said Sam Bird.

John Butcher fingered a musket.

'Doan mind,' laughed Mary. ''Tis shelter for the little 'uns, an' 'tis very welcome!'

'Can we stay here, Mama?' Charlotte asked excitedly, pointing to the huts.

'Maybe for a little while, sweetie,' Mary said. She put Emanuel, who had begun to cry, to her breast. From the bow, Will looked hungrily at Mary's full breasts. It had been many weeks since he had enjoyed the rights of a husband.

They landed by the huts and searched the shelters. They were empty, but the remains of a fire were scattered between the huts and the trees.

Soon after they took possession of the huts, Mary and the others saw two naked female savages, each with a young child and one carrying a firebrand, emerge from the trees that lined the shore.

'Doan shoot, John. Or you, Chips!' Mary called, raising her hand as Butcher and Jimmy Cox reached for their muskets. ''Tis mothers an' their babes.'

John Butcher brandished the musket like a staff, and the alarmed women ran back into the trees.

'I'll talk to 'em,' Mary said. She walked to the edge of the forest with Emanuel carried in a sling across her chest and Charlotte on her hip. '*Go-mul*. Friends,' Mary called, hoping that the warmth in her voice would make up for not knowing their language. 'We'll not 'urt 'ee.'

Within minutes the two women reappeared with the firebrand, and Mary beckoned to them to bring it forward. When they did so, she used it to start their own fire. The native women engaged in nonstop chatter that Mary couldn't understand but which she guessed was about Charlotte and Emanuel, whom the women pointed at and touched. Mary also pointed at their children, trying out the Port Jackson tribe's word for children, '*Go-roong*'. But it was no use. Mary's children, in turn, took an interest in the black children.

'I want to play with this one.' Charlotte said pointing to one of the black babies. 'What's his name, Mama?'

'I doan know, sweetheart,' Mary said, fanning the fire.

'Ask them,' Charlotte begged, hugging the little black boy like a doll.

'I can't, Charlotte, because we don't speak their language,' Mary replied.

'Well, learn it, Mama. Like you learn me to do things,' she persisted, kissing the little boy.

'You've a way with savages, Mary Bryant, you have,' James Martyn said kindly, after the women walked off. 'Well, children bring women together, and they are mothers an' children, jus' like us.'

While Mary attended to the fire, Will, Bill Moreton, Willy Allen and Jimmy Cox ran the cutter up the beach and set to to repair the leaking seams. Late the next morning, a great number of naked savages appeared at their camp. Mary attempted to approach them in a friendly manner, as she had the two women the day before, but trigger-happy Jimmy Cox and John Butcher fired off their muskets, and the frightened savages fled into the bush. As the natives appeared to pose no real threat, and the fish and fresh water were plentiful, the crew of the cutter stayed on shore for two days and two nights.

Will and Mary took the opportunity provided by the huts to spend the nights in each other's arms. Their physical passion for each other hadn't dimmed, despite the rigours of their journey. They then talked late into the night about their chances of returning to England and their hopes for the future.

Leaving Halifax Bay behind, they continued past Rockingham Bay following the coast, now trending west of north. Bill Moreton thought they were now sailing through a belt of trade winds, which enabled them to make steady progress northwards towards Cape York. 'In the tropic, now,' he told the crew. He waved seawards, to the east. 'The great reef to the east certainly makes the seas a mite flatter.'

Yet, within a few days, a gale struck the boat, giving them the worst weather they had encountered. The cutter managed to keep sailing on through the violent, heaving seas, the miserable conditions dogging them for days. It seemed they would never reach the northern tip of this huge island continent. Although not worried for her own safety, Mary feared for her children. Charlotte cried miserably, and she couldn't keep Emanuel dry while she fed him. The rain was relentless, making it impossible to light a fire. For days, they had eaten no cooked food and existed mainly on raw rice.

Finally at 17 degrees south, they reached a forested island not far from the mainland, which Bill Moreton said was part of the great reef on the chart and should be called Green Island, as it was so lush with vegetation.

'Mus' land again, Will,' said Mary. 'We'em runnin' low on food an' water, an' us needs a rest.' All of them were haggard from the poor food, fatigue and lack of sound sleep, and their bodies were covered with saltwater boils and festering cuts. They bore little resemblance to the joyful crew that had snuck out of Port Jackson under cover of darkness all those weeks ago.

'Surf's high,' Will said.

'Doan matter,' she said. 'Gotta land, Will.'

'Likely there'll be no savages, as it's an island. But there's reefs, too,' Moreton added, pointing. 'It'll be a risk.'

'Nay. Doan matter!' Mary repeated.

James Martyn looked around them. 'Aye. Must land,' he agreed. 'Little 'uns have to walk ashore.'

Will looked at Moreton. The ship's officer nodded.

Using every ounce of his ability, and standing up forward with Will, the steady navigator guided the boat through the treacherous reef, with only inches to spare between the wooden hull and the jagged rocks that reached out menacingly from either side. Will gave a cheer when they landed safely on the beach. He instructed Sam Bird to take the painter up the sand and make it fast to a rock. 'Wouldn't want to lose it, Birdy,' he teased. 'Or you'd never have that big black beard of yours stroked by your sweetheart in sweet Surrey.'

Mary breathed a sigh of relief and handed the children down to James Martyn. They sat on the sand, exhausted. She asked the crew to unload everything on to the dry sand so that they could set up camp, dry out and take a break. John Butcher and Jimmy Cox stood guard.

Willy Allen and Nat Lilly set off to collect some firewood. As they walked, they sang an old song they had learned on the *Lion* hulk. When they returned with armloads of dry branches, Mary struck the flint, lit a fire and cooked what was left of the rice in a little of their remaining gallon of water. James, Will and Jimmy went in search of fresh water, but returned to the makeshift camp empty-handed.

As if to make up for the lack of water, the men found some large turtles caught on the reef that had nearly smashed the cutter. It was their first fresh meat in many days. With their bellies full, they rested. Mary admired the sights and sounds of the wonderful birds on the island, which ranged from rainbow-coloured parrots to gigantic pelicans. Then, much to their delight, it began to rain. They quickly spread out a sail to catch the raindrops. Not only would they now have fresh water, but the rain would wash the salt from their ragged clothes.

With no savages in sight and so much fresh meat and water available, they decided to stay awhile on the island. They rested for some days, eating turtles as they caught them. Charlotte, watched by Emanuel, caught crabs, which she delighted in throwing into the pot of boiling water. Mary dried some turtle meat for the voyage ahead, and found some bell pepper fruit and sarsaparilla leaves for making tea. She and Charlotte also found some baby fowls, which they plucked and cooked.

After they had all gathered their strength, the crew put to sea again, sailing north. They passed a great number of green and verdant islands. Although they called in on some of these islands in search of turtles, no more were to be found. Instead, they found ample supplies of shellfish. Some of these turned out to be bad, making some of the crew violently ill. They also found plenty of fresh water on these many lush islands that were mercifully free of savages.

The cutter sailed on, day after day. As they weaved their way through the channel between the great reef to their right and the never-ending coastline to their left, they passed the many seamarks charted and named by Captain Cook. Eventually, they came abreast of the estuary of the Endeavour River at latitude 15 degrees south, where Cook had repaired his ship the *Endeavour* after she struck the very same coral reef they were navigating through in their cutter.

'Must 'a' been a good seaman, that Cook,' Bill Moreton commented, 'to beach and repair his ship 'ere.'

'Good craftsman, too,' Jimmy Cox said, 'with good tools and all. Never left nothing behind, eh?' he said with a laugh, still thinking of the handsaw he had dropped on the night of their escape.

'But I doan think we'll be goin' into that Endeavour River,' Will called from the bow. 'We've got to make up time and get to the top of this bloody great big continent.'

With a good, steady sea breeze, the cutter sailed north inside the great reef for days without stopping, passing by Cape Melville, Cape Weymouth and Cape Grenville, all named by Cook, and then headed for Cape York. Finally, with a shout of joy, Will called out: 'Thar she blows! Tip of the continent: Cape York!'

'You sure, Will?' Mary asked. Emanuel was asleep at her breast and Charlotte on her lap. 'My God, I hope so. We must have nearly reached latitude 10 degrees south.'

'Mus' be the top,' Will said, looking at the expanse of milky-blue water to the west and northwest, devoid of land for the first time, apart from some islands.

'Thereabouts, but may be another bay,' Bill Moreton cautioned. 'I can't be that definite of the position.' He checked his chart. 'That's it, alright,' he said, looking up and checking his compass. 'We've reached latitude 11 degrees south and that's the end of New South Wales to the north. Now we can sail west, through the Endeavour Strait.'

'Cape York,' said Sam Bird. 'Highwayman Dick galloped from London ter York, didn' 'e?'

'Aye, so 'tis said,' John Butcher nodded. 'Leastways, he *rode*. I doubt he galloped. 'Tis a fair distance.' Willy Allen grinned.

'Governor won't catch us now!' Jimmy Cox shouted. 'We're leavin' the east coast forever!'

'I done my calculations,' Bill Moreton announced. 'We have done very well, like. We've run down some 1300 miles of our northing. But, with the courses of northeast and northwest, an' the tacks 'n' all, more 'n likely we've sailed about 1500 miles north from Port Jackson now. Aye! Fifteen 'undred miles in this damned cockle. An' my arse feels it, too! Right you are, Will. We'll assume it's Cape York and alter accordingly. Mary, lass, put your helm down. We'll wear and steer west a quarter north.'

So, after many weeks of sailing north, the cutter finally turned west and, running before a strong southeasterly wind headed into Endeavour Strait.

'Is this still New South Wales?' Nat Lilly asked Moreton.

'Aye, it is, indeed, Nat. Makes Yorkshire seem small by comparison.'

'Is large, for sure,' Nat agreed.

'Three cheers for the Old Dart, where we are now all headin',' Will called out. 'Hip, hip, hip an' a tiger!'

'Mayhaps you Cornishmen should give a cheer when we pass Prince of Wales Island,' Moreton said, looking up from his chart.

'An' why is that, Master Moreton?' Mary asked.

'Because the southern point is named Cape Cornwall!' he said with a laugh.

'Oh, 'tis a wonderful omen,' Mary cried. 'It will give us strength for this next stage.'

The little cutter, with its elated crew of escaped convicts, headed steadily westwards across the northern coast of the great island continent. Prince of Wales island passed astern and disappeared, providing a huge boost to their morale. The crew members were the happiest that Mary had seen them since the morning after their escape from Port Jackson, and she felt contented. She and Will had done the right thing by bringing them away on the cutter.

But then, rather than sail straight across the top of the Gulf of Carpentaria, which Mary argued was the safest and shortest route to Timor, Bill Moreton wanted them to head south so that they wouldn't lose sight of the coastline. After all, he explained, he only had a quadrant to navigate by; for taking proper sights right out at sea he needed a sextant and, ideally, mathematical tables with both.

Mary felt strongly that it would be a mistake to follow the coastline, and said so to Will.

'Mary, lass, let Master Moreton say. He's the navigator, he has the chart and the instruments — or, as you heard, lack of 'em,' Will said, shaking his head.

'I doan want us to lose sight of the coast, Mary,' Moreton repeated. 'We doan have any chart now to indicate the exact distance across this gulf, it's not been explored yet. May be many, many days, an' we can't carry that amount of water.'

'As you wish,' Mary said, hugging her children and shaking her head.

But after following the coastline south for just a few hours, the exhausted crew sailed directly into the path of a large fleet of native canoes rigged with makeshift sails and packed with warriors who shouted angrily at them and waved their spears in a threatening manner.

'See them!' Will shouted. 'Never seen so many.'

'Take a look at their sails,' said Moreton. 'They're made of matting. I ain't seen that afore. These tribes are a cut above their southern brothers, eh?'

'Let's give 'em somethin' to swallow, Chips,' called John Butcher.

'Righto, Long John. I'm ready,' Jimmy Cox replied, lifting his musket.

'One, two, three,' Butcher called, 'an' fire!'

The shots rang out, the puff of smoke wafted up, but the balls dropped harmlessly into the water as the savages continued their advance.

'There be too many,' Mary said. 'An' they be different savages. More of 'em, more spears, an' more canoes.'

'They'll go. Watch us,' Butcher said. He and Jimmy reloaded and fired, missing their targets again. But the warriors weren't frightened, and maintained their course, powered both by paddles and the small matted sails.

'Let's flee,' Mary said. 'We'll escape 'em if we change tack, Will.'

'Aye, right y'are. 'Bout now! Headsails!' Will shouted. The cutter turned to the northwest, picked up a strong wind immediately, and raced off ahead of the warriors in their canoes.

''Tis better,' Mary said, looking back. 'We have no business bein' here in their world, anyway.'

Before long the wind dropped, and more war canoes full of savages began to draw closer; these craft were lighter and had more rowers. 'We mus' row as well,' Will ordered. The six oars were shipped in the tholes, including the substitute oar that Jimmy Cox had made, and the men rowed hard in the sweltering heat. But they were weak from their long voyage, and before long the warriors closed on them again. As they came closer, they fired arrows and threw spears at the cutter, none of which found their mark. The crew snatched up those that floated close by the boat; they may become a last line of defence, the men thought, should the warriors come alongside.

Bill Moreton then spotted a possible route by which the cutter might shake off the pursuing canoes. The navigator suggested an alteration to starboard, heading to the north in order to sail around the back of one of the islands there. Will changed course again, reaching across the gulf to the windward side of the island. Gradually, they left the canoes in their wake. They then came on to the wind, where they stayed, to slip around the northern coast of the island. They had given the more-cumbersome canoes the slip.

'Someone is watching over us, to be sure,' James Martyn sighed loudly. 'Thank you, God, for our deliverance.' He crossed himself fervently.

'Long John, you and Chips better reload those muskets,' Bill Moreton said to Butcher and Jimmy Cox. He then turned to Mary. 'Well, ye have your way, lass. I believe I'd rather die for want of water than have my gut decorating one of them savages. West it is, 'cross this gulf. An' ye, Paddy Martyn, ye save your prayin' for rain an' a short passage.'

'Did you mind the coloured chalk an' jew-jaws they had?' James replied. 'Sure, I never seen 'em with so many shells around their necks afore.'

'In all my time at sea, I ain't seen nothin' the likes of them savages,' Willy Allen said, shaking his head.

'Proud buggers, ain't they?' added Sam Bird. 'And bleeding good sailors.'

For days, they sailed westward across the gulf. Mary rationed the water and divided up the diminishing supplies of food. Thank God, she thought, she had been able to find the edible plants. But by the time they reached the western shore of the gulf, they were so short of water they had to land immediately near a point named on the chart Cape Arnhem. Here they located a small cove as a likely outlet for a stream, and sailed in. On beaching the boat, the exhausted crew members were staggered to find a village of around 20 abandoned huts, near a watercourse with fresh, though brownish-coloured water. After they had slaked their thirst, they inspected the village. Each of the huts was large enough for up to six people, perhaps, made of bark with a grass roof. There was no sound apart from the screech of some cockatoos in the high treetops above.

'Glory to God, they're almost civilised,' James Martyn said. 'Would you look at 'em? Compare well to them humpies the savages had at Port Jackson.'

'Happen they're as good as some of the settlement's huts they offered us,' Bill Moreton said.

'Shall us stay?' Will asked. They all wished to rest ashore awhile, but feared those northern warrior savages.

'No,' said Mary finally. 'Place 'tis spooked. Hark to them crazy screeching birds that are warnin' us. 'Tis bad, 'ere.'

'Is gloomy, for sure,' Nat Lilly agreed. 'I's not easy.'

'Ghosties an' ghoulies,' said Willy Allen.

They agreed to stay only long enough to search for food, to collect herbs and sarsaparilla leaves for Mary's special tea, and to take crabs and fresh water from the watercourse. Mary also found a bush similar to one Arabanoo had shown her. She named its round yellow fruit 'coastal bearded heath', as it reminded her of a plant found on Bodmin Moor. Then they put to sea again and sailed north past the islands at the northwestern tip of the gulf before turning to the west and into the wide expanse of the Arafura Sea.

'The Hollanders call it Arnhem Land,' Bill Moreton said, gesturing at the forbidding-looking hills on the southern horizon. 'I believe we're in their soundings now. This is the northern tip of

New Holland and is Cape Wessel. I suggest we sail direct for Timor now, parallel to this northern coast, but out far enough to avoid savages. Only a shade north of west.'

'Doan wan' to follow the coast closer along anymore, Master Moreton?' Will asked.

'Nay, Will. Happen coast dips to the south again soon anyway, according to the Hollanders. I want to keep well north of the Cobourg Peninsula, an' we've seen enough of them savages, I believe. If we ration the supplies an' water, like, an' sail direct for Timor Island, will be half the distance.'

'Sure, let us sail direct now,' James Martyn agreed. 'Time to get this over with.'

'We're low on wood, but fine with water,' Mary said. 'Food'll last if we'em strict. We'll last.'

'How far?' Will asked, looking over Bill Moreton's shoulder at the creased and torn chart.

'Nigh on 300 mile from Cobourg Peninsula, I reckon. A week, if this breeze holds. Maybe more if it fades.'

'We'll catch a fish or two, I'm thinkin',' said Will. 'I'm for it. You others?'

'Aye, aye,' came the chorus from the cutter.

And so, for the ensuing days, the crew of the cutter sailed west by north, and then west, fortunately with the south-east wind on their quarter, giving them steady progress through the tropical Arafura Sea. It was perhaps as well that they had decided to make a dash for Timor, as they saw on the southern horizon many flotillas of canoes packed with savages. The cutter's course put them out of range of pursuit, for which the crew was thankful.

Miraculously, some days later, Bill Moreton announced: 'If ye cast a careful look ahead now, in the west, like, I believe ye're looking at Timor Island. That green smudge on the horizon.'

'Thanks be to God. Yet are you certain, now, Master Moreton? Maybe it's another island of these Indies?' James Martyn said.

'Nay, put it in your diary, Paddy. We have raised Timor, in the Dutch East Indies,' Will confirmed. 'Look at them green treetops on the horizon.'

'If that be so, Master Bryant, why 'tis time 'ee called for three cheers for the best crew ever sailed the governor's cutter,' Mary called, her smile cracking the parched skin of her lips.

''Tis fine, Pixie,' Will said. He pulled off his cap and, waving it aloft, cried: 'Three cheers, lads 'n' lasses, to the cutter — one for all and all for one!'

As one, the relieved escapees joined in the chorus, while young Charlotte chimed in with a cheer of her own.

As the Dutch island grew larger on the horizon, the elated crew began to ready themselves for their arrival. They talked excitedly about what they would do when they went ashore, having successfully made their escape from New South Wales.

'A glass of Holland's will suit well,' Moreton said, greatly relieved that his navigation had seen them to their destination.

'Pint of ale 'twill do me,' said Will. 'Maybe two pints. An' rum.'

'We 'ave no pennies,' Mary cautioned the men. 'Them Dutchies may not take kindly to us.'

'No damned Lowlander'll keep me from ale!' Will declared. 'And I have that fancy watch our navigator Master Moreton 'as been using which I kept back from Capt'n Smit to sell on arrival to 'elp us all get started. That'll buy a few beers'

'Mus' 'ave a believable tale,' Mary said. 'Us'll be shipwrecked. A likely enough tale. What say ye, Master Moreton?'

'Aye, 'tis as good a tale as any. Happen it'll be the only tale they'll take. No mention of Sydney Cove, mind. No tales of transportation. We're honest sailors. Lost at sea, we are. Exactly like Bligh.'

'Should we go in now, or wait?' Will asked. 'Which would be safer?'

'I say we go now,' Mary the fisherman's daughter said, 'in case a storm comes up.'

'In we go, then!' Will shouted to the wind.

'Shipmates, one and all,' Mary said, 'we done it just like Capt'n Bligh hisself.' She thought of how proud her father would be of her and her shipmates on the cutter.

'It has been all for one and one for all, in true Cornish style,' Will said.

'But now we 'ave to stick together e'en more than at sea,' Mary warned, 'an' all stand by 'at same story. Musn't let 'em think we was convicts. We must behave well and break none of 'ere laws. 'Member we is all poor shipwrecked sailors from 'n English ship sunk in Arafura Sea,' she said.

'Name o' the ship was…?' Moreton asked.

'The *George*,' Mary said thinking of the half penny around her neck. 'After His Majesty King George no less. Good enuf, eh?'

'Easy to remember,' Will said. 'And no madder than our mad farmer king hisself, eh?'

Their story agreed upon, on 5 June 1791, 69 days after escaping from Port Jackson, the cutter with its nine convicts and two young children aboard sailed into Coupang, the trading port of the Dutch East Indies settlement on Timor.

CHAPTER 8

Liberty lost

*In the Dutch settlement of Coupang, Mary and the
others recover from their ordeal at sea while awaiting passage
on a ship to England. When they do set sail, however,
they are in leg-irons once more, after Will Bryant reveals that
the cutter's crew were not shipwrecked crew but escaped convicts.
Mary's family is decimated by fever before she sets foot
again on English soil.*

The Dutch settlement of Coupang was a hive of activity.
Commercial boats plied backwards and forwards across the
harbour, traders hawked their wares, and people went about their
business in the waterside buildings and warehouses, all modelled
on the Dutch design.

''Strewth, but we look a sight!' Sam Bird said. 'Beards, long 'air, dirty an' torn clothes.'

'Jus' like shipwrecked should be,' Mary reminded him. 'Doan you forget that.'

They were attracting a lot of attention. Before Jimmy Cox or John Butcher had even clambered on to the wharf to make fast the painters fore and aft, spectators had begun asking them questions in Dutch, which none of them could understand. On stepping ashore, Mary and Will found an English-speaking seaman who agreed to take them to the residence of the governor of the settlement. On arriving at the gate of the official residence, they requested an audience with Governor Timotheus Wanjon.

'Pray tell, how exactly are you in Coupang?' the governor asked, upon receiving Mary and Will and the children, and Bill Moreton and James Martyn, in an ante-office. He spoke excellent English, and looked them up and down in some amazement. The men removed their caps, and Mary took off her salt-stained bonnet and gave it to Emanuel to play with as she moved him from one hip to the other.

'We're shipwrecked sailors, Y'Excellency,' Will said on cue, having practised saying his story, and he dipped his head to knuckle his forehead. 'English. Brig *George,* of Plymouth. We were overwhelmed in the Arafura Sea, sir.'

'How unfortunate for you, yet how fortunate is your survival,' Governor Wanjon responded formally. 'But your master? Has he not also survived?'

It was Bill Moreton who answered this unexpected question. 'Aye, the whole crew took safely to the boats, sir, including master. The two boats were quickly separated, like, an' we fear his boat may have capsized. The storm was mortal strong, sir. Barely survived ourselves.' He glanced at the others, who nodded their heads and shuffled their feet.

'Well, certainly we must pray for his survival. I will order a mention in the evening service.' The governor took a pinch of snuff, raised his head and sneezed violently. 'Another of your country's seamen and his loyal crew overcame great odds to reach this same harbour, in an open boat similar to yours, oh, barely two years ago, after a dastardly mutiny by some scoundrels on his vessel the *Bounty*. It was shortly after I was pleased to commence this governorship. A Captain Bligh, I recall. It is the age of miracles at sea, apparently. Perhaps we shall have another miracle when your master arrives. Let us hope so. Meanwhile, as I say, we shall pray for his deliverance.' He looked them over again, taking in their tattered and emaciated condition. 'Yet, you have the appearance of having suffered even more than Bligh at sea,' he said, raising his eyebrows.

'Sure, the storm was fearful bad, Your Excellency,' said James Martyn.

'Aye. It blew for many days before finally we were forced to abandon ship. We fought for the ship, Excellency,' added Bill Moreton.

The governor nodded. 'I am no sailor myself, yet I am familiar with the perils of the main, as I think you English term the *zee*. The storm passed us here at Coupang,' he said. 'At any rate, we have become used to caring for English sailors.' He sniffed. 'You are, no doubt, aware of the frequent hostilities of late between our two great nations, not to mention our competing claims for the Cape Town base? But, you shall be our guests, of course. We shall feed and accommodate you, and doubtless find some suitable garments with which to conceal your near-nakedness. I will charge it to the English government as usual. In the meantime, I shall make enquiries for your future occupation. Meaning, of course, a passage home, at the first opportunity,' he said kindly. 'Now, if you will excuse me, I must continue with my duties. The affairs of the colony are ever pressing, I fear.' He offered a mere shadow of a bow and left them in the care of a young aide-de-camp.

Back at the cutter, they handed out the fresh water they had collected from the town pump and told the other crew members that a government official would be arriving to take them to their accommodations. They repeated the story they had told the governor, so that everyone could maintain the fiction that they had been shipwrecked.

'Yet, he forsook to ask our master's name,' said Bill Moreton. He took another gulp from his mug of cool, fresh water. 'We must be very careful. I fear His Excellency is no fool.'

When the aide-de-camp, Jan Van De Merver, arrived at the cutter he organised for it to be moored, then escorted the party to a house, which he said they could use as their quarters until an English ship arrived to take them home. He then took them to a drapery, where he arranged for them to be issued with new clothes, and to an inn, where he left them to eat their fill.

'Now for some ale,' Will said eagerly. 'We're safe here. Dear God, but I'm thirsty!'

'Aye, mayhaps, Will. Mus' mind our tongues, though, an' not gossip with the strangers here,' Mary said. She filled a tin plate with food for Charlotte, warning her not to eat too quickly. And she fed Emanuel his first solids. Now that they were back in civilisation, Mary decided, she would start to wean the infant, to give herself a rest and strengthen his tiny frame.

Looking up from his meal and surveying the Dutch settlers who were going about their business all around them, Will said: 'We're free now, lass. Doan fret your pretty little head, Pixie.'

'That aide-de-camp did mention the small matter of us workin' for our keep, now,' James Martyn said, in between taking large mouthfuls of his food. When he had finished, he took out his journal and started to write.

'Time ye stopped all your letterin', Paddy,' John Butcher said. 'The voyage is finished.'

'Oh, sure, Long John, but it's a long way to Dublin, I'm thinkin',' James replied. 'I shall still keep a record of what happens.'

As the days passed and they had their fill of food and rest, their strength returned. Before long, Jan Van De Merver had assigned the men jobs on the plantations or the wharves. The children soon regained their strength and enjoyed playing with other children, though Mary cautioned Charlotte not to talk with her playmates about their time at sea. Now that she wasn't breastfeeding

Emanuel, Mary also got her strength and energy back, and her spirits lifted.

Mary and Will enjoyed lying together once again, though Mary felt that Will no longer considered himself bonded to her. She suspected that he thought them no longer married in the eyes of the law, the banns not having been read before their marriage at Sydney Cove, where different rules applied. She had grown very fond of Will, despite their marriage having been one of convenience for them both. Would he take the opportunity now, she wondered, to reclaim his single status along with his freedom?

By September 1791, they had all grown fat and relaxed while waiting for a Europe-bound vessel to take them home. One day, an English-speaking Dutch ship's captain, Hank Jansen, came to see Will, who was planting some fruit trees on the government farm. 'He has arrived!' he called out excitedly. 'He has arrived! Jan Van De Merver sent me to tell you. Such glad tidings! Gott, what a seaman he must be!'

'Arrived, Cap'n Jansen?' Will said, pleased to have a reason to put down his spade. 'Who has arrived?'

'Your captain,' the Dutchman said, beaming.

'Captain?' Will said. The day was hot, too hot for digging, and Will wondered if he was dreaming.

'Yes. The captain of your ship!'

Will suddenly felt very angry. If there was a captain of the cutter, then it was *he*. Well, he and Bill Moreton, perhaps. Leastways, he reminded himself, he had always been the leader of the escape, even before they'd reached Botany Bay; he'd talked with Mary of plans to escape as far back as when they were on the *Dunkirk*. If Moreton was now saying *he* was the captain … Will stared at Captain Jansen, who was somewhat confused by Will's response. 'Us doan 'ave a cap'n!' Will said, and returned to his digging. 'Doan know what 'ee talkin' 'bout.'

When Captain Jansen told the aide-de-camp of Will's reaction to the news that the captain of his ship had also survived their shipwreck, Van De Merver was also perplexed. Will Bryant's reaction was very strange indeed, he thought. The English were odd — every Dutchman knew that — but still, he became suspicious.

A British captain had indeed arrived in Coupang that day, in a ship's boat with his crew, having lost his ship when it struck a reef and sank in the Arafura Sea. They had sailed and rowed for many weeks until they arrived in Dutch Timor. This latest shipwreck arrival introduced himself as Captain Edward Edwards, Royal Navy. He considered himself extraordinarily lucky to have survived and to have reached Coupang. Unsurprisingly, despite the time lag, the Dutch authorities had assumed Captain Edwards to be the very same captain of Will Bryant and his crew, for whom they had been waiting and praying following their shipwreck in the Arafura Sea. They also assumed that Bryant would be happy to hear of the survival of his captain and the others of their crew. The governor certainly saw Captain Edwards's arrival as something of a miracle.

Not imagining for a moment that another ship could have been wrecked where the cutter's crew had said they were shipwrecked, Will hadn't understood the Dutch captain's news. He told Mary of the visit from Jansen that evening as they sat down to a meal with the children.

'Them Hollanders have trouble with the heat, lass,' he laughed. 'Cap'n Jansen says today our cap'n's arrived!' Two tankards of ale had soothed his anger at Jansen. It must have all been a misunderstanding, he decided.

'Faith! What do he mean, I wonder?' Mary said.

'Doan know. I told 'im we doan 'ave a cap'n,' Will said. He quaffed another ale.

'You says what?' Mary asked, confused.

'Well,' said Will. 'This 'ere Holland cap'n says some English cap'n arrived today, an' 'e thought 'e was *our* cap'n. But we doan *'ave* a cap'n. So I told 'im 'e weren't our cap'n. See. That's end of ut, 'tis.'

'But us told 'em we lost our cap'n, remember?' said Mary, becoming alarmed.

'Aye, lass, I know. But 'e weren't real, were 'e?' Will poured himself another beer, his fourth.

'Nay, William,' she said, calling him by his full name, which he disliked. 'But I believe you should've gone down to meet this 'un, if only pretendin' to see if 'e were our cap'n or otherwise.'

'Nay, nay! This new cap'n 'll say he weren't our cap'n, woan 'e!' Will protested.

'Doan matter, Will,' Mary said. 'You should've gone an' seen, an' then said 'e weren't our cap'n an' you was sorry our real cap'n must've drowned. It seem strange, otherwise, to the gov'ner.'

'Strange? *You're* strange, woman! *You* go an' see this cap'n, why doan you? Sick of all these damn'd cap'ns. We doan 'ave a cap'n, see?' Will shouted. 'An' if'n we do, 'tis me! Understand?' He slammed his tankard down, so that beer slopped on to the wooden table. Emanuel began to cry, and Charlotte ran to her mother's side. 'I'm goin' to yon inn for some decent ale!'

Both children were now crying. Will glared at them, then stood up, pushing his chair back violently. 'This ale is pig's piss! These Hollanders givin' us world's worst ale, after all we bin through.' He stormed out.

The next morning, it was all over Coupang. Their secret was no longer a secret; it was the main news of the day, together with the arrival of Captain Edwards, RN.

'What the hell has happened?' Bill Moreton asked James Martyn, who was scribbling in his book. 'Have ye also heard what's being said?' He had brought fresh bread to the men's quarters, and had heard the news at the bakery.

'Aye, I've 'eard it meself I 'ave. Well, it's true, Master Moreton. Hard to believe, to be sure,' James replied wryly. 'But Will an' Mary had words last night, then he got drunk at the inn an' went an' informed against hisself, his wife, his children, an' us all. He told anyone who has ears that we're escaped convicts. Sweet Jesus, yes!'

'Fuck him! What a wild, hot-headed fool! After comin' so far, like,' Moreton despaired. 'And to think we trusted 'im.'

'Aye, 'tis a damned shame now. Unfortunately for us, stayin' quiet for a while didn't suit our Will Bryant,' James said. 'Mind,

Mary can be a handful at times, there's no doubtin' that. So strong-willed. But not as bad as bloody Bryant.'

'I'll top the bastard!' John Butcher said, priming the musket.

'And I'll wring 'is neck, I will,' Willy Allen moaned. 'I've never 'ad a cap'n betray me afore.'

'Then it's only a matter of time,' Moreton thought to himself. He shook his head. 'Where is he?' he said aloud.

'They've bolted into the forest,' James replied.

'Forest? Oh, aye, jungle, ye mean. Well, no matter. They won't get far. It's an island, all said an' done.'

Will Bryant's drunken outburst had betrayed them all. Only Jimmy Cox refused to condemn Will until he had talked with him. But if it *was* true, Jimmy decided, he would now go it alone.

In a clearing in the forest, where Mary and Will took a moment to rest the children, Mary turned to her husband. 'Why did you do that, Will? Why?' She couldn't believe that he would jeopardise the freedom they had fought so hard for.

'I dunno, Mary. Somethin' jest come over me, ut did.' He stared at his feet.

'But *what?*' Mary stood her ground. 'You've got ten people's lives apart from yours that could be lost, an' yer say that somethin' come over yer? Must 'ave been madness.'

'Must 'ave been the grog, too,' he said, looking defeated. 'I wanted these Dutch people down at the inn I've bin drinkin' with to stop lookin' down on me. To know I wasn't just cap'n of a cutter 'scaped from a wreck, but done the whole voyage from Port Jackson. Then they'd stop treatin' me like a peasant.'

'That's exactly what Jack Sheppard did. Haven't you learned anythin' I've told you?'

'What's 'e gotta do with ut?'

''E was the best at escapin' from gaols all time, but gave hisself away gettin' drunk and boastin', jest like you.'

'How'd 'e end up then?' Will asked.

'Tyburn. They sent 'im to the tree,' Mary spat. 'Where we could go now, thanks to you.'

Around midday, the governor sent grenadiers to arrest those of the convicts who had remained at their quarters. Although John Butcher and Jimmy Cox wanted to use their muskets, Bill Moreton and James Martyn cautioned that they would be treated even more harshly if they did so. The men were marched off to Coupang's fortress prison, where they were locked in cells. Their names — James Martyn, Jimmy Cox, Sam Bird, William Moreton, Willy Allen, Nat Lilly and John Butcher — were recorded in the gaol register.

After interviewing Captain Edwards, who denied any knowledge of Mary and Will's party and said that he knew of no other English ship in the region, nor of any missing captain, Governor Wanjon had already concluded that the cutter's crew were impostors. But now that Will Bryant had recklessly told the truth, the governor had no choice but to imprison the escaped convicts.

Captain Edwards also had a remarkable tale of his own to tell. He had been despatched from Britain in command of HMS *Pandora*, under orders of their Lordships of the Admiralty in London, to seize or sink the captured *Bounty* and take or execute the mutineers responsible. He had sailed first to Tahiti, where he had found and arrested some of the men. He had ordered that they be shackled in a cage on deck, while the *Pandora* made the return journey to England where the mutineers would be tried. Edwards had found no trace of the *Bounty*, nor of the leader of the mutiny, Fletcher Christian, who some said sailed off in the *Bounty* searching for an uninhabited island. Finally abandoning the search for the remaining mutineers, Edwards was returning home when the *Pandora* ran up on an outer reef while attempting to reach the Endeavour Strait. She took water fast and started sinking. Edwards had launched three boats, not concerning himself overmuch with the mutineers, whom he left to drown as the ship started to sink. But one of the junior officers, taking pity on the men, unlocked the cage, enabling the mutineers to get out before the *Pandora* sank and swim to the boats. Seconds later, the *Pandora* slid off the reef and sank. In what became the third passage by longboat over the same stretch of water that Captain William Bligh and Will Bryant had traversed, Captain Edwards's three boats — containing the *Pandora*'s crew and also *Bounty* mutineers — sailed and rowed through the Endeavour Strait and the length of the Arafura Sea to Timor. On arriving in Coupang, Captain Edwards had put the mutineers in chains and imprisoned them in the fortress.

*　　*　　*

It was very bad luck for the escapees from Sydney Cove that their well-laid plans and courageous bid for freedom had been ruined by an unlikely series of coincidences, but it nevertheless spelt the end of their escape attempt. Within days of fleeing from Coupang, Mary and Will and the children were tracked down by the Dutch authorities. Outnumbered and unable to flee with the children, the pair surrendered. Escorted back to Coupang under arms, they were locked up with their shipmates from the cutter and the mutineers from the *Bounty*.

Mary considered their predicament. On being returned to England, they, like the mutineers, would all likely hang. She refused to accept that she had survived everything that life had thrown at her up to now, only to be put back in irons on a prison ship bound for London and the gallows. She must try to escape with the children. Perhaps if she pretended to be sick, she might be taken to the hospital, from where she could escape? But, try as she might, she was unable to come up with a plan. For now, she decided, she would submit to her fate in the hope that something would occur to save her from the rope.

''Tis best to bend along with this Cap'n Edwards an' his men,' she said to James Martyn after coming to the decision to bide her time.

'Aye, I see no other way,' he agreed. 'But, I's surprised to hear *you* say that, Mary.'

'Well, 'tis hard, Paddy. Yet 'tis best to be locked away by my own countrymen than these Hollanders. I mind what they does to their folk. Remember Cape Town?'

Martyn nodded, recalling the wheel, the cut hands, the broken bodies.

A few days after they were imprisoned, Captain Edwards came to interview them to confirm their stories and record their details.

'So, you are the woman who has caused all this trouble,' he said, having summoned Mary last and alone to a room where he sat at a table. After taking down her details, he said: 'I fail to understand why you would leave the security of a British colony and put to sea in a small boat. Surely you were endangering the lives of your children?'

'Aye, sir,' she replied. 'But Port Jackson settlement was runnin' out of food, an' governor 'ad many mouths to feed an' few farmers, sir. Knew we could feed my children better with fish till we found a settlement where there was food.'

'I don't believe a word you say, madam. You are an escaped convict, and you shall be punished for that crime as well as for your original crimes,' Edwards said.

'An' my children?' Mary asked.

'Convicts all, it appears to me. However, I shall not be the judge at your hearing. My advice to you is to put yourself at the mercy of the court. Along with the *Bounty* mutineers. Though precious mercy *they* can expect. That is all.'

Mary decided to keep her distance from Captain Edwards, whom she found cold-hearted and without compassion. He had told her that he would be taking the cutter's crew and the mutineers back to England for trial, as soon as he could find a vessel for the voyage. There, he said, they would probably hang.

While they waited to be transported back to London, Governor Wanjon insisted that the prisoners work to pay for their food. Mary and her party were given work in the settlement's vegetable gardens. Mary was permitted to take the children, and she was delighted when Emanuel took his first steps outdoors instead of in their dark cell.

On 6 October, Captain Edwards announced that he had chartered a suitable vessel and they would soon be setting sail to return to Britain. Early one morning, the Dutch prison guards marched the escapees down to the very same wharf where they had arrived on their cutter, and rowed them out to a Dutch East India ship named the *Rembang*. The Dutch officers and seamen ushered Mary, Will and their companions down below, where they were put in double irons. Mary's heart sank, as did her companions'. With both legs in clamps, their prospects were very bleak, they realised.

'To think it has come to this,' Bill Moreton said, sighing loudly. 'To have survived the boat passage, those storms, navigating all those reefs. Week after week, like. Now, at our first town, back in irons. And it need not have happened, but for one drunken loudmouth. 'Tis enough to make a man weep.'

'Aye, for certain, Master Moreton,' said James Martyn kindly. 'But it's better than being taken by those savages.'

'An' from being drowned,' Nat Lilly added.

'An' you saved us from such a fate,' James said. 'Pray those good English judges take pity on us, after what we have suffered.'

'May we survive so long,' Bill Moreton replied. 'I have a sense of foreboding. The mutineers and yon captain have a sorry habit of losing their vessels.'

'Hush, Master Moreton. Doan think worst thoughts,' Mary interrupted. 'Do you think we'd be spared from all 'em storms in the cutter just to be drowned at sea on next voyage? Not likely. Never fear, we'll get through. I'm not the drownin' kind.'

But it was as if Bill Moreton's premonition had conjured forth the furies, as on the first leg of the passage to England, before even the *Rembang* had reached Batavia, a ferocious typhoon engulfed the ship. The island of Flores was on their lee. The sky was rent by lightning, and thunder rolled about them. The ferocious wind tore at the sails, reefed down to a topsail and foresail only, and the vessel laboured in the whipped-up shallow seas. Sails, handed and furled along their yards, were torn in sections from their gaskets and shredded by the steel fingers of wind. Seamen were plucked from their feet and disappeared forever overboard. The combined crew of the *Pandora* and the *Rembang* fought for control of the ship against the typhoon. It was the most horrendous storm that either Edwards or the Dutch captain of the *Rembang* had ever encountered in all their years at sea. They couldn't steer, pump the bilges, or prevent the vessel being driven towards the lee shore of Flores, where the beach and rocks would pound the vessel to matchwood within minutes. Below-decks in their cells, the prisoners held on for dear life and Mary did what she could to comfort the children.

The typhoon hadn't yet reached its full intensity. As the raging wind heaved the sea into a vicious surf, creating a maelstrom of weather and shrieking noise, spirits quailed. Some of the horrified Dutch seamen panicked and slipped below-decks, away from the mind-numbing noise, to the relative quiet below, their wits shredded like the sails above. Seeing already a wearied and battered crew now further depleted by this loss of the terrified Dutchmen, Captain Edwards turned to the Dutch captain where they stood together on the poop.

'With your permission, Captain,' he shouted, his mouth barely an inch from the other's ear. 'I'll release the mutineers and convicts from below. Despite their sins, and God knows they'll burn in hell for 'em, they are mostly good seamen. The extra hands might yet save us.'

'As you wish!' the Dutch captain shouted back against the wind. 'We are so short of hands I'd accept an offer from the devil himself, but are these prisoners worse than the devil?'

'They could be, but I recommend we release them till Batavia!' Edwards shouted in response. It was the Dutchman who was in command; he, Edwards, was a mere passenger. He tried to phrase his words accordingly. 'If you have fears of a mutiny it means you still have a ship!' he shouted. 'If you do not wear your ship soon, you'll have no ship to concern yourself with, sir.'

Edwards waved his hand to port, to the lee coast of Flores, and the surf now booming above the shriek of the storm. It was an action more eloquent than any words. The captain looked at

227

Edwards once more and nodded. Edwards immediately beckoned his lieutenant.

'Right, go below and release the mutineers and the convicts,' he instructed. 'All but the woman and her two children.'

'But what do I tell them, sir?' the lieutenant asked.

'Tell 'em that they are being released on my orders so to work the ship, to save themselves from destruction. They shall submit to being shackled when that is done. I will attest in my report that they have performed their duties as ordered and helped save a vessel from foundering. I will promise no more. If any demur, leave 'em shackled. Release only those who agree.'

The lieutenant shouted, 'Aye, aye, sir!', touched his sou'wester and went below.

A loud crack reverberated through the fabric of the ship. Both captains immediately looked aloft. The fore-topgallant mast had toppled sideways, taking the main with it; the two masts swept blocks and rigging before them and threatened the reefed fore-topsail below. With the forestay gone, the foresail whipped, slashed and tore itself to pieces in a minute. With the wind presently on their starboard quarter and the vessel running before the typhoon, the loss wasn't too serious. However, they would need a foresail in order to come closer on to the wind, so that they could steer away from the dangerous coastal rocks. The Dutch captain waved the men forward. The *Pandora* seamen were already fighting their way aloft to clear and secure the confusion there. Edwards saw the first mutineer arrive on deck. He waved to attract his attention and went down the companionway to meet him on the main deck.

'You're aware of your terms?' he shouted.

'Aye, aye, sir,' the man replied. It was Morrison, bosun's mate. Another joined him, then another, each knuckling his forehead. They were all immediately drenched as a wave came surging along the waist, and hung on to the main shrouds to stay on their feet.

'Very well. Aloft with you and help clear the raffle there. The fore and main topgallants have snapped. Up with you!' Others he sent forward to help the Dutchmen set another foresail. He kept the eight convicts on deck; some manned the pump, others released lines and made fast, as required by those working aloft. 'Which are the real seamen of you?' he asked Bill Moreton, who indicated Will, Sam Bird and Willy Allen. Edwards beckoned them. 'Can you steer?' he shouted. They all nodded. 'Assist at the wheel. We need all the hands we can get. Smartly now!' Edwards followed them back to the poop. The two captains nodded at each other.

The Dutchman bent his head to Edwards's ear. 'I shall wear ship very shortly,' he said. 'Stand by!'

Edwards nodded and returned to the main deck to pass the order.

The combined crews, mutineers and convicts fought for the *Rembang,* and saved her in the nick of time from being smashed on the rocks. Within five hours they were out of danger, sailing clear, the tangle aloft secured. The cowardly Dutchmen below were routed out and sent about their tasks again, the majority being put to the pump. In another four days, the *Rembang* was brought safely into the harbour at Batavia.

*   *   *

Not that Batavia, capital of the Dutch colonies, could be considered a safe haven. The city was prone to the deadly Batavia fever, which killed a large number of the sailors who visited the unhygienic and stinking port. The fever was also decimating the population of the settlement. Even as the *Rembang* came alongside the wharf, a corpse floating amidst the faeces, urine, dead dogs and rotting rubbish bumped against the hull. The convicts and the mutineers were by this time back in irons.

The captain of the *Rembang* ordered that the sick members of his crew be taken ashore to hospital. Any of the English crew or prisoners who became ill should also be taken to hospital, he said, so that they wouldn't infect others with the deadly disease. But it wasn't long before germs carried in the air and on the water reached the *Rembang* and other crew members on board contracted Batavia fever. Mary had hoped that the few remaining herbs she had gathered in New South Wales, when brewed to make tea, would keep them free from the disease. Charlotte woke her one morning by tugging at her sleeve. 'Mama, Mama. Mannie won't play with me. Make Mannie sit up and play with me, Mama.'

'Alright, sweetie,' Mary said, scrambling off her bunk and shuffling towards her sleeping son's cot. But Emanuel was lying panting in a muck sweat, hot and feverish. 'Will,' she called. 'Wake up! Summat wrong with Emanuel.'

'Looks like the poor blighter's got fever,' Will said, when he saw his son's weak state. 'Bloody fever, it doan spare nobody. See if'n get 'im to hospital.'

Will persuaded the Dutch master who was in charge of the ship while it was in port to allow Mary to take Emanuel to the dockside Dutch hospital under escort. An English-speaking doctor, Wilhelm Janstoon, examined the sweating, feverish child.

'Ja, it is fever,' he announced. He clucked and shook his head. 'It is not good, no.'

'What can be done?' Mary pleaded.

'There is no cure,' the doctor replied. 'Once contracted, the fever must run its race. Few survive, most die. Ja, we lose thousands every year.'

'Is there nothin'?' she cried.

'Oh, ja. The only way to stop fever is not to come to Batavia,' he said philosophically.

This is it, Mary thought. The cruellest blow of all. Her heart ached for her tiny son, but again she steeled herself so that she could be there for him, care for and comfort him, during his final days.

Mary sat watch day and night beside Emanuel's bed in the overcrowded hospital. She mopped his brow, and fed him water and some food when he could bear to swallow. Then, on 1 December 1791, barely three weeks after the *Rembang* had arrived in Bavaria, Mary and Will Bryant's little son died of the fever.

'Poor little blighter,' Will said, when Mary returned to the *Rembang* with the sad news. He began to cry. 'What 'e went through. Not even 18 month. Most of his time spent in gaol an' in a bleedin' boat, to die in this 'ell'ole. Oh, Jesus!' He clasped his head in his hands, perhaps realising that it was his own actions that had put the boy in harm's way. 'My son. My own son.' He sat in his irons, weeping in a way that Mary had never seen, not even when he had been flogged in Port Jackson.

After burying their son's tiny body in the burial ground next to the hospital, a simple wooden cross over the pathetic mound recording his name and age, Mary and Will were escorted back to the ship. There was nothing Mary could do to console Will. The light that used to twinkle behind his eyes was extinguished. Distraught and distant, he retreated so far into himself that Mary didn't know that he, too, felt unwell. It was only when he broke into the telltale sweat and began to tremble that she knew, and feared the worst.

'Why, oh why, didn't ye tell me, Will?' she cried.

'Doan want you to worry, Pixie,' he wheezed.

He was taken ashore to the hospital, where, a day or so later, the fever appeared to have broken. He sat up in the hospital bed and leaned against the wall. 'My Pixie. You're the best wife a fisherman could've had. Us done it, lass. We got clear away. The first ever.'

'Aye, we did that, my Cornish smuggler man, thanks to you. Clear away,' Mary replied, taking his hand. 'You were cap'n, an' we'em got 11 of us clear away from Sydney Cove.'

He smiled gently. ''Twere a voyage, an' no doubtin' that! Jus' like Bligh. Better, maybe.'

'Will,' Mary assured him, 'our'n were best.'

'Doan mind dyin' now, lass,' Will said. 'Now we're out of Sydney. Bastards! Doan you let 'em take you back there, Mary.

Doan you let 'em ever drag you back to bloody Port Jackson. Promise me you'll keep tryin' to escape. Promise me!'

'I promise. I shan't go back, Will, that for a fact!' She shook her head.

'Keep a-chewin' them herbs to keep away fever,' Will said. 'Wish I'd a listened to 'ee, Mary. Leave the others if you mus'. Make sure you get away.'

'We'll get through,' she said. 'an' we'll get to Launceston. See your family, tell 'em how you did. They be proud of you, Will Bryant.'

Will lowered his voice. 'Take the last coins. Here.' He passed a few coins to his wife. 'Get Chips to chisel on me cross "Will Bryant, Smuggler from Cornwall",' he said proudly. 'No use for you, lass, you not readin', but give this to Chips.' He handed her a slip of torn paper with writing on it.

'Why! It's just like my mark!' Mary exclaimed, pointing to the 'WB' at the foot of the terse sentence thinking of how she signed her name MB. ''Cept the first bit is upside down. How close our marks are, Will.'

'Aye, 'tis true. Promise me, Mary. Chips,' Will said, his strength fading.

''Course, Will,' Mary said, holding back her tears as she had when Emanuel was dying. 'Promise. Swear to God. Next to our son, Emanuel.'

Will nodded, and sank back into the pillow. He smiled wearily. 'Such a voyage!' he mused. He drifted quickly into a restless, fevered coma and never spoke again. Late that night,

22 December, Mary lost the man who, more than anyone, had helped her to realise her dream. Finding the bosun's locker empty below-decks, once she was back on board ship she locked the door from the inside and wept tears of grief.

Will was buried the following morning, to reduce the chances of the fever spreading. Jimmy Cox chiselled the epitaph Will had requested on to a cross similar to Emanuel's, and it was planted in a graveyard soon to become overgrown with tropical plants and weeds. Mary persuaded the kindly mate of the *Rembang* to allow her a little while in the sailors' chapel by the sea. While he waited outside the portal, Mary entered and found herself alone and able to think. She had been through so much with this brave man who had led the cutter out through the Sydney heads on their daring escape. Now he had been struck down by this insidious fever and had left her. She would have to face her future with only Charlotte by her side.

She knelt before the cross in the empty church and opened her heart. She farewelled the souls of her son and husband, and cried until she had no more tears to shed.

When she returned to the *Rembang* Mary found relief in talking with James Martyn, who had been a comfort to her since they were fellow prisoners in Exeter Gaol. She also brewed up the last of the herbs she had gathered, in the hope that they would protect her and Charlotte from the fever. She vowed that she would carry out the promise she had made to Will, to try and escape.

Concerned that he might catch the fever himself or lose his precious *Bounty* mutineers, Captain Edwards chartered berths on three ships to take his human cargo to England — the *Horssen* and *Hoornway* for the escaped convicts, and the *Vreedemberg* for the mutineers. Edwards feared that the two groups were sufficiently desperate and ingenious to work together, and determined not to give them that opportunity. To minimise the risk of any trouble by the convicts, he split them up, putting Mary, Charlotte, James Martyn, Jimmy Cox and Sam Bird on the *Horssen*, and Bill Moreton, Willy Allen, Nat Lilly and John Butcher on the *Hoornway*.

Already mourning the loss of her husband and son, Mary was heartbroken when, shortly after leaving Batavia, as they followed the coast towards the Strait of Sunda, Jimmy Cox, Will's best mate and her long-term friend, disappeared overboard. He had managed to free himself during the night while they were still close to the shore with its twinkling lights, and was seen to clamber over the bulwark and down to the chain plates. He called out, 'They'll never turn me off, the bastards!', then leaped into the sea. There was no attempt made to heave to and send a boat. Mary prayed that Jimmy, who was a very strong swimmer, had made it to land. A skilled carpenter should be able to find work anywhere, she thought. Mary knew that Chips was a determined man who had been trying to escape since he was first transported to America on the *Mercury* in the early 1780s — after all, he was a lifer. But she would miss the friend she had first met on the *Dunkirk* four years before.

Neither Sam Bird nor the cutter's navigator, Bill Moreton, were as lucky. Both had contracted the fever in Batavia and died in quick succession as the ships entered the Indian Ocean. Moreton's death meant that they no longer had a navigator, Mary realised, so there would be little point in trying to escape by boat now, especially as none of the *Bounty* mutineers could navigate.

Only six of the original 11 escapees on the cutter were still alive, and five of those were headed for the gallows, among them the three Second Fleeters. Nat Lilly wished only to see his family again; Willy Allen yearned to resume working as a free sailor; and John Butcher regretted leaving Port Jackson and talked about going back as a soldier or farmer.

For once, the weather favoured the fleet of three Dutch ships, and they sailed without further incident to the east of Ceylon and across to Cape Town, arriving there on 18 March 1792. Edwards could now offload his unhappy human cargo.

Shortly after the little convoy arrived at the Cape, Mary heard that some officers of the First Fleet who had sailed to Botany Bay in 1787–88 were also in port en route to England. They were travelling from Port Jackson on HMS *Gorgon*, having finished their tour of duty. Much to Mary's surprise and pleasure, Captain Watkin Tench was among them. It was Tench who had told her about Timor in this very port in 1787 and who had befriended her on the outward voyage.

Mary was further pleased to hear that Captain Edwards intended to send all the remaining convicts back to England on the *Gorgon*, together with the *Bounty* mutineers. She would receive a good welcome from Tench, she believed. In the event, as well as Tench, there was the friendly Lieutenant Ralph Clark from the *Friendship* and Sergeant John Easty from the *Scarborough*, both of whom she remembered with affection. Their time spent together in the colony of New South Wales gave them a bond that Mary lacked with Captain Edwards.

Having heard of Mary's surprising arrival on board the *Gorgon,* Tench wasted no time in tracking her down. He was still writing his book about the new colony and was anxious to record the story of her escape.

'So, it is indeed the very Mary Broad!' he said, entering the cell where she was being held.

'Aye, Captain Tench. It is I,' she sighed.

'I hear that your husband, Mr Bryant, has gone,' Tench gently said. 'Was it at Batavia? I heard you called there.'

'It *was* Batavia. Poor Will,' she replied. 'The fever also took our son Emanuel,' she said, turning her face away.

Shaking his head sadly Tench appraised Mary's condition. 'I have no doubt you have been through a great deal since that night you absconded from Sydney Cove,' he said. 'I have to tell you that in that settlement you are assumed drowned at sea or killed by the natives. And, yet, I find you here in the Cape!'

'Sir, 'tis pleased I am to see you. The same ship, but different destinations. You goin' home, an' me to gaol,' Mary said.

'Be kind enough to tell me what you can remember of your travails, your adventures, and I will do my best to give an honest account of your story in the book I am intending to have published in England,' Tench said.

'But, please, Captain Tench. So much has happened. Can we discuss it during the voyage, as we'll have the time?' Mary asked.

'Of course,' he said. He looked at Mary with something approaching wonderment before continuing in the formal writer's vein she remembered from before. 'But I do confess, Mary Broad, I couldn't now look at you and your little band of adventurers without pity and astonishment. You have mounted such a heroic struggle for liberty, combating every hardship and conquering every difficulty, but by a vicious play of fate you have miscarried in that struggle.'

'We had both good and bad fortune but it is kind of you to see both sides, from your position as a marine,' Mary said.

'Before we leave the Cape, I'll order some fruit and vegetables for you and little Charlotte,' Tench said, closing his book and disappearing up the companionway.

Once the *Gorgon* sailed, her skipper, a Captain Parker, promised that he would 'assume their good conduct on his ship from their previous meritorious conduct in the voyage from Timor to Cape Town and he would not place them in irons'. However one slip, he added, and they would be clapped back in irons. But as Mary said to James Martyn, no one in their little gang had the will to try anything anymore.

''Tis still hard, Paddy,' Mary said. 'Bein' dragged back to England as prisoners 'stead of free.'

'Aye, for sure. Yet, I believe we won't hang.'

''Twas your words in Exeter Gaol, too,' Mary said.

'And was I right then, Mary?' James said. 'Sure, there'll be an outcry if they were to turn us off after our troubles. Especially you, lass, with your daughter an' all. I think your Captain Tench would be most grieved should you swing, 'an 'e might even protest on your behalf.'

'I could certainly use some 'elp when it comes to me trial this time,' Mary said wistfully, thinking back to her first hearing at the Exeter assizes.

The *Gorgon* departed Cape Town on 6 April 1792 and sailed without incident through the South Atlantic. There were few features apart from the British islands of St Helena, which they sighted on 18 April, and Ascension, five days later, where they paused for a few days to take on supplies. As they approached the equator the temperature rose, and a number of the children of the officers and seamen fell ill. Every few days, another child died and was buried at sea.

Then Charlotte, too, became ill. The ship's surgeon suspected a recurrence of the Batavia fever, perhaps carried dormant since they had left that pestilent town. The fever — if, indeed, that's what it was — soon wasted Charlotte's body and she lapsed into a coma. A few days after Mary's 27th birthday, on a day of incessant rain, her remaining child died in her arms. Mary was distraught. After a committal service, Charlotte's body, swathed in canvas, was lowered over the side of the ship. Mary turned away as the tiny form slid off the polished plank and splashed as it entered the water. It was the same ocean on which the child had been born. 'God giveth, God taketh away,' Mary said to herself bitterly.

Utterly alone, Mary had once again to steel herself and contemplate her uncertain future. It was a pity that she and her fellow escapees had been thrown together with the *Bounty* mutineers, she thought, as the government might think they were all as bad as each other. She was sure that some of the mutineers would hang. But she was determined that she wouldn't give up; she had promised Will that she would keep fighting for her release. She hoped that James Martyn was right again, and that they wouldn't hang. She may have a longer sentence now, but if she ever did get out of prison she would be a lot closer to home than Port Jackson and it would be far easier to get back to her family and to Richard Thomas as a free and unencumbered woman. It was the first time in months that she had thought of Richard. She still had her half of the penny he had given her. Was he waiting for her still? Was her father still alive? What had become of her sisters? Had her mother lived for much longer after Mary's arrest?

As Mary looked out across the ocean that was carrying her towards England, her indomitable spirits lifted.

CHAPTER 9

Grace and mercy

*Once again Mary finds herself in gaol awaiting sentencing for
her crimes but when the story of the escape from Sydney Cove
captures the attention of a London newspaper, Mary's case is
taken up by the author and lawyer James Boswell.*

On 18 June 1792, on a bright summer's day, HMS *Gorgon* tied
up off the old wharf at Purfleet, in the River Thames, several
miles east of London. Mary had journeyed halfway around the
world, and back again. She had tasted freedom for only a few
months in the years since her arrest for highway robbery. It seemed
now that she would never taste it again.

Two days after their arrival, the notorious *Bounty* mutineers
were escorted down the gangplank to a longboat and rowed across

to HMS *Hector*, where they were to be held until their trial. Soon after, three constables arrived by boat with a warrant signed by Sir Samson Wright to collect Mary, James Martyn, Willy Allen, Nat Lilly and John Butcher. After showing their papers to Captain Parker, who signed the necessary authority, the constables went below-decks and took custody of the prisoners. They were placed in the boat that would take them to Newgate Gaol.

As the boat travelled west up the Thames, Mary had her first glimpse of greater London. A vast number of ships, both naval and merchant, clogged up the river and obscured her view of the wharves and buildings that lined the banks. It was a far larger and busier port than any she had seen.

Convict hulks were tied up midstream every mile or so. Mary wondered if the convicts on board would be transported to New South Wales, and how many would die on the hulks and be thrown overboard to join the bodies that bumped alongside their boat from time to time. Little had changed, she thought. The sight of rotting corpses strung up on gibbets and heads on pikes as they approached the Tower of London sent a shiver through all five escapees.

On reaching Puddle Dock at Blackfriars, Mary and her companions were taken ashore and marched to Newgate Gaol, the grim façade took up a long stretch of Newgate Street. As they passed through the massive gates, Mary recalled that Jack Sheppard had escaped from these very walls. The thought also reminded her of Will's last words and she vowed never to give up hope, however dire her circumstances appeared to be. They were ushered into a cell already crowded with felons of all types, from housebreakers to pickpockets.

'Same old stinking cells, cold stone floors and filthy straw. Don't look too promising, does it?' Willy Allen said.

'At least we'll get regular meals,' John Butcher said. 'And slops we get 'ere can't be any worse than all that salted meat on *Gorgon*. It'd have to be fresher.'

'It better be good, as we won't be gettin' away from here in a hurry, eh?' Nat Lilly said.

'Jack Sheppard did, and more than once,' Mary reminded them.

'Well, Mary, I think it's best if we lay low,' James Martyn said, 'and hope for a bit of mercy.'

The following Saturday, Mary and her companions were put into leg-irons, led out of their Newgate cell, placed in a cart and driven through the thriving centre of London. Mary was agog at the sight of all the activity around them as they made their way down Fleet Street and The Strand: horse-drawn carts jostled with hackney cabs, and street vendors cried out their wares to pedestrians, who pushed and shoved their way along the crowded thoroughfares. At Bow Street Magistrate's Court, they were brought before Nicholas Bond, Esquire. Mary was the first of the five escapees to be questioned.

'Record these details for the Newgate Prison manuscript register, Snivels,' Magistrate Bond said in a droning voice to his clerk of court. 'Are you ready, Snivels?'

'Yes, sir,' the clerk said, giving a nervous cough. He picked up his quill and dipped it in the inkwell.

'The first one's name: Mary Bryant, although originally convicted in Exeter assizes in 1786 as Mary Broad. Age 27. Height 5 foot 4 inches. Grey eyes. Brown hair. Sallow complexion. Born in Cornwall. Widow.'

'Description completed, sir,' the clerk said.

After recording the others' details, the magistrate announced that the five convicts had been found guilty of absconding from one of His Majesty's prisons and would be held in Newgate until their punishment was determined by a hearing at the Central Criminal Court in the near future. Their likely punishment, he reminded them, was death. They were then escorted from the courtroom and returned to Newgate.

'Don't fear, my good friends,' James Martyn said when they were back in their cell. 'The government already has its hands full with the *Bounty* mutineers. I don't believe they would have the nerve to turn us off as well.'

'Well, we didn't rebel against a captain of one of His bleedin' Majesty's ships and cast the captain adrift, did we?' Nat Lilly said. 'So, I'm hopin' to see my family again.'

'It all depends on the whim of the judges at the time,' Mary said. 'Our lives are worth nothing to them. People have heard about the *Bounty* mutiny, but no one has ever heard about our plight. No one would be any the wiser if we were turned off tomorrow.' Although it was uncharacteristic of Mary to fear the worst she suddenly felt she could not take anymore on her own, especially with Will and both her children gone. Her normally unbreakable spirit had been dampened by their visit to the magistrate's court, seeing the contrast between their chained selves and the Londoners who were free to walk the city's streets. But as it turned out, those same Londoners were soon to learn of their adventures after a reporter from a weekly newspaper, *The London Chronicle*, bribed the escaped convicts' turnkey, who went by the name of Drayton, and paid them a visit in their Newgate cell where he interviewed them. And this became the turning point Mary was hoping for.

A few days later, on 30 June, there was a commotion outside their cell. A group of turnkeys surrounded Drayton, who was waving a newspaper. He showed it to James Martyn. 'You're the talk of the town!' Drayton said. 'There's almost a whole page of *The London Chronicle* devoted to your story.'

'What's it like?' James asked. 'Did the reporter make us out to be villains?'

'Not at all,' Drayton said. 'In fact, you've come up smelling roses, you have — regular heroes, you might say. The paper even recommends a bit of mercy for your souls,' he laughed. 'Here, take a copy. It's called "Escape of Convicts from Botany Bay". You can keep it.'

'Is it really a whole page, James?' Mary asked. 'I hope it doesn't mention all our names, or say where we are from, or make us appear as bad as the *Bounty* pirates,' she said, biting her lip. 'I just hope my family doan hear about ut down in Fowey. I doan want to bring anymore shame on my poor father, nor on Richard.'

'Doan break your little heart just yet, Mary,' James said. 'Sit down, and I'll read it to you.'

Mary took a seat on a bench.

'Well, Drayton's right. It's called "Escape of Convicts from Botany Bay" and it describes our escape as "wonderful and hazardous".'

'What else?' Mary said nervously.

'Well, it says things like: Bryant stole the governor's cutter, a six-oared boat with an old lugsail and persuaded a Dutch Captain Smit to let him have a quadrant and a compass for which he paid the captain what money he had.'

'Too much money, I say,' John Butcher interrupted. 'What else?'

'It says we had to sail 1300 miles and the "monsoon wind set in and the wind was contrary", which was right,' James said. 'And it also says, "the weather was extremely tempest like".'

'Well, he got that right,' John said.

'It says, "the savage natives wherever they put on shore came down in vast numbers with intent to murder them" and we used our muskets, "firing over the heads of these multitudes on which they ran off with great precipitation".'

'That weren't true,' John said. 'We had to fight 'em, didn't we? Some savages cared nothin' for musket fire, eh?'

'Let me continue,' James said. 'The article also says we had "continual rain" and to lighten the boat they had to "throw overboard all their wearing apparel" and so "were continually wet".'

'That's true enough,' Willy Allen said. 'Well, not *all* our clothes, and anyway, we gave some to the savages.'

James read the rest of the article to his companions, who continued to express their agreement or disagreement with the reported version of their experiences.

'It says, "These poor people being destitute of necessities several gentlemen gave them money",' James read.

'I haven't seen any money,' John said.

'Well, it has been deposited for us with Drayton, the turnkey, apparently,' James said. 'But it's true a donation fund has been started for us all.'

'Is that it?' Mary asked.

'No, it finishes off saying what our crimes were,' he replied.

'With all our names and towns?' she asked, wincing.

'No, Mary. It just says "Mary Bryant" for you, and you was charged at Exeter assizes,' he said. 'It doesn't mention the name "Broad" anywhere, nor the place of Fowey.'

'Nobody from Fowey would know that was me,' she sighed with relief.

'It then says, and this is worth listening to, "They declared they would sooner suffer death than return to Botany Bay. His Majesty, who is ever willing to extend his mercy, surely never had objects more worthy of it." That's how it finishes,' James said, putting down the paper.

Since their arrival back in England, Mary hadn't wanted to contact her family in Fowey. She planned to wait until she knew what her fate would be, if the news was good. Although she was named as Mary Bryant in the newspaper account, she continued to worry that Richard and her family might somehow connect the story with her.

Despite Mary's fears, it was this very story published in *The London Chronicle* that alerted the person she and the others needed to help them: a defence lawyer and author named James Boswell. Some days later he picked up the weekly newspaper and read the article after taking breakfast at his central London club, Boodles, with an old colleague, Sir John Page.

'My God,' he cried, on reaching the end of the article. 'His Majesty certainly never had objects more worthy of his mercy, indeed. He cannot hang a woman like that — that's the stuff we Britons should be breeding from. She is a modern Boadicea, not a bandit,' he said. 'She must be saved.'

'Well, why don't you go to her rescue?' Sir John said, looking up from his paper. 'You seem to have a passion for the underdog, especially penniless criminals, no matter how slim their chances.'

'But she warrants it, Jack, this Mary Bryant. Read the story yourself. What she has done is wonderful.' He thrust the *Chronicle* at his old friend.

'The case may not be worth the candle, James,' Sir John warned. 'But perhaps you could write her biography, as a companion to your scholarly work, the *Life of Samuel Johnson*?' He laughed. 'Although I hear that's not selling too well.'

'I only published it last year, dear friend. It takes time for a book to get established, as you well know.'

'Well, it sounds like your girl from Botany Bay could even be a better story,' Sir John said, turning his attention to the article. Boswell farewelled his breakfast companion and left the smoke-filled room for the streets of London and headed for Newgate Gaol.

On hearing that their case was to be heard at the Old Bailey the following day, Mary found a quiet corner where she hung her head in despair. She had heard that three of the *Bounty* mutineers had been condemned to die. The judges could decide to impose the death sentence on her and her fellow escaped convicts, too, she thought, hanging being the usual punishment for the crimes they had committed. She thought back to the time she had spent in Exeter Gaol in 1786 awaiting execution. At the last minute, her sentence had been commuted to transportation. But six years later, Mary wondered if she could dare hope for a similar reprieve. She was worried this time the authorities would consider she had shown how ungrateful she had been for that 1786 reprieve by escaping and so insist that she be hanged once and for all.

Mary's thoughts were interrupted by the sound of the turnkey unlocking the heavy door to her cell. 'Mary Bryant?' he called.

'Aye. 'Tis Mary Bryant,' she replied.

'Gen'l'man to see you.'

The turnkey escorted her into an adjacent, less gloomy cell where a well-dressed, rather portly man stood clutching a newspaper.

'Mary Bryant?' the visitor asked.

'Sir,' Mary nodded.

'I am James Boswell, a defence lawyer and I wish to take up your case, if you'll be kind enough to tell me the facts of the matter.'

After listening to Mary's account of her arrest for highway robbery, transportation to Sydney Cove, escape and recapture, Boswell scoffed at the likelihood that she would be hanged, along with her fellow escapees.

'Hanged? For what?' he said. 'For sailing halfway around the world, battling savages, losing your husband and children, fighting on and on? Things have changed since you left England six years ago. You have rights now that you didn't have then. An American revolutionary by the name of Thomas Paine has just published a book called *The Rights of Man*, and it's all that anyone talks about in the coffee houses. Thanks to the successful revolutionaries in France and America, times are changing dramatically. People's rights are being taken more seriously. In France, poor people like you are being treated the same as rich people before the law,' he explained.

'Even escaped convicts?' Mary asked.

Boswell nodded. 'Just this year, the Danes have abolished the slave trade. They are the first country to do so. They will lose a lot of cheap labour, but they have given the slaves their freedom. I must hurry off now to look further into your case, and that of your fellow escapees, before tomorrow,' he said, signalling for the turnkey.

Back in her cell with the others, Mary was surprised that anyone could be interested in her case, let alone a lawyer who seemed confident of securing her release. She told James Martyn of Boswell's timely visit. 'Do you think I can trust him, James?'

'Well, there is nothing wrong with his Christian name,' he smiled. 'And if he is keen to help us four as well, as you say, he can't just be after you as his mistress. Nice to have somebody on your side now that Will's gone. But, you should listen to your heart.'

'I'm going to trust him,' she decided.

The following day, 7 July, Boswell arrived at the Central Criminal Court at the Old Bailey to hear the verdict. He was pleased to see that members of the press were present, as most of the newspapers were clamouring for Mary's release. As the court was situated next to Newgate Gaol, Mary and her companions had been escorted there on foot, fettered as usual. When it was their turn to appear before the judges, they were ushered into the court, where a panel of judges heard the case against them. They then explained that the law recommended the death penalty for such offences, but, as it was an unusual case, they would postpone their verdict. There were extenuating circumstances, the judges said, including no small degree of public interest in the case that may in time permit some measure of mercy to be exercised. His Majesty the King, the judges added, had the discretion, if he so chose, to 'extend his mercy to these objects now before the court'. With nothing decided, but with a little more hope, the escapees were taken back to their cell in the neighbouring gaol.

James Boswell believed that his best legal option was to campaign for a pardon, initially just for Mary, for whom there was much public sympathy, and then for her accomplices. He believed that the current political climate might induce the King to look favourably upon such a petition.

By early August, there was still no word from the judges, and Boswell continued his campaign to secure the escapees' release.

'How are you going with that girl of yours from Botany Bay?' Sir John Page asked Boswell when next they dined together at Boodles.

'Slower than I anticipated, I'm afraid,' Boswell said.

'Surely you haven't exhausted all your connections in the government yet?' Sir John asked, taking a mouthful of wine.

'Such as...?' Boswell asked.

'Henry Dundas, the secretary of state, for one. Didn't you go through university with him?' Sir John asked.

'By jove, that's a capital plan. Yes, I did.' Boswell raised his glass. 'To old school friends.'

Boswell made an appointment to see the secretary of state on 16 August, but the secretary failed to appear. So Boswell returned to his home in Great Titchfield Street, where he wrote to the Right Honourable Henry Dundas, saying:

I staid in town a day longer, on purpose to wait on you at your office yesterday about one o'clock as your letter to me appointed; and I was there a few minutes before one; but you were not to be seen. The only solatium you can give me for this unpleasant

*disappointment, is to favour me with two lines directed Penrhyn
Cornwall assuring me that nothing harsh shall be done to the
unfortunate adventurers from New South Wales, for whom I interest
myself, and whose very extraordinary case surely will not find a
precedent. A negative promise from a Secretary of State I hope will
not be withheld, especially when you are the Secretary, and the
request is for compassion.*

In September, *The London Chronicle* reported that six of the *Bounty*
mutineers had been condemned to death by a court martial. They
were due to be hanged the following month from the yardarm of
the *Brunswick* in Portsmouth Harbour, where the *Bounty* had
originally sailed from in 1787 shortly after the First Fleet. Three of
the six, the paper reported, had been recommended for a royal
pardon. But, as John Butcher said, 'That would depend on the
King, and we all know how mad he is.' Still, Mary and her
collaborators were encouraged that four of the ten had been
acquitted altogether. On 24 October, they learned that the King
had, in fact, granted a pardon to the three mutineers. 'Perhaps the
king isn't so mad after all, John,' Mary said.

Five days later, the three mutineers who had been found to
have played a key role in the mutiny were hanged as planned. 'They
had to be hanged as an example to other would-be rebels,' James
Martyn said. 'According to *The Chronicle*, those revolutionaries
who rebelled against the French King the same year as the
mutineers took over Captain Bligh's *Bounty* have now run amok
and imprisoned the King of France himself.'

'How did they do that?' John Butcher asked.

'The soldiers marched into his palace armed with firearms and arrested him and his family, just like that,' James replied.

'When did the buggers do that?' Willy Allen asked.

'Just last month. And the paper says the King and his family could be guillotined.'

'That's why the government here is determined to make an example of revolutionaries who rebel against authority on one of His Majesty's ships,' James explained.

'I wouldn't have thought it would matter over here,' John said.

'But the paper says there are plenty of French revolutionaries over here, could be some in this prison. The revolutionary French government is now offering to help poor people anywhere who want to overthrow their King,' James said, brandishing the newspaper the turnkey had given him. 'In fact our parliament is just makin' up a new law to ban aliens coming to live 'ere,' he said authoritatively.

'There'd be plenty of rebels here who hate mad Farmer George and would love to see him go the way of King Charles I,' John said, referring to Britain's seventeenth-century revolution.

James cut in. 'There aren't too many Cromwells stepping forward this time, Long John. Although, since this French revolution, there's been so many riots in London our government's scared the mob might run amok 'ere. That's what's working against rebels like us gettin' a pardon,' he concluded.

*   *   *

With the months dragging by and Boswell having little luck in his endeavours on their behalf, Mary and her companions were disappointed to hear of another potential setback in late January 1793. Drayton, the turnkey, came rushing up to their cell, waving a copy of *The London Chronicle*.

'They've done it!' he panted.

'Done what, who?' James Martyn asked.

'Cut off 'is head!' he said. 'Clean off,' he said, drawing a finger across his fat throat. 'The King himself!'

'The king is dead? Mad Farmer George? I don't believe it. I know he was mad, but ...' John Butcher said.

'No, the King of *France*,' Drayton said. 'They put him to the guillotine. Louis XVI lost his head. It rolled into a basket.'

'Poor bastard,' Nat Lilly said.

'All these outrages are going to make it harder to forgive law-breaking rebels like us, who this government would see as the same sort of rebels as them French ones,' John said. 'It just turns 'em against escapees like us. They don't want to take a risk.'

'Well, we'll see,' Mary said. 'Time will tell. We weren't political rebels; we were just tryin' for our freedom, which Mr Boswell says is our right nowadays.'

Then, at last, there was some news that could work in their favour. In early February, Drayton appeared with the latest issue of *The Chronicle* and announced, 'It's war! The frogs have declared war on us.'

'They have, too,' James said, taking the paper and reading the headline of the main story. 'The revolutionary government of

255

France has declared war on the monarchies of Britain and Holland. Well, it's on for young and old now.'

'Aye, and they'll need the likes of us to fight their war, too, won't they?' Willy Allen said brightening up. 'If they let us out, we can become sailors and soldiers for His Majesty's forces against France.' The old sailor rubbed his hands excitedly at the prospect of signing on to a man-of-war again.

'The recruiting officer might just think an old seadog like you is a bit old at 50-something,' John said.

'I knows more 'an any young midshipman I do and anyways, *you're* not too old, Long John. They could let *you* out to become a soldier against the French,' Willy replied.

'I'd do it to get out of this bloody stinking hole,' John said. 'But I've got me heart set on that land back in New South Wales, where they give soldiers a farm, they do.'

'I certainly wouldn't want to leave my family to fight the bloody French revolutionaries,' Nat said. 'I'm safer in here. At least my family knows I'm alive in here.'

'I think it will help with our pardons,' Mary said. 'Because they will be emptying gaols to save money to put into the war effort.'

On 2 May 1793, the day after Mary's 28th birthday on a warm spring day, an unfamiliar voice called into the cell: 'Which one of yer is Mary Bryant?'

Mary looked up from her sewing. 'Sir, it is I,' she said, stepping forward. 'What is it?' she asked, wondering if the judges had changed their minds and decided to hang her after all.

'It seems you is to get a pardon, missy.'

'A pardon?' Mary said with a start, dropping her sewing on the cell floor as her head began to spin.

'Follow me,' the man said, unlocking the cell door.

Mary was shown into the office of the gaol manager. 'Name?' he barked.

'Mary Bryant, sir,' she replied as if in a dream.

'Stand before me, Mrs Bryant,' he said. 'I 'ave 'ere a piece of paper that says you've got your pardon. We have received a letter from the secretary of state, the Right Honourable Henry Dundas, which says: *"By His Majesty's command* — that's King George III, that is — *Mary Bryant is to be granted a free and unconditional pardon due to some favourable circumstances humbly represented to us on her behalf inducing us to extend our grace and mercy unto her."* So now put your mark here, woman, as I 'ear you don't know yer letters,' the manager said, pointing to a blank space at the bottom of the page.

Although unable to read let alone focus on the page Mary wrote her 'MB' mark in the place his grubby finger pointed to.

'Right, now you collect yer things and I'll arrange for the turnkey to come and get you and escort you to the gate directly.'

Returning to her cell in a daze, Mary knew who had represented those favourable circumstances and her heart went out to James Boswell, whose letter of 16 August 1792 had finally had the desired effect. Eleven months after her ship tied up at Purfleet, Mary could leave Newgate Gaol a free woman.

'Oh, Paddy,' she said, hugging James Martyn who had been a comfort to her since those long-ago days in Exeter Gaol.

'Go, Mary, before they change their minds. Our time will come. You know how much faith I've always had. That's something we have always shared,' he said, patting her head in farewell.

'You should finish writing all your notes out clearly now, James, so there is a true record,' Mary said.

'I will, offer the turnkey something to get some paper and ink for me,' he replied.

'Don't forget about us, Mary, will you?' John Butcher said. 'Tell 'em I'll earn my keep back in Botany Bay, too.'

'I will, Long John, and I won't leave London until you get your pardons.'

'I'll miss you, Miss Mary,' Willy Allen said, with a tear in his eye. Mary hugged him and wished him well on his next sea voyage. Finally she farewelled Nat Lilly, saying it would not be long before he was back in the bosom of his family. She then scooped up her things and left the cell for the last time.

Walking in a trance out into the broad daylight as a free woman at last, Mary nearly fainted. Fortunately Boswell stood waiting for her at the prison gate and was able to take her things and give her the fatherly hug she needed to steady her down. His face bore a beaming smile. 'We did it, Mary!' he said, pulling back from the hug and holding her at arm's length. 'It took longer than I'd hoped, but we finally got you your pardon.'

'Well, *you* did, Mr Boswell,' Mary said with a great sigh, shaking her head. 'I don't know why or how, but you worked as hard with the paperwork as we did in the cutter.'

He hailed a passing hackney coach. 'I have rented a room for you in Little Titchfield Street, near my house, where you can rest before deciding what to do as a free woman.'

'I doan wanna do nothin', until we 'ave got a pardon for James, Nat, John and Willy,' she said. 'I'm very grateful for the room, but all I really want is to help get 'em free pardons as well,' she said, climbing into the coach. The thought that she was now a free woman and riding through London in a coach made her feel quite dizzy. Her head was spinning the way it did the night she drunkenly held up that other coach near Plymouth, which suddenly came back to her. Overcome with emotion she gripped Boswell's arm for support. It was all she could do to maintain her composure until they reached the house where Boswell had arranged for her to stay. After he had shown her to her room and left her to rest, she lay on the bed and wept until she had no more tears left to weep. She then fell into a sound sleep, the deepest she had had for years.

The next morning, Mary found herself at a total loss. She didn't know what to do or where to go, so she stayed in her room, as if she were a prisoner there. Boswell brought her meals and was her only company. She had always planned, when she returned to England, to go straight home to Fowey, but now she felt unable to leave London until her companions were released. She decided to try to earn some money to pay for her journey to Fowey and asked Boswell to help her find customers with garments that needed repairing. Fortunately, as a widower, he had a pile of his own that he gave her to get her started.

Boswell hoped that some of his colleagues might agree to contribute something to Mary's keep. One of those he called on just after Mary's release was Lord Thurlow, the former lord chancellor, who, after some initial reluctance, gave Boswell a handful of coins after hearing her remarkable story. That night, Mary was surprised to find Boswell knocking on her door and looking hurt and very dishevelled.

'What's 'appened to ye?' she gasped. Boswell was covered in blood and grime, and his normally immaculate clothes were torn.

'A gang of footpads,' he wheezed. 'They came out of a dark lane and attacked me.' He leaned towards her for support.

'Please come in, Mr Boswell. Come into the kitchen,' Mary said. She helped him into a chair by the fire. 'Here, drink this,' she said, handing him a cup of hot tea she had just made. 'It'll warm ye up and calm ye down.'

'I was just walking home along Great Titchfield Street,' he said, groaning as she dabbed at a wound on his head, 'when they demanded my money. I gave them what I had, including some coins I had been given for you, Mary,' he said.

'Stop talking and drink yer tea,' Mary said. 'I don't want any money, anyway.'

'Then they knocked me down,' he said, 'and searched my pockets while I was on the ground.'

'Ye poor thing,' Mary said. 'But ye'll be alright. No bones broken.'

Before long he had recovered sufficiently to return home. 'But this time I'll escort ye,' she said firmly.

'You are a good woman, Mary,' he said.

Although Mary thought nothing more of it, a few days later Boswell returned and read her an account of the attack that had appeared in *The London Chronicle*. Her name wasn't mentioned, for which Mary was grateful. She didn't want her family to learn yet that she had returned from New South Wales. Her obligations to her four companions in Newgate came before her own concerns, she felt. She would bide her time. When her business in London was finished, she planned to ask Boswell to write to her father and Richard.

However, on the morning of 18 August, the first word was brought from Fowey when Boswell opened his door to a visitor.

'Morning, sir. Mr Boswell, is it?'

'Yes.'

'Castel is my name, sir. I am a glazier from 12 Cross Street, Carnaby Market.'

'How may I help you? I don't need any glazing done,' Boswell said.

'Well, you see, sir, I used to live in Fowey,' he said. 'And I got a letter from the family of Mary Broad, and her family have been reading in the newspapers about an escaped convict from Botany Bay named Mary Bryant and how you have been helping her,' he said. 'And they were wondering, seeing as how their Mary was transported to Botany Bay and was a good sailor knowing about boats and all, if it was their Mary. Bryant being a Cornish name as well.'

'Well, I'm not so sure,' Boswell said cautiously, having just been robbed himself. 'Have you any proof that you are representing the family?'

'Yes, sir. Look here.' Castel pulled out a folded letter. 'Mary Broad's sister, Elizabeth, has written asking me, as an old friend, to give her the news of the family.'

'Let me see that,' Boswell said, and quickly scanned the contents of the letter. 'That seems genuine enough,' he said. 'So, what do you want me to do?'

'Well, sir, her sister Elizabeth from Fowey wants Mary's youngest sister, Dolly, to come and see her,' Castel said.

'It's a long way for Dolly to come from Fowey,' Boswell said, 'on the chance that this is the same Mary.'

'No, she is here, sir, working as a domestic servant in London, and wants to meet with her long-lost sister, Mary,' he said.

'Well, before you get anybody's hopes up, I will take you to see Mary myself. If she recognises you, then we will take it further,' Boswell said.

'Good, sir. And it will be worth her while, because I've also heard that Mary Broad's father, William Broad, has been left a large sum of money – no less than £300,000.'

'Well, I must say that sounds extremely unlikely for a poor fisherman. In any case, Mary cares little for money,' Boswell said. 'But I will get my hat and coat and take you to see her.'

Although Mary didn't recall ever meeting Mr Castel, formerly of Fowey, he obviously knew her village and its fisherfolk as well as her family extremely well, judging by the stories he told as they drank tea in her kitchen. His main errand, he told Mary, was to pass on the message that Dolly wanted to see her as soon as possible. When he told her that her father had been left a very large sum of money, Mary showed no interest in the matter, as Boswell had predicted.

That night, Mary responded to a knock on her door, to find Mr Castel and her youngest sister, Dolly, standing before her. 'Mary, is it really you?' Dolly cried, bursting into tears and flying into her sister's arms.

'Oh, Dolly! Yes, it is — greatly changed, I am afraid. And is this really you, Dolly, after all these years?' Mary held Dolly as if she would never let her go.

Mary thanked Castel, who left the sisters to catch up on all that had happened since they had last seen each other. 'I don't know where to start,' Mary said. 'I haven't seen you since you took that message home to tell the family I had been arrested.'

'Oh, that seems like a lifetime ago,' Dolly said.

'But first, tell me, how is our father?' Mary said, holding her breath.

'Father is fine. He rents part of the house to another family, who look after him. He still wears that old smock and smokes his funny old pipe. He goes out on the boat from time to time, but mainly he fishes from the wharf now,' Dolly said. 'Oh, how he has missed you! He always said that, wherever you were, he knew you would be looking after yourself and that one day you'd come back home.'

'Thank God,' Mary said. 'And Mother?' she asked apprehensively.

'She was very sick when you were arrested, wasn't she?' Dolly replied.

'Yes. Last time I saw Father, when he came to visit me in gaol, he said she was fading fast,' Mary said.

'Well, she died soon after that, but peacefully, poor dear. It was a relief not to hear that terrible coughing hurting her so much. We buried her in the graveyard at St Fimbarrus with a nice little headstone,' Dolly said, wiping away a tear.

'What about Elizabeth?' Mary asked.

'Well, she was the first sister to marry,' Dolly said, not knowing about Will Bryant. 'She married a nice local man, Edward Puckey, and they live down there and have started a family, so you are already an auntie,' Dolly said with a smile.

'And Jane?' Mary asked.

'She's still in the district but had to move to St Austell to get work,' Dolly said.

'And do you remember Richard Thomas, the farmer?' Mary asked as nonchalantly as possible. 'He kindly brought our father to see me in gaol.'

'I know who you mean,' Dolly said, pausing to think. 'I remember getting a message to him after you left, but I don't know what's happened to him, as I left Fowey so long ago myself.'

'I see,' Mary said, hiding her disappointment.

'But, oh Mary, it's so good to see you, and to know you are alright after all you have been through. What was it like?'

'Let's talk about what happened to me another time, Dolly,' Mary said firmly. 'You look so grown up now. Last time I saw you, you were just a girl.'

And so the two sisters talked on into the night. Having got leave from her employer, Dolly stayed that night and from then on visited Mary at Little Titchfield Street as often as she could get time off.

Now comforted by frequent visits from Dolly, who also brought her sewing work to do, Mary waited while Boswell tried to obtain pardons for her companions. Little progress was made until the war against France began to gather momentum. Then, throughout England, a widespread recruiting campaign was organised to raise a large army with which to fight the new French military leader, Napoleon Bonaparte, who was gaining ground against Britain. Desperate for soldiers, the government relaxed its prison policies and began releasing inmates who could serve in the war.

As a result of the government's policy changes and Boswell's efforts on their behalf, James Martyn, Willy Allen, Nat Lilly and John Butcher were all granted pardons. On 2 October, Boswell called on Mary to tell her the news she had been waiting for: her friends would be freed the following month and she need not worry about them as he had supervised the transfer of the charity funds from the turnkey Drayton which would be divided four ways between them. 'Now, you realise that this leaves you free to put yourself first and to go home to your family?' Boswell said.

'So it does,' Mary said excitedly, thinking of seeing her father and sisters again but not daring to hope too much about Richard.

*   *   *

A few days later, Boswell arrived with a letter from Mary's married sister, Elizabeth, inviting Mary to stay. 'You will be very warmly received indeed,' the letter said.

'So that's it, Mary,' Boswell said. 'Now that I have secured the release of your companions, this invitation is what you have been waiting for. May I organise your conveyance to Fowey?'

'Please do so,' Mary said.

'I will organise a vessel for you myself,' he said. 'It's much safer to go by sea than coach in these troubled times,' he smiled. 'And more your sort of transport anyway, eh, Mary?'

'Yes, I'd rather sail than go by road,' she agreed.

'But is there anything I can get you before you return to Fowey?' Boswell asked.

'Well, there *is* one thing,' she replied coyly.

'What is that?' he asked.

'A silk bonnet. I would love to have a silk bonnet, but I doan know where to get ut,' she said.

The next day, Boswell went with Mary to Petticoat Lane, where she purchased, using her sewing money, a bonnet very similar to the one she and her companions had stolen from Agnes Lakeman all those years before.

On the morning of 12 October, Boswell knocked on Mary's door and announced, 'I have fixed for you to sail for Fowey in the *Ann and Elizabeth*, under the care of a Master Job Moyse.'

266

'Thank you, Mr Boswell,' Mary said. 'When does she sail?'

'Tomorrow morning, but you need to be on board after dinner tonight. I will take you to the wharf.'

'Tonight!' Mary said. 'I would be grateful to travel with ye to the wharf, sir.'

That evening, after dining on his own at home and refusing other social engagements, Boswell collected Mary in a hackney coach. They rode in silence down to Beales Wharf, Southwark, where Boswell bought Mary a meal before she was due to board the vessel. As she finished her tea, Mary said to the man who had secured her release from prison: 'Mr Boswell, I wondered if ye would accept a gift from me, for all ye have done?'

'Of course, Mary. But I expected nothing.'

'I 'ave been saving these,' she said, opening her box and taking out a small paper packet. 'I want ye to 'ave 'em.'

'What are they, Mary? They smell strange,' Boswell said, undoing the packet.

'Sarsaparilla leaves from New South Wales, which I took on our cutter to make tea. They are not valuable,' she said biting her lip to contain her emotions, 'but they 'ave come a long way.'

'That they have, Mary,' Boswell said, looking wistfully at his charge for the last time. 'I shall really treasure them as I will our friendship.'

A shrill whistle then came from the boat. The moment had come for Mary to leave her saviour and confront her future. Turning her face to one side to conceal her tears, Mary gave the portly Boswell a strong hug that expressed her gratitude and affection, then picked up her box and walked up the gangplank without a backward glance.

The next morning, Mary stood on the foredeck at the bow of the *Ann and Elizabeth* as it sailed silently down the Thames and away from Newgate. It was the moment she had been dreaming of for years — setting sail for Fowey Harbour as a free woman.

Some days later, again on the foredeck sailing west off the coast of Cornwall, she watched her home town materialising out of the mists. She gulped and shook her head in disbelief — the dream had indeed became a reality. Stiffening her back and riding in with the ship as it rolled with the incoming tide into Fowey Harbour, she stood then as proud as any figurehead on any ship that had ever returned with a rich prize from beyond the seas.

CHAPTER 10

Joining the halves

*Safely back in Fowey, Mary is thrilled to see her father again,
and sets out to find the man who had been keeping her
going all this time, hoping not only to join up their half
pennies but also the rest of their lives.*

Not long after she stepped ashore from the *Ann and Elizabeth*
Mary found her father dangling his fishing line into the water
at Town Quay, in Fowey's bustling little harbour. She had been
directed there by the middle-aged woman who answered the door
of Mary's former home at Lostwithiel Street.

'Father!' she called out, on spotting his familiar old blue
smock from behind. 'Father, I'm back!'

'Mary?' he exclaimed, recognising her voice as he turned around, dropping his line and pipe. 'My lost daughter. Ye's back 'ome!' He broke into sobs. 'Give your old father the hug he's been waiting all these years for,' he said, embracing her.

'Oh, Father,' Mary said, burying her face in his smock and feeling she had finally come home. 'I 'ave missed ye so bad,' she sobbed. 'I'm so relieved to see ye is alright.'

'Here, let's have a look at ye,' he said, holding her at arm's length. 'You don't look that different. A little older and more weather-beaten, but still my beautiful Mary.'

'I feel older, Father, after what I've been through,' she said. 'But I never stopped believin' I could get back 'ome somehow.'

'Well, ye must tell me yer story shortly. But I never gave ye up fer dead neither. After I seen ye in gaol, I knew ye could survive. I knew ye'd get back. Ye seemed so strong and unbeaten — like a real proud Broad of Fowey. I told everyone ye'd come home, I did. And here ye are. Mind, ye know yer dear mother's gone, eh?' he said gently.

'Dolly told me when I seen 'er in Lunnon,' Mary said.

'So, ye seen yer sister Dolly, and got the family news, eh?' he said, stooping to pick up his pipe and line. 'Well, come wid me now and tell me everything.' He took her hand and led her to the Old Lugger Inn.

'Dolly told Elizabeth somethin' 'bout you comin' back in a six-oar cutter wid a lugsail,' the old sailor said excitedly. 'Bigger 'n our old fishin' boat, eh?' he laughed. 'But ut made me so proud to hear of ye doin' 'at — all that boatin' I taught ye.'

'I couldn't have done it otherwise,' Mary said. 'I never forgot that teachin' of yourn and how ye said a boat always gives ye freedom.'

After listening to Mary's story, William said: 'I doan care what you did breakin' the law. They was cruel to transport ye just for that — so unjust. You were just tryin' to 'elp yer family as we Broads always have wid smugglin' and in 'em old days even wreckin' fancy ships. Nobody ever deserved to get back 'ome to Fowey more than 'ee, my dear daughter. And,' he added meaningfully, 'I suppose you'll be wantin' to see that young farmer who took me to see you in yon gaol?'

'I s'pose he's married by now?' Mary asked.

'I got no idea. He come down from the moor once or twice till yer mother died and brought us food from 'is farm. Then, when she went, we didn't need 'elp, with me workin' agin, so he just sort of vanished back up the moor,' he said.

Reassured that her father was well, Mary then followed an increasingly strong impulse to seek out Richard without delay. Leaving her box at her father's house, she set off for Lostwithiel to talk with a Reverend John Baron, whom Boswell had suggested might be a suitable person to help her. She took a boat upriver, past all the familiar landmarks that brought back memories of previous trips there en route to Bodmin Moor. Alighting at the Lostwithiel jetty, she made straight to the church of St Bartholomew, where, as luck would have it, Reverend Baron was polishing the brass cross.

'Reverend Baron,' she said, approaching him.

'Yes, madam? How may I help you?' he said, looking up from his polishing.

'I 'ave a letter for 'ee, Reverend, from a lawyer, Mr Boswell, of Lunnon,' she said, handing him a piece of paper. 'And if it wouldn't be too much trouble, I would like 'ee to write a short letter for me.'

'Well, first let me read this one,' he said, leading her into the vestry, where he lit a candle and read Boswell's letter.

After a few minutes, Reverend Baron said: 'I see, you really have had some adventures, haven't you, Mary? This Mr Boswell speaks very highly of you, indeed. So highly, he is going to send you an allowance of £5 every six months, on condition you behave yourself, and he wants me to manage the funds. And I am happy to do so. Now, tell me about this letter you want written.'

Mary dictated the letter to Reverend Baron, who wrote it out in his neat hand as follows:

Dear Richard,
I have got back now, after many hardships, and still remember our
agreement to meet that Sunday. So if you still feel the same way
please place the other half of this coin I am sending you together
and leave by the Hurling Stones on the moor this Sunday.
Your old friend with the bonnet
MB

'Is that all?' the reverend asked. 'It doesn't make much sense to me, Mary.'

'Yes, Reverend,' Mary said. 'That is all I want to say.'

'Will he know who "MB" is?'

'Well, Reverend, that is my mark. Anyway, he will know because I will put this 'alf-penny in the letter as well.'

'Very well,' Reverend Baron said. 'Here is your letter. But you'll have to make haste, as Sunday is tomorrow.'

'Thank you, Reverend,' Mary said.

'I will contact your Mr Boswell,' the reverend said. 'Come and see me again in six months. And Godspeed with finding your Mr Richard.'

Clutching the letter, Mary set out for the moor and Woodland Farm, where she thought local farmhands would know of Richard's whereabouts. As she travelled across the moor memories of falling in love with the strong young farmer with the deep brown eyes flooded back; her heart started beating rapidly. But she still had no idea whether he had waited or married somebody else. When she reached the gate of Woodland Farm, she gave a coin and her letter to a young swain she saw leading a cow, who said that Richard was indeed working nearby and agreed to deliver Mary's letter. Some time later, she arrived at the hamlet of Minions, where she took a room for the night and waited.

The next morning, Mary made her way to the Hurling Stones on the moor. So much had happened since the last time she had seen the stones, perhaps she and Richard were now quite different people. As she approached the stones her heart skipped a beat, for there in front of the first stone she saw a white envelope. Her heart beating quickly, Mary picked it up. On the front it had the only letters she knew, 'MB'. She tore it open. If this was a letter, she thought, she wouldn't be able to read it. But the only thing inside was the 1765 penny stuck back together — her half and Richard's now rejoined.

Looking around her, she saw him standing quietly beside one of the Hurlers a short distance away. He was much taller than she remembered, finer looking and older. But as he walked slowly towards her she saw he had the same kind demeanour, open face, deep brown eyes and the smile that she had first fallen for. They looked at each other, saying nothing, just seeing how they felt about one another, both hoping that same old love was still there. Within seconds it was clear nothing had changed. Richard shook his head, overcome with emotion. She thought he might cry, perhaps thinking she looked so much older and careworn. They seemed frozen in time, like the Hurling Stones in the field behind them. Then without a word they both stepped forward, arms wide open, and embraced for what seemed hours with Mary's tears silently moistening his old farmer's smock. With her head nestled into his chest like a cutter in a safe harbour and feeling his solid protective strength she breathed the greatest sigh of relief, feeling that after all she had been through she was at last in good hands and could now let go.

Finally, Richard pulled back and spoke. 'Mary! Oh, Mary! Is it really you, after all these years?' he said, shaking his head in disbelief.

'Yes, Richard it is,' she said, looking into his eyes. 'Greatly changed, but still me inside.'

'I don't know how you did it, but thank God I never gave up hope waiting for you to get back. From the time I saw you so calm in that gaol, I always knew you'd have the strength to do it,' he said proudly.

'Well, apart from righting the wrong of the unjust punishment, I had good reasons, Richard, with my father and 'ee,' she said, 'and the comforting 'alf penny 'ee gave me that day also helped.' She smiled, hugging him again, 'Remember that old Cornish saying how we could not die till the two halves were rejoined?'

'Of course. I have the same faith in willing things to happen despite all obstacles, but let's sit down,' he said beckoning to a fallen stone. 'I want us to talk before we go off anywhere.'

By nightfall, having talked all day without stopping, Mary and Richard felt the intervening years had slipped away, leaving them where they had left off all those years ago.

On their way back to Woodland Farm, Richard explained that his father had died and had left this small farm to him.

'Fact is, Mary, I have always hoped you would be the one that would come back and join me on the farm.'

'Of course, I will, Richard. I wouldn't have had the strength to come back had I not hoped for that to happen,' she said, pulling him into her arms again. 'You know how I love the moor and I've certainly 'ad enough of boats and the sea so I doan mind leavin' Fowey and the fishing. I'd love to help 'ee with the farm.'

Agreeing that they had always meant to end up together, and her capture and exile had only delayed things, Mary and Richard decided then and there to become man and wife, and selected a date on which to marry. Mary said she would ask Reverend Baron to marry them, and that she would arrange everything with her father and sisters whom she had also been longing to see again and must go to with the good news.

On the appointed day, Richard waited at the altar at the little church of St Bartholomew in Lostwithiel with Reverend Baron as Mary and her dear old father walked up the aisle towards them. Tears filled his eyes when he saw that his beloved Mary was wearing a pretty silk bonnet, as she had promised she would all those years ago.

Postscript

After Mary and Richard got married they worked on the farm where they lived happily ever after. Today there are many people in Fowey and the surrounding districts who are proud to have the blood of the Broad family in their veins. The rumoured inheritance of £300,000 proved to be unfounded. William Broad spent his twilight years fishing from the Town Quay.

James Boswell was true to his word and continued to send an allowance to Mary via Reverend Baron who confirmed Mary's good behaviour. This allowance continued until Boswell died in 1795. He also helped Dolly to find a better-paying job in a household in London where she met and married the butler.

James Martyn finished his *Memorandums*, which became the only first-hand account of the convicts' escape from Sydney Cove. After he was pardoned, he returned to his home county of Antrim, in Ireland, where he resumed work as a stonemason.

Nathaniel Lilly was reunited with his wife and two children in London and resumed work as a weaver.

Willy Allen served on a warship that fought in the war against Napoleon.

John Butcher successfully applied for a position as a private with the New South Wales Corps. He sailed out to Port Jackson as a free man and soldier, arriving in very different circumstances from those in which he had left. In September 1795, after persistent written applications for a block of land he succeeded. Even in his first letter from London he claimed he was 'capable of bringing indifferent lands to fruitful production', so was granted 25 acres of the finest land in the vicinity of Parramatta. Butcher successfully farmed the land for the rest of his life. He married a former convict and together they raised a family of free children in the new colony in whose future he so firmly believed.

It is possible that Jimmy Cox made it to shore in the Dutch East Indies, where he may have changed his name and nationality and resumed his living as a versatile carpenter.

Sailors who visited Batavia reported they had seen the wooden crosses for Emanuel and Will Bryant in the hospital graveyard and confirmed that Will's did indeed carry the inscription 'Will Bryant, Smuggler from Cornwall'.

Catherine Fryer and Margaret Shepherd worked out their sentences in the colony, married fellow convicts and eventually became free citizens in the new land.

Convict Peter Paris did get away from Botany Bay with the French captain, La Perouse, but these French ships *Astrolabe* and

Boussole were wrecked off the island of Vanikoro where all the survivors, including the escapee Peter Paris, were killed and eaten by the natives when they struggled ashore from the wreck.

Mary and her party were the first to find coal at Newcastle. Once it was known about this coal, settlers were sent to develop the area and Newcastle eventually became a coal-producing and industrial centre of New South Wales.

Despite the misgivings of the early colonists and the many years of hardship, the 1788 English settlement in New South Wales did survive, due in no small part to the early efforts of the governor, Arthur Phillip, and of course those hard-working convicts who remained. In time this penal colony grew into the nation of Australia.

The Escape Crew

March 1791

Group A:
First Fleet convicts from the *Dunkirk* and *Charlotte*

MARY BRYANT (née BROAD), 25
Baptized 1 May 1765 daughter of fisherman and mariner William Broad and Grace Broad. Grey eyes, brown hair, sallow complexion, five foot four inches, 'one knee bent but is not lame'. Strong Cornish accent. Convicted at Exeter assizes in 1786 of highway robbery for stealing a silk bonnet and sentenced to death. Sentence commuted to seven years transportation. Imprisoned on the hulk *Dunkirk*. Transported to New South Wales on the *Charlotte*. Illiterate. Strong constitution. Survived.

WILL BRYANT, 31
Fisherman and smuggler from Cornwall. Convicted at Bodmin in 1784 for 'resisting revenue officers'. Imprisoned on the hulk *Dunkirk*. Transported to New South Wales on the *Charlotte*. The colony's main fisherman. Spoke with a Cornish accent. Black hair. Wore pony tail. Captained the cutter they escaped in. Died in hospital in Batavia of fever on 22 December 1791.

CHARLOTTE SPENCE, 3

Child of the Exeter turnkey, Charlie Spence and Mary Bryant. Born on the First Fleet ship *Charlotte* at sea in 1787 en route to Botany Bay. A chatterbox. Loved to catch crabs. Died at sea on the *Gorgon* 4 May 1792 en route to England.

EMANUEL BRYANT, 1

Child of Will and Mary Bryant. Born at Sydney Cove in April 1790. Died in Batavia on 1 December 1791.

JAMES 'PADDY' MARTYN, 40

Irish stonemason. Five foot nine inches tall. Dark, sallow complexion, black hair turning grey, grey eyes. Lisped (so preferred to write). Kept a journal of the escape, his 'Memorandums' (now in the British Museum). Religious. Stole old lead and iron screw bolts (20-pound weight) from a wealthy lord. Convicted at Exeter assizes on 20 March 1786. Befriended Mary as father figure. Imprisoned on the hulk *Dunkirk*. Transported to New South Wales on the *Charlotte*. Survived. Pardoned from Newgate Gaol in 1793. Returned to stone mason work in Ireland.

JIMMY 'CHIPS' COX, 34

Cabinetmaker from East End of London. Best mate of Will Bryant. Wore an earring in right ear. Convicted of a burglary carried out on 27 July 1782 (stole 12 yards of thread lace worth 41 shillings and two pairs of cotton stockings worth four shillings from Thompson Brothers' dwelling). Tried and sentenced to death on 11 September 1782. Commuted on 10 September 1783 to transportion for life. Transported to America on the *Mercury*, but escaped after a mutiny. Re-captured and imprisoned on the hulk *Dunkirk*. Became best friend of Will Bryant.

Transported on the *Charlotte* to New South Wales . Lover of Sarah Young. Carpenter on the escape boat. Jumped overboard in Straits of Sunda in a bid for freedom. Attempted to swim to shore. Fate unknown.

Group B
First Fleet convict from the *Alexander*

SAM 'BIRDY' BIRD (alias John Simms), 32

Surrey labourer from Wandsworth. Dark complexion, stout, five foot seven inches tall. Wore a bushy beard. Convicted on 7 July 1785 at Croydon assizes for using force and arms and breaking open a warehouse with his brother James at Wandsworth, where they stole 1000 pounds of saltpetre worth £30 and ten hempen bags of goods worth five shillings from Bridges Brothers. A handy sailor. A joker. Transported on the *Alexander* with rebel escaper John Powers who got away temporarily at Tenerife then led a mutiny off Cape Town. Only had 16 months to serve when escaped. Died at sea between Batavia and Cape Town.

Group C
Second Fleet convicts arrived June 1790

WILLIAM 'BILL' MORETON, 33

A financial fraudster from Newcastle. Dark complexion, thin, five foot nine inches tall. Had a tattoo of a square-rigged tall ship on both upper arms. Former second mate, mariner, brilliant navigator and able-bodied seaman. Convicted in Newcastle for obtaining money on false pretences. Imprisoned on the hulk the *Justitia* in July 1789 (the month the French Revolution started). Transported to New South Wales on the *Neptune*. Escaped after only nine months in the colony. An intelligent loner taken on by Mary and Will Bryant for his navigation skills. Responsible for guiding the cutter safely to Timor. Died at sea of the fever between Batavia and Cape Town.

WILLY 'SILLY WILLY' ALLEN, 51

Professional mariner. Mate of Nat Lilly. Born at Kingston-upon-Hull. Five foot 11 inches tall, hazel eyes, bald, dark complexion. Convicted in July 1787 at Norwich for stealing 29 handkerchiefs from a Norwich shop. Held in Norwich Castle. Imprisoned on the hulk the *Thames* at Woolwich, then imprisoned in the hulk *Stanislaus* at Portsmouth then on the *Lion* (with Nat Lilly). Transported to New South Wales on the *Scarborough* (also with Nat Lilly). Assigned servant to Marine Captain James Campbell. Escaped after only nine months in the colony. One of the most experienced and competent sailors in the escape crew. Survived. Pardoned from Newgate Gaol in 1793. Returned to sea as a seaman and served in the war against Napoleon.

NATHANIEL 'NAT' LILLY (aka LILLIE), 36

Born 1753 in Suffolk. Five foot eight inches tall, grey eyes, black hair, sallow complexion. Wore a moustache. Jewish. A weaver by trade. In 1783 arrested and held in Newgate Gaol, then tried in Bury St Edmunds assizes for highway robbery (like Mary), but acquitted for lack of evidence. Sentenced to death in March 1788 at Bury St Edmunds for burglary, during which he stole a silver-cased watch, two silver tablespoons and some fish net. Seven witnesses betrayed him for a £40 reward. This death sentence was subsequently commuted to transportation for life. Was imprisoned on the *Lion* hulk at Portsmouth (with Willy Allen), then transported to New South Wales on the *Scarborough* (with Willy Allen). Escaped after only nine months in the colony. Survived. Pardoned from Newgate Gaol in 1793. Reunited with his wife and two children in London.

JOHN 'LONG JOHN' BUTCHER, 48

(alias William Butcher, Samuel Broome, John Brown)

Born in 1743 in Kidderminster, Worcestershire. Labourer or farmer. Six foot one inch tall, red hair, grey eyes, fair complexion, walked with a limp. Stole three pigs from a John Harsbury, as reported in *The London Chronicle*. Convicted at Shrewsbury, then sentenced at Shropshire assizes in July 1788. Transported to New South Wales on the *Scarborough*. Escaped after only nine months in the colony. Was the main armed guard on the escape boat responsible for security. Pardoned from Newgate Gaol in 1793. Successfully appealed in writing to return to the penal colony as a soldier and land-owning farmer and returned to develop his property, marry and raise a family in New South Wales.

Sources

Ainsworth, Harrison, *Jack Sheppard, A Romance* (Richard Bentley, London, 1840)

Aughton, Peter, *Endeavour: The story of Captain Cook's first great epic voyage* (Cassell & Co., London, 2002)

Bateson, Charles, *The Convict Ships* (Library of Australian History, Sydney, 1983)

Burnum Burnum (ed. Sainty, G.R), *Wild Things Around Sydney* (Sainty & Associates, Sydney, 1989)

Borough of Restormel, Fowey, Mevagissey & St. Austell Bay, *The Real Cornwall* (Dowrick Design & Print, St. Ives, Cornwall, 1982)

Chapman, Don, *1788 The People of the First Fleet* (Cassell, Sydney, 1981)

Clark, Ralph (eds Fidlon, Paul and Ryan, R.J), *The Journal and Letters of Lt. Ralph Clark 1787-1792* (Australian Documents Library, Sydney, 1981)

Clark, David, *Poldark Country* (Bossiny Books, Bodmin, 1977)

Cobley, John, *Crimes of the First Fleet Convicts* (Angus & Robertson, Sydney, 1970)

Cobley, John, *Sydney Cove 1788, vol 1* (Angus & Robertson, Sydney, 1962)

Cobley, John, *Sydney Cove 1789-90, vol 2* (Angus & Robertson, Sydney, 1962)

Collins, David (ed. Brian Fletcher), *An Account of the English Colony in New South Wales* (A.H. & A. Reed, Sydney, 1975)

Currey, C.H., *The Transportation, Escape and Pardoning of Mary Bryant* (Halstead Press, Sydney, 1983)

Du Maurier, Daphne, *Vanishing Cornwall* (Penguin, Harmondsworth, England, 1967)

Edwards, Captain Edwards, *Voyage of H.M.S. Pandora. Dispatched to arrest the mutineers of the 'Bounty' in the South Seas 1790-91* (Francis Edwards, London, 1915)

Faull, Jim, *The Cornish in Australia* (AE Press, Melbourne, 1983)

Flynn, Michael, *The Second Fleet: Britain's Grim Convict Armada of 1790* (Library of Australian History, Sydney, 1993)

Foot, Sarah, *Views of Old Cornwall* (Bossiny Books, Bodmin, 1981)

Gilbert, Thomas, 'The Logs of the First Fleet, Charlotte' (Admiralty, Captain's Logs, 51/4375, unpublished)

Green, Christina, *The Mysterious Moor* (Ideford Publications, Newton Abbot, Devon, 1978)

Harris, Max (ed.), *1918 Dictionary of the Vulgar Tongue* (Bibliophile Books, Adelaide, 1981)

Headley, John, *Cornwall* (Estate Publications, Tenterden, Kent, 1981)

Hunter, Captain John (ed. John Bach), *An Historical Journal of Events at Sydney and at Sea* (Angus & Robertson, Sydney, 1968)

Iggulden, David, *Sailing Home. A Pictorial Record of the First Fleet Re-enactment Voyage* (Angus & Robertson, Sydney, 1988)

King, Jonathan, *The First Fleet: The convict voyage that founded Australia* (Macmillan, Melbourne, 1982)

King, Jonathan, *The First Settlement: The convict village that founded Australia* (Macmillan, Melbourne, 1984)

King, Jonathan, 'Journal of visit to Fowey' (Private Papers, unpublished, 1983)

King, Jonathan, 'Journal of the First Fleet Re-enactment Expedition 13 May 1987 – 26 January 1988' (Private Papers, unpublished, 1988)

King, Jonathan and John, *Philip Gidley King* (Methuen, Sydney, 1981)

King, Philip Gidley (eds Fidlon, Paul and Ryan, R.J.), *The Journal of Philip Gidley King, Lieutenant, R.N. 1787-1790* (Australian Documents Library, Sydney, 1980)

Lind, Lew, *Sea Jargon: A Dictionary of the unwritten language of the sea* (Patrick Stevens, Cambridge, 1982)

Martyn, James (aka Martin, James), 'Memorandums: The log of the escape voyage' (British Museum, unpublished, 1791)

McBryde, Isabel, *Guests of the Governor: Aboriginal residents of the first Government House* (Friend of Old Government House Site, Sydney, 1989)

Pottle, Frederick, *Boswell and the girl from Botany Bay* (William Heinemann Ltd, London, 1938)

Shepherd, John, *Georgian Times* (Owlet Books, London, 1977)

Spreadbury, I.D. (aka Kerdroya), *Fowey: A brief history* (Osborne Press, St. Blazey, Cornwall, fourth edn, 1983)

Sweeney, Christopher, *Transported in Place of Death* (Macmillan, Melbourne, 1981)

Tench, Watkin, *Sydney's First Four Years* (Library of Australian History, Sydney, 1979)

Thompson, E.V., *Discovering Bodmin Moor* (Bossiney Books, Bodmin, 1980)